PHILOSOPHY
PRACTICE

PHILOSOPHY PRACTICE

An Alternative to Counseling and Psychotherapy

Shlomit C. Schuster

Westport, Connecticut
London

Library of Congress Cataloging-in-Publication Data

Schuster, Shlomit C., 1951–
   Philosophy practice : an alternative to counseling and
psychotherapy / Shlomit C. Schuster.
     p.   cm.
   Includes bibliographical references and index.
   ISBN 0–275–96541–4 (alk. paper)
   1. Philosophical counseling.   I. Title.
BJ1595.5.S38   1999
100—dc21   99–13432

British Library Cataloguing in Publication Data is available.

Library of Congress Catalog Card Number: 99–13432
ISBN: 0–275–96541–4

First published in 1999

Praeger Publishers, 88 Post Road West, Westport, CT 06881
An imprint of Greenwood Publishing Group, Inc.
www.praeger.com

Printed in the United States of America

The paper used in this book complies with the
Permanent Paper Standard issued by the National
Information Standards Organization (Z39.48–1984).

10 9 8 7 6 5 4 3 2 1

Copyright Acknowledgments

The author and publisher gratefully acknowledge permission for use of the following material:

Shlomit C. Schuster, "Philosophical Practice and Its Effective Rhetoric of the 'Sane,'" *Agora, Zeitschrift für Philosophische Praxis* 8–9 (1990): 15–16. © 1990 *Agora, Zeitschrift für Philosophische Praxis*.

———, "Philosophical Counselling," *Journal of Applied Philosophy* 8 (1991): 219–223. © 1991 The Society for Applied Philosophy.

———, "Philosophy as if It Matters: The Practice of Philosophical Counseling," *Critical Review* 6 (1992): 587–599. © 1992 *Critical Review*.

———, "The Practice of Sartre's Philosophy in Philosophical Counseling and in Existential Psychotherapy," *Iyyun: The Jerusalem Philosophical Quarterly* 44 (1995): 99–114. © 1995 *Iyyun: The Jerusalem Philosophical Quarterly*.

———, "Report on Applying Philosophy in Philosophical Counseling," *The International Journal of Applied Philosophy* 9 (1995): 51–55. © 1995 *The International Journal of Applied Philosophy*.

———, "Philosophical Counseling and Humanistic Psychotherapy," *Journal of Psychology and Judaism* 20 (1996): 247–259. © 1996 *Journal of Psychology and Judaism*.

———, "Philosophical Narratives and Philosophical Counselling," *Journal of the Society for Existential Analysis* 8 (1997): 108–127. © 1997 *Journal of the Society for Existential Analysis*.

———, "Yoetz Philosophi (Philosophical Counselling)" first published in *Journal of Applied Philosophy* 8 (1991): 219–223. Second publishing in *Emda* 7 (1999): 56–59. © 1999 *Emda*.

For Susan Sontag

Die Philosophische Praxis ist ein freies Gespräch.
Gerd B. Achenbach, *Philosophische Praxis*

Contents

Acknowledgments

I want to express my gratitude first to my parents for their faithful support of my endeavors. Thanks also to those who were matriarchs and patriarchs to me in philosophy practice. Particularly I am grateful to the practitioners who gave of their time in discussions or correspondence with me, among them Gerd B. Achenbach, Gert de Boer, Elliot Cohen, Nicholas Coleman, Maurice S. Friedman, Will Gerbers, Ad Hoogendijk, Ida Jongsma, Peter T. Kemp, Hans Krämer, Ekkehard Martens, Petra von Morstein, and Eite Veening. That I could make use of journals and books from different libraries in Israel and abroad contributed much to this research project, and so I thank these libraries: the Hebrew University of Jerusalem Bloomfield Library for Humanities and Social Sciences, the Jewish National and University Library, the Koninklijke Bibliotheek in The Hague, and the New York Public Library. I want to honor and thank all my counselees for their courage in venturing into this old–new domain of philosophical counseling, and in particular those counselees I have written about, although they will hardly recognize themselves in their case histories. Last but not least I would like to thank the acquisitions editor Elisabetta Linton and others at Praeger Publishers and the Greenwood Publishing Group, as well as copy-editor Sharon Pabst of the John Beck production group, for their interest and assistance in contributing to the realization of my writing project.

PART I

THEORETICAL
VIEWS

CHAPTER 1

Philosophy as an Alternative Practice

In order to understand the world, one has to turn away from it
on occasion; in order to serve men better, one has to hold them
at a distance for a time.

Albert Camus, "The Minotaur"

This volume is mainly a report on practicing philosophy in counseling sessions with individuals; it tells about the new profession of philosophical counseling, which is an alternative to psychotherapy and psychological counseling. I do not believe that psychological counseling can legitimately lay claim to the notions of counseling and counselor as it predominately does.

I use different names for philosophy practice with one or two individuals—philosophical counseling, philosophical consultation, philosophical psychoanalysis, philosophical practice, or philosophy practice. The last two names are also used as general terms for philosophizing with groups. All these expressions form an array of the activity of philosophizing in particular settings, but these are not proper nouns to be coined, receive a trademark, or obtain title protection. These abstract nouns belong to universal philosophical terminology. However, compound proper nouns, such as the Achenbachian, Sartrean, or Grimesian philosophy practice, indicate that the intellectual property rights to these type of practices belong to the persons named in these compound nouns.

This book may seem initially to be of a complex design, but the motifs through which I describe the practice of philosophical counseling are mainly three in number:

1. The historical setting of philosophical practice in classical and contemporary philosophical practice.
2. The justification of the nonclinical approach of philosophical counseling by placing it in a framework of philosophical and clinical critiques of psychotherapy.
3. Case histories from my own practice.

Because the aim of my writing is to interest a public unschooled in philosophy, as well as philosophers and scholars from other disciplines, I have limited the theoretical discussion to a survey of the most elementary features of philosophical practice.

Philosophical counseling as a nonclinical approach to well-being is of interest to mental-health workers, for personal and professional reasons alike. For example, the psychologist and the physician who came to me for philosophical consultation felt a need to know themselves and life beyond the standards of their professional knowledge. They wanted to advance their scientific and clinical understanding of themselves through philosophical verification, intuition, and ideas. In contradistinction to the disciplines having endings in "-logy," such as psychology, sociology, and anthropology, which all have the aim of discovering scientific, substantial knowledge: Philosophical activity attempts to go beyond scientific established knowledge either by criticizing scientific "truths" or through an intellectual quest that in the future may lead to the establishment of new scientific knowledge. In our so post-Enlightenment age there still exists the scarce but highly educated person who clings to scientifically obtained knowledge as if it is the ultimate, absolute revelation of the truth. Though I much value the intellectual heritage of the Enlightenment, history and common sense teaches that science and philosophy cannot outdo each other in ever renewing or supplanting discoveries and inventions.

Whereas scientists use the empirical method for establishing truth, philosophers need only think. Edmund L. Erde characterized the juxtaposition of philosophy and science as follows: "In short, science makes us active members of a community of events; philosophy makes us active members of a community of ideas."[1]

There seems to be no beginning to the time when people started consciously looking for truth, knowledge, and a right way of conducting their lives. Searchers for truth and knowledge today should consider the answers of those who searched before us. Now more than ever before, there is a need to continue this tradition of questioning and searching for the answers that may be obtained by philosophical inquiry as an art for its own sake. Although twentieth-century analytical philosophy has shown little concern for the meaning of life and how to live, it has not prevented other philosophers from looking for such a philosophy. Nevertheless, analytical skepticism and criticism of philosophical thought in general has had practical consequences: It is a sobering influence on the wild imaginations of old-fashioned metaphysicians. The purpose of philosophical criticism is to correct or, in a medical metaphor, to "cure," although not so much to cure philosophers and others from philosophizing as to teach critical self-reflection. A critical attitude is necessary in philosophy as well as in science, economics, politics, religion, and all other areas of knowledge and daily life.

Questioning and searching for answers has a value in itself that often exceeds the answers ultimately found; the exercise of reaching a particular goal is often as valuable—if not more valuable—than the attainment of the goal. Not daring to question, or not integrating new knowledge with old worldviews and existing knowledge, may debilitate the great capacities and possibilities of the human intellect. Philosophical practice as an alternative to psychological counseling and therapy can provide a place for examining the self, life, and the world, and aims at restoring a childlike wonder to our existence. Aristotle considered wonder to be the beginning of philosophy, while Wordsworth called the child the best of philosophers. The Harvard philosopher Stanley Cavell finds that we learn from the child-philosopher to leave the childish behind: "The child is a philosopher because we are to learn from the fact of childhood. . . . These will be philosophical ways of letting childhood go. . . . Putting aside childish things becomes the achievement of intellect."[2] The goal of philosophical counseling is such cultivation of the intellect; playful wonder turns into philosophizing as an art of living.

My own experience as a student of creative therapy (a psychoanalytic variation of occupational therapy and psychodrama) in the early seventies was one of disappointment with the psychotherapeutic establishment. The many questions that I did not find answers for in psychotherapeutic theory and practice were answered, to my surprise, when I studied philosophy in the eighties. Still later I found more answers in the ideas of Gerd B. Achenbach about the practice of philosophy.

This book presents many ideas that will be familiar to academic philosophers; however, philosophical counseling offers a new style and approach for well-known academic exercises. This new style of philosophizing turns philosophy into a private or public revolutionary happening. Academic philosophy today is often somewhat provincial; it is either analytic, existential, phenomenological, postmodern, or historically oriented. In the context of this book the word "philosophy" does not mean one specific provincial kind of reflection or method, but philosophy in its widest universal sense. A suitable definition of philosophy as used in this book is "the study of the most general and abstract features of the world and categories with which we think: mind, matter, reason, proof, truth, etc. In philosophy, the concepts with which we approach the world themselves become the topic of enquiry."[3] In addition, philosophy can be divided into various subfields such as logic, ethics, metaphysics, epistemology, and the history of philosophy; or into specialized areas such as philosophy of the mind, of religion, of science, of law, of art, of language, of medicine, of mathematics, or of film.[4]

Although philosophical counseling has many predecessors, it has recently emerged as a new phenomenon in the discipline of philosophy; it is the contemporary attempt to unite philosophical thought with the activities of life. This merging of philosophical theory and real-life practice takes place in conversations people hold with a philosophical practitioner who possesses the expertise that is beneficial to them. The word "counseling" in the phrase "philosophical counseling" has its etymological origin in the literal, neutral meaning of "giving advice." Experts in the fields of law, literature, tax, politics, and gardening each give their advice autonomously; beauty, tax, or financial counselors are not interdisciplinary specialists, but simply counselors in their specific fields. Likewise, the philosopher–counselor is an autonomous counselor. The etymological origin of the word "practice" is found in classic Greek philosophy as "praxis," meaning "action," "act," "practice," or "experience."[5] Philosophical practice as counseling is not a hybrid of philosophy and psychology, but philosophy "proper"; this in spite of the fact that in our post-Freudian and postmodern world, the idea of the autonomy of thought seems scandalous. The philosopher with such a sovereign praxis has become an entrepreneur and is no longer dependent on universities or psychological associations for making a livelihood. Philosophers' independence of academic institutions may not only be beneficial to them and to their clients, but may also positively affect the development of academic philosophy. However, a small group of U.S. philosophy professors seem to feel daunted by philosophy practice as a free-market enterprise and aim through legislation and state certification to monopolize philosophy practice by bringing it under the supervision of colleague professors and mental-health specialists. It is obvious that such political restriction concerning the different types of philosophy practice is doomed to fail, because it contradicts the Universal Declaration of Human Rights (Articles 18, 19, and 20) and the First Amendment of the Constitution of the United States.

The growing interest in philosophy among mental-health workers led to the founding in 1989 of the Association of Philosophy and Psychiatry in the United States, and the Royal College of Psychiatrists' Philosophy Group in Britain. Although antipsychiatry and existential psychotherapy have always had a strong philosophical inclination, for "straight" psychiatry and psychology to be profoundly interested in philosophy is something new. As a philosophical practitioner I am pleased and encouraged by this new clinical interest in philosophy, but at the same time I find it of paramount importance to develop further the nonclinical contribution of philosophy to well-being, which is philosophical counseling.

In Chapters 2, 3, and 4, I present a theoretical description of philosophical practice and its narratives; I clarify here the historical origins of philosophical counseling and how it is different from therapeutic approaches. In Chapters 5 through 12, I present narratives originating in my private practice of philosophical counseling.

Chapter 2 is a comprehensive historical sketch followed by a detailed account of modern attempts to improve life through philosophy. I describe those contemporary practitioners who were helpful to me in developing my own views on philosophical counseling: Achenbach, Hoogendijk, Veening, Nelson, von Morstein, and others. I present a description based on the written works of, or of those written about, these practitioners and on personal interviews and letters with some of them.

Many people who think, speak, and write about philosophical practitioners refer to them as though they were therapists in the usual sense of the term. However, the point made by Gerd B. Achenbach, the founder of this new profession, and his followers is that philosophical practitioners are not therapists, though what they have to offer can be an alternative and a supplement to psychotherapy.

A possible reason for misunderstanding philosophical counseling as therapy might be the mistaken ascription of almost any problem or affliction to a pathological state of body or mind. The misuse of such words as illness, disease, and sickness is all too common. One need not have read Freud's *Psychopathology of Everyday Life* to be aware that, generally speaking, talk and action are no longer accepted naively. In our post-Freudian world, psychopathology is seen as hidden everywhere. Thomas Szasz, Susan Sontag, David Cooper, and Ivan Illich, among others, have critically analyzed the metaphors of illness in various disciplines of knowledge and situations in life.[6]

The general use of phrases such as "the average neurotic" to refer to ordinary people show how far reaching this influence, which
I call "psychopathologization," has become in the understanding of
people. That that psychopathologization is less innocent than is
generally believed is shown by the research of Mordechai Rotenberg.
Rotenberg says that "Nomen est Omen," or, to name is to indicate.[7]
When an unapparent mental illness is given its medical name, and
this name is accepted by the person suffering, the person starts to
identify with the particular affliction as a medical fact. A physically sick person may *have* a cold or an ulcer or even AIDS, but a
mentally sick person *is* his sickness. The concept of a mental sickness incarnates: One *is* a neurotic, a psychotic, or a hypochondriac. It
can be claimed that the neurotic is so labeled because he has a neurosis, but if the same person had a headache, he would only become a
"headache" if he complained endlessly about it. Rotenberg showed that
people who consider themselves possessed with an evil spirit have
a better self-image and a greater chance of becoming a "healthy"
self. This is because when the demon was believed to have left them,
these people often returned to their former ways of life as "normal"
people; no longer did they "have" the evil spirit. On the other hand,
those who see themselves as having a mental illness or disorder
often remain hospitalized or in treatment for the rest of their lives.

In Chapter 3, I describe my formulation of the theoretical side of
philosophical counseling. My own practice may be termed "transtherapeutic" because it consists of activities that are not therapy,
yet can nevertheless induce well-being. In an age where it is said
that therapeutic methods have triumphed, there are very few people
who can conceive new understandings, an "other" awareness, or
change, correction, or development in human thought and behavior as anything but therapy. Consequently, in this chapter and in
following chapters, it is necessary to justify my nonclinical and
noninterdisciplinary approach by extensively describing some of
the problematic aspects of the all-invasive therapeutic culture.

Therapy has become the most powerful ideology of the twentieth
century. The latest expression of the urge for therapy is the "recovery movement." One can describe this movement, as David Rieff
did, as guided by a new narrative which replaces the "rags-to-riches"
narrative of former American generations. In the new narrative,
terms "such as 'character,' 'weakness,' and 'individual responsibility' are no longer deemed appropriate. Those who drink too much,
take drugs, or destroy themselves (and their co-dependents) in other
ways suffer either from a disease (like alcoholism) or . . . of the
faulty upbringing to which they were subjected as children."[8]

Apparently, not only is the twentieth century preoccupation with
therapy enhanced by the enthusiasm of physicians and social sci-

entists, but, according to Victor Frankl, the secularization and de-humanization of society confronts doctors and psychiatrists with "meta-clinical problems"—that is, human philosophical questions rather than neurotic symptoms. Those persons who in former days would talk to some clergyman about philosophical questions now call on a mental-health worker or physician.[9] Unfortunately, these professionals often do not recognize such quests for meaning as being of a philosophical nature.

In 1942, in the introduction to an anthology of classical works, *The Consolation of Philosophy*, Irwin Edman could still claim that "through the centuries certain books have been sources of consolation and fortitude for troubled spirits in troublous times, in personal crisis, or in public calamity; they have been both anodyne and refreshment."[10] At the end of the twentieth century, many people seem to have forgotten this old home remedy and only look to psychotherapy and drugs for relief.

That the word "therapy" has become more or less meaningless (since almost anything is the proper subject of therapy and almost anything can be called therapy) is not just to be blamed on medical "imperialism." The therapy craze can be understood as an unhappy configuration of social developments and scientific progress.

Therapists with an awareness of the new use of the word "therapy" try to justify it in different ways. For example, Ernesto Spinelli, inspired by Wittgenstein and Nelson Goodman, defines therapy as an "open concept": "The varying forms or categories of therapy do not possess sets of characteristics shared by all members of the category 'therapy.' Rather, category members are united by 'family resemblances' the varying similarities of which overlap and crisscross one another."[11] Spinelli finds it more useful to ask "*When* is [it] therapy[?]" rather than "What is therapy?" There are also those therapists who, in spite of being professional psychotherapists, admit to performing a different trade—for example, Emmy van Deurzen-Smith, psychologist, psychotherapist, and philosopher. As an existential counselor, van Deurzen-Smith has no aim to cure people in the tradition of the medical model. Life is seen as an art and counseling as an art tutorial: "Assisting people in the process of living with greater expertise and ease is the goal of existential counselling."[12] However, in the few pages van Deurzen-Smith dedicated to the subject philosophical consultation in the more recent book, *Everyday Mysteries*, she welcomes philosophical counselors' claims not to be therapists, but firmly locates herself in the psychotherapy realm when applying philosophy to her own work.[13] With due respect to van Deurzen-Smith as one of the founders of the British existential analysis movement, it seems to me that her theory is not free of an intellectual dilemma.

If one accepts the above definitions of therapy, is it possible to classify philosophical counseling as psychotherapy? Most therapists will clearly answer "No." Included in most all possible definitions of psychotherapy is the rule that therapy is therapy *when* it is done by a professional, accredited therapist. To be recognized as a professional therapist by the psychotherapist "family," one must have followed the family rites of initiation.

Judy Tame, the director of Lifeplan, an organization which aids people in finding and developing their personal philosophies, finds that "most of those psychotherapies that reject the medical paradigm—as well as those that accept it—still want to create a mystique around the art of helping by setting up lengthy pseudo-medical training which produce accredited 'experts.'" While Tame writes with appreciation of van Deurzen-Smith's brand of existential counseling, she still criticizes van Deurzen-Smith's "simple," "down-to-earth" method of practical philosophizing because it is "dropped incongruously into a medical environment thus barring all those potential 'therapists'—whom van Deurzen-Smith in one place calls 'consultants'—who have no desire to train or work in a mental hospital or GP's practice."[14]

The therapy mystique maintains its sway even over those who are highly critical of the profession. Is this because of the prominent status of therapy? Is it because the therapist–patient relationship is experienced as personally gratifying to the therapist? Or is it because of the faith most people have in the medical profession? According to Tame, the research of Aaron Estersen and Windy Dryden has shown that nonaccredited counselors are not less helpful than accredited, psychotherapeutic counselors. Accordingly, Tame concludes that the preference for the pseudomedical training is a result of the status given to the therapist.[15] (In spite of this ardent critique, Tame's latest writing gives the strong impression that she too joined the accredited guild of psychological counselors.)

The pseudomedical way of training obviously creates a lasting alliance between counselors and the medical model of helping people. Nonetheless, there are those who escape the ambitions of the therapeutic professions. My personal experience as a dropout student-therapist is that there is a way back from psychotherapy, although it demands a conscious and continuous effort to avoid old therapeutic thinking habits and ambitions. I find there exists a real difference, not just a semantic or a conceptual one, between using the word "therapy" to describe the practice of psychotherapists and using the word "counseling" as it is employed in philosophical practice. Philosophical counselors describe their practice as a philosophical way of "helping" or "caring" for people; these are indeed open concepts, without the connotations of development, growth, recovery, and cure that the word "therapy" has.

That therapists continually go beyond the literal meaning (or the closed meaning) of the word "therapy" was criticized by the psychiatrist Thomas Szasz as being the medical and therapeutic pretensions of psychiatry and psychology. Szasz finds that the medicalization of many personal and social problems is caused by the lack of an operational, meaningful definition of bodily and mental illness.[16] His main objection, however, is not against medicine or psychiatry, but against medical and psychiatric coercion. The analogy Szasz makes between medical and religious coercion is even more helpful for understanding in depth the influence medicine and psychotherapy have on modern society, because it compares this influence with the influence of religion on society in the Middle Ages.

I suggest that not only should medicine and psychotherapy renounce coercion, but that people's rights to freedom of or from medicine (and this includes psychology and psychotherapy treatment) should be established in law just as the freedom of religion has been legalized. Whereas the right of freedom of religion is widely acknowledged (although not as widely observed) the right of freedom of medicine is still in debate. Concrete examples of the rights discussed in this recently begun debate are the refusal of medical treatment by terminally ill patients, the refusal of electroshock treatment by mental patients, the refusal of blood transfusions or immunization, and the right to suicide. This debate can, and from my viewpoint should, be extended to many other areas of life that are greatly influenced by medicine and psychotherapy.

In many countries patients have legal rights to refuse medical procedures because of the right of a patient needing to provide medically informed consent: "Informed consent is a legal duty and its fulfillment is to be judged by legal standards instead of by the standards of practice of the medical community."[17] Social pressure, customs, and standards may nevertheless effectively overrule this right when patients are ignorant of it or do not dare to assert their right. Whereas one may refuse medical procedures in treatment, to resist the influence of clinical intelligence where its verdicts have been socially implemented is a completely different matter. For example, consider job-selection procedures using diagnostic or psychometric screening methods. Does a person have the right, for reasons of conscience, to refuse a Rorschach test? At present such a refusal would imply risking one's job opportunity, as it makes the person suspect of trying to hide some secret. Moreover, who is qualified to make decisions about the limits of the medical and psychotherapeutic sphere of influence? Is it the medical professionals and those who have passed the psychometric or other diagnostic tests designed by clinicians and psychologists?

Within the medical profession the boundaries of medical influence are becoming more and more a topic of discussion. An example is the question of whether to treat a depressed person suffering from diabetes: "The question for clinical management was whether he was to be detained . . . or whether his refusal of treatment was 'informed' and he was capable of making this judgement." These types of questions are shown to be professional dilemmas for which decisions "are likely to remain vexed as ever."[18] But, as they did show in their research, an "ethically educated view" is the preferred course in taking action, and not a "blind paternalism."

The philosophical counselor's place in the conflict of interests between physicians, psychologists, and patients is that of a neutral philosophical educator. The philosophical counselor ought to work in a no-man's land—between the diagnostic views of therapists and the free interpretations of the agnostic, between medicine and ethics, between the sciences and the arts. The philosophical practitioner may feel at home in this wasteland; unlike many of their predecessors, their rights to philosophize are safeguarded.

Though this book is not concerned with the clinical interpretation of human problems, in Chapter 3 I discuss the use of philosophy as therapy and show how this differs from philosophical counseling. I do not ignore the importance of different clinical approaches, nor is this ignored by most of my clients. If clients are looking for a clinical approach, they can easily contact a doctor or psychotherapist. Methods to help people can be different, even if the problems are the same: "Surely it is not too much to ask philosophers and psychiatrists to approach problems involving the same *material* set of reality or the same subject matter (seen from *formally* distinct points of view) in a spirit of mutual respect, understanding and cooperation?"[19]

It is true that Bertrand Russell considered issues such as appearance and reality, the existence and nature of matter, idealism, knowledge, and truth and falsehood to be "problems of philosophy." However, Russell thought that the way in which these problems are solved bears on all other problems of life: "The mind which has become accustomed to the freedom and impartiality of philosophical contemplation will preserve something of the same freedom and impartiality in the world of action and emotion."[20]

Obviously, some issues seem easier or better treated by one practitioner than another. For example, chronic insomnia seems to be best helped by a psychiatric prescription. In contrast, an ethical dilemma seems a typical issue for philosophical counseling. Most people indeed find their way to a psychiatrist or a philosopher, guided by such common-sense division of tasks. But often problems are not so typically this or that in that they are either fit for psychotherapy or for a nonclinical philosophical approach. For example, few psychotherapists would trace insomnia back to an ethical conflict; rather, they trace it to a conflict between the superego and the id. A philosophical analysis seems to be most appropriate when one assumes that an ethical conflict is the source of the insomnia. In such and other cases, philosophical counseling can help the person resolve or accept the conflict. If the insomnia was indeed caused by an ethical conflict, the return of a sound night's sleep can be expected after this conflict has been talked through.

Likewise, persons with, for example, a chronic or terminal disease may benefit from a philosophical understanding of their situation concurrent with their medical or psychotherapeutic treatment. Each approach is helpful in its own particular manner. The different approaches can be useful in complementing each other, but each has its own independent value. Philosophical, psychotherapeutic–philosophical, psychological, psychiatric, and medical approaches can all be beneficial to a person suffering, for example, from anxiety, depression, insecurity, or stress.

A good example of a philosophical understanding of anxiety is Paul Tillich's analysis of the subject. According to Tillich, anxiety is an inescapable human phenomenon that has been recognized as such by philosophers from Plato to Nietzsche and the existentialists. Tillich stressed the concept of courage as the way to overcome anxiety. When anxiety is not recognized and accepted as something everyone has to encounter, pathological anxiety is likely to develop.[21]

Tillich's analysis proved itself valuable in my philosophical practice. A woman in her early fifties came for consultation because she felt very depressed. She explained that she had had an affair with the man of her dreams, but she was trying to put an end to it. She didn't know yet what was going to happen; she was thinking of giving him a call. However, she was certainly not going to marry him, but maybe just see him now and then. She had been married and divorced and for many years had had flirtations with men who were not really her type. Just before she had met her "ideal partner," she had been sick for a few weeks. In those weeks she made up her mind to make a change and to get married again. She was getting older, and she needed a more secure way of life. The week after she made this life plan, she met *him*. They had been an ideal couple until he told her that he had had the impression she was younger than she actually was, and he only wanted to marry a younger woman. She was heartbroken, and her world seemed to have come to an end.

It seemed to me that an "ideal partner" would not be so concerned about her age. She might be very hurt and disappointed now, but she could yet meet her truly ideal partner, who might even be years younger than herself. That did not give her much comfort, but she started to listen eagerly when I pointed out that if she had not made these plans for the future she would probably not have taken this disappointment so badly. I found it remarkable that this all happened right after she decided to get married again. My impression was that she was not so much mourning a lost lover as a seemingly lost future. I asked her if some of her pain and depression was not caused by anxiety: fear of the future, old age, loneliness, dying. I suggested that if she would first face these existential anxieties she might be free to reconsider her wish to marry and be able to overcome her depression. I introduced her to Tillich's understanding of facing anxiety with courage. She agreed to read Tillich's *The Courage to Be*. My interpretation that her depression was mainly caused by existential anxiety helped her to calm down and to be somewhat comforted about the end of her latest affair.

Indeed, Tillich distinguishes between "normal" and "pathological" anxiety. Should the philosophical counselor also make this distinction? As I pointed out before, Szasz demonstrated the lack of a satisfactory definition of mental and physical illness. Moreover, he, Anthony Quinton, David Cooper, Michel Foucault, and others have shown that diagnoses are often based not so much on scientific knowledge as on political, cultural, religious, social, and economical considerations.[22]

The verb "to diagnose" is laden with medical significance. In a nonclinical vocabulary, to diagnose is defined as "to establish or verify, as the cause or nature of a problem."[23] One can identify the cause of noise in a motor, of failing an examination, or of being sad. In the nonclinical sense of "to diagnose," philosophical counselors do diagnose: They identify through philosophical means the cause or nature of the client's problem. Such a philosophical verification is in a sense a diagnosis, but is very different from a medical diagnosis and can in particular cases even lead to the "depsychoanalysis" and "dediagnosis" of clients. Depsychoanalysis and dediagnosis are useful for clients who think about themselves in psychoanalytical or diagnostic terms only. These procedures help such clients understand from where they got their self-concept. The counselor can then discuss with them whether that particular self-concept is necessarily true or whether they might wish to choose (or discover) another self-concept. The counselee thus becomes engaged in philosophical self-diagnosis or self-verification.[24]

Another example shows how dialogue, as depsychoanalysis, can take surprising turns. A woman in her mid-thirties, unmarried, and seeming to be desperately looking for a partner, came to see me. She had been hospitalized during a psychotic breakdown ten years earlier. She said that she knew what her psychiatrists wanted to hear from her, and because of that, she did not tell them what was bothering her. However, she knew she could tell me anything since she understood that I was not interested in hearing any particular story. I had told her that I consider the Oedipus complex to be merely a myth, and that as a philosophical practitioner, I have no preconceived ideas about her psychological or mental reality. This made it possible for her to tell me about what she herself had perceived as an Oedipal bond to her father, which she had wanted to keep secret from her therapists. Since I showed a neutral attitude toward her explanation, she did not experience telling me her story as exposing a secret of immense importance.

I did indeed question whether her father's erotic interest in her as she perceived it was really so personal and whether it actually had the influence on the rest of her life that she thought it had. Was it not possible that her father just liked women in general and not her in particular? This seemed to me not unlikely since she said that he often had left her and her mother at home and went alone to bars and discotheques. In spite of my skeptical view of her "Oedipal" situation, my client found it extremely helpful just to talk about her childhood relationship with her parents, and in particular about her father. My attempt to depsychoanalyze her "Oedipal" relation by questioning and criticizing Oedipal theories seemed to have a liberating effect on her. She did not criticize my attitude and neither wanted to discuss the right or wrong of Oedipal theories; she just wanted to get rid of the fear of having this idea by talking about her father.

Whether what happened subsequently was due to her new openness about her childhood relationships or to some other fortunate situation is difficult to say. What can be said is that after almost a year and a half of telling me stories about her father, she met a suitable partner whom she later married.

It seems to me that counselors who use Gerd B. Achenbach's nonclinical philosophy approach and avoid the generally accepted clinical diagnoses must nevertheless distinguish between the clients they can help and those they cannot. As a criterion for discerning which persons I can help, I consider the client's ability to engage in dialogue. Some existential analysts, such as Ludwig Binswanger, find the ability to engage in dialogue an indication of well-being. Philosophical counselors cannot help persons suffering from severe functional cognitive defects or those afflicted with serious communicative disorders—those who cannot understand a common-sense explanation, cannot respond to simple questions, or fail to express themselves at all through ordinary language. For such people, philosophical counseling might only be helpful after a successful medical or psychotherapeutic intervention. Consider, for example, the elderly man who consulted me, repeating his complaints of restlessness and embedding these complaints in a long monologue about his past. If I asked him to explain something he had said or if I remarked on something he had said, it was if he could not hear me. Trying to make him aware of his talking only to and for himself consequently did not improve our dialogue. It was obvious that I could not help this client with philosophy and that a psychiatrist might have been the right primary or supplementary caregiver. On the other hand, empathetic listening can be a great help to those in distress.

Another criterion for determining whether philosophical counseling is to the advantage of a client is by verifying that the counseling relationship contains the following factors: a personal relationship of warmth and trust, reassurance and support, desensitization by sharing the problem or question, attainment of understanding and insight, and reinforcement of adaptive responses. Garfield and Bergin found that experienced counselors with different orientations appear to be equally effective in helping their clients. Therefore they concluded that factors common to various forms of therapy and counseling—the factors mentioned—may be more important in the counseling approach than the specific procedures used.[25] To exercise these common factors (which I explain as humane, common-sense behavior) is not only beneficial in therapy, but would be in any profession, including philosophical counseling.

It seems to me that many patients and many psychotherapists are playing games with one another. They are continually looking for new therapy games, and new therapy games, and again new therapy games. The therapy market is filled with countless new approaches. Philosophy as therapy, clinical philosophy, and philosophy combined with therapy all have been games on the therapy market for more than half a century. The antipsychiatrist Ronald D. Laing analyzed what he called "some" situation—possibly the therapy situation—as follows.

"They are playing a game. They are playing at not playing a game. If I show them I see they are, I shall break the rules and they will punish me. I must play their game, of not seeing I see the game."[26]

Philosophical counseling is different: In philosophical counseling therapy games can be named, confessed, talked through, and brought to an end. Many of my clients who had been in therapy wanted to talk through the experiences they had had with their therapists. For some, the games had been beneficial, for others not.

And what about philosophical counseling: Is it not a game as well? Or is it a game about other games? Isn't the philosophical counselor playing a game, albeit a nontherapy game, as well? If so, philosophical counselors would do well not to learn to say with Laing: "I must play their game, of not seeing I see the game." But whether or not philosophical counseling is interpreted as another game, for many people it has been a relief to be able to find something other than therapy to deal with their problems.

In Chapter 3 and 4, I discuss ideas taken from the works of Martin Buber, Jean-Paul Sartre, Michel Foucault, and Karl Jaspers that are important for philosophical practice. Since my approach is pragmatic—in the literal sense of the word—and eclectic, ideas of other philosophers as well appear throughout the description of my practice. However, the eclecticism I propose denotes conceptions that do not contradict each other. As Michael Zdrenka well observed, the way I practice philosophy is quite similar to that of Gerd B. Achenbach.[27] It would seem regrettable to me if philosophical counselors lose consistency in their approach and combine the most different and contradictory methods in their sessions. Although one may defend a relativistic eclecticism in theory, the practice of it seems to me a confusing experience for the counselees as well as for the philosophical counselor. And, though a thorough grounding in theory is of paramount importance for the expertise of philosophical practitioners themselves (though not that important to the counselee), an elementary knowledge of philosophical counseling, as found in this book, would seem to me to be beneficial to the counselees.

Most people under the influence of pathology metaphors can only perceive philosophical practitioners as therapists, rather than counselors striving to integrate philosophy into all areas of life. Such integration occurs when a person has mastered philosophical skills and attitudes and knows how to use these in daily life. It is likely that such a person–philosopher (cf. Plato's king–philosopher) will handle problems at work, family life, politics, business, and the like with their philosophical equipment. Integrating philosophy in all areas of life could be done in philosophy classes in elementary schools, high schools, and at colleges. At present such elementary philosophical training is lacking worldwide. However, the public teaching of philosophy would not be sufficient for the integration of philosophy in solving very complex or delicate personal problems. A face-to-face relationship with a philosopher as a philosophical guide seems needed in situations that are confusing or painful or so complex that a person alone cannot understand the situation.

Philosophical practice or counseling can be adapted for people under psychiatric or medical care by taking into account not only their medical, religious, artistic, or sexual needs, but also their philosophical needs. Philosophical counselors working in cooperation with health practitioners—but without adopting the therapist's tools and methods—might prefer to be called philosophical "therapists" instead of just philosophical therapists. Since it is likely that the implication of the quotation marks will sooner or later be lost, and would not be present in verbal communication, it might be best to adhere to the initial terminology for philosophy practice. In that way, accredited therapists using philosophy in their treatments will also have a name of their own: philosophical therapists.

"What's in a name?" some may ask. However, to keep its own value, philosophical counseling would have to remain a nonclinical approach even when used within a clinical framework such as a mental hospital. Cognitive therapy, existential therapy, clinical philosophical–psychology, rational psychotherapy, and other hybrids of therapy and philosophy each have their own value, but it is different from that of the nonclinical philosophical approach. As I see it, clinical psychologists with a supplementary degree in philosophy who use philosophy along with their psychotherapeutic treatment should not be called philosophical practitioners or counselors. Psychotherapists such as Cyril Vink and Will Heutz in the Netherlands,[28] who do not separate philosophy practice from their psychotherapeutic discourse, remain within the professional framework advocated by most existentialist and humanist psychotherapists: They may use specific concepts from Achenbach, while other psychotherapists use Plato's, Nietzsche's, Heidegger's, or Sartre's ideas in therapy. For psychotherapists to become philosophers or philosophical practitioners, they need not only a degree in philosophy but a *philosophical conversion*, such as of the kind that Jaspers and Michel Foucault underwent. (For more details on these conversions see Chapter 4.)

The use of philosophy in psychotherapy and medicine in general is not new. The use of philosophy in the treatment of patients in hospitals has been described by Oliver Sacks.[29] Sacks considers philosophical thought a substantial aid in treating patients. He believes that inquiries such as "How are you?" and "How are things?" are metaphysical expressions and that his patients' search for their lost health is a metaphysical search for the elixir of life. Leibniz's "caritas sapientis," the combination of wisdom and care, is, according to Sacks, the most important factor in his medical treatment. The idea of combining medical care with philosophy goes back to ancient times. Hippocrates, in the fifth century B.C., advocated combining philosophy with medicine.

Outside the walls of medical institutions, however, philosophical practice leading to personal improvement is at its best when it is not regarded as "therapy." Formal therapy is not necessarily the only way to produce "therapeutic" results; therefore, calling philosophical practice philosophical therapy would needlessly limit the open and neutral position of philosophical practitioners.

Some do not understand that an adjective has not precisely the same meaning as a noun. Accordingly, they understand the adjective "therapeutic" to be the same as the noun "therapy"; they argue "something is therapeutic because it is therapy." If, however, one compares other adjectives and nouns, it is clear that they do not necessarily have the same meaning. For example, consider "comedy" and "comic." Although these words derive from the same Greek root meaning "to revel," comedy is a dramatic or literary composition of a humorous character. Comic is not the same as comedy: One may encounter comic situations or ideas—that is humorous, laughable situations or ideas—anywhere, not only on the stage or in a book. Likewise, therapy is not just something that can be found anywhere, but a scientifically discovered or designed method of curing, while the therapeutic can occur spontaneously to induce well-being. Therapeutic changes in people can occur during a vacation in a distant country.

Take the following example. Some travelers visit an ancient city. They enjoy one another's company, and the explanations of the licensed tour guide are interesting and informative. The travelers feel much better than before they went on vacation. Have they undergone therapy? Even when a medical practitioner advises a patient to go on a vacation (except for a vacation in a health resort or sanatorium), this would not be considered therapy, since therapy is not a vacation; so, what is therapeutic is not necessarily therapy. People who still want to maintain that part of Spinelli's definition of therapy, that claims therapy is when there is the guidance of a therapist or clinician, could argue that when a physician advises a patient to go on a vacation, the vacation then automatically becomes therapy.

I envision the place for the philosophical counselor as an open no-man's land or neutral area between philosophy, psychology, medicine, and other disciplines. This open domain could become a closed territory belonging to "philosophy modified by psychology" or "medicine with a philosophical objective," if the philosophical counselor gave up the position of neutrality. But giving up this neutrality would mean forsaking those people who have "seen it all" in the therapy realm and need other options, leaving them and others who are disappointed with or dislike therapy in a conceptual desert without any guidance. Moreover, as I showed before, the questions people bring to physicians and psychotherapists are often meta-clinical matters; treating them as clinical matters and not as philosophical issues makes it difficult to understand these problems as they are.

Though philosophical practice outwardly shares several aspects with the various psychotherapies, philosophical practice is the polar opposite of therapy. In its refusal to be therapy, philosophical practice in theory seems to have the approval of scholar and former psychoanalyst Jeffrey Masson. Masson sees therapy in itself as harmful: "Psychotherapy cannot be reformed in its parts, because the activity, by its nature, is harmful. Recognizing the lies, the flaws, the harm, the potential for harm, the imbalance in power, the arrogance, the condescension, the pretensions may be the first step in the eventual abolition of psychotherapy that I believe is, one day in the future, inevitable and desirable."[30] Masson's acceptance of conversations with friends—not therapists—is more than just a trivial choice of somebody to talk to. Chad Varah's extensive experience in suicide prevention teaches that friendship is more effective in this area than therapy or counseling.[31] As I show in Chapters 3 and 9, I find the subjects of friendship and suicide prevention relevant for philosophers to investigate and practice.

Whereas the words "philo" and "sophia" may remind the philosopher and a few others of friendship and love in relation to wisdom, nonphilosophers often believe that philosophers can only argue for cold, detached, intellectual relationships and a laissez faire attitude regarding suicide. Indeed, David Hume considered suicide acceptable, though quite a few other philosophers thought the opposite. The role of suicide prevention for philosophical counselors is in helping people to make a rational reassessment of the reasons for and the ethical meaning of such a radical deed: not prohibiting suicide, but requesting of those who contemplate suicide to postpone it and think it over with a philosopher. There are also people who are looking for reasons not to commit suicide. An example is the woman who called my first-aid philosophy line and asked me if I could help her find reasons not to commit suicide. Because of financial difficulties it seemed to her that life was not worth living. But how could she know if this was really true?

Emile Durkheim, in his application of the sociological method to suicide, showed that very few poor people commit suicide, though there is "a correlation between the fluctuations of economy and suicide: Suicide rates rise quite steeply in times of economic depression."[32] It is not so much the material circumstances as much as it is the *change* itself for the worse, or sometimes even for the better, that triggers a suicidal tendency in a person. This sociological insight into suicide seemed relevant to me in the situation of the woman who called me, since under different circumstances life was meaningful to her. Her question seemed to me not so much "When does life stop being worth living?" as how to bear her difficult economic situation and what to do about it. She agreed to my changing her initial question, which I was unable to answer, into an inquiry as to how she could cope with her present situation. She had lost her job, and as a middle-aged woman, she had experienced great difficultly in finding another one. I argued that even though it was difficult, it was not impossible. If she kept on looking for a job she would probably find one eventually and thus improve her difficult circumstances. The argument she was looking for against suicide were words of encouragement.

Therapy often seems inappropriate in cases where so-called "patients" are generally in good mental health, such as the desperate woman just described. Living without the correct understanding—or wisdom, if you will—can lead to a painful state of body and mind. If this is the case, why should we continue to interpret suffering as the symptom of an illness, complex, or infirmity? Since there is no scientific guide to the subjective state of human beings and their inner world, it is impossible to determine conclusively whether people are psychically invalid or handicapped.

Nevertheless, philosophical counselors cannot assume that suffering is primarily caused by a lack of wisdom. Looking for wisdom and suitable understandings can eliminate pain or make it easier to bear. A nonjudgmental openness and the practice of wisdom by testing it in lived reality can help people in distress to find appropriate solutions.

Paul Goodman, a social philosopher and unlicensed Gestalt therapist, considered the "erotic forces of nature" to be the cure for those problems that people usually visit a psychotherapist for. Accordingly, he advised therapists "to stand out of the way" by not doing therapy and to allow "nature to heal."[33] Philosophical practitioners can follow this dictum by not attempting to "heal" but rather by letting the clients define and find their own health through the discussion of questions such as "What is health?," "What is illness?," and "What is an 'Oedipal' situation?"

Chapters 5 through 12 can be compared to what are called case studies in psychology. These and the shorter illuminating stories in other chapters, are selected from notes taken of conversations with the hundreds of counselees I have spoken with since 1989. What distinguishes these stories from most case studies is that they are descriptive narratives. They are subjective and imaginative records of events that occurred in my philosophical practice. Fictional attributes were added to ensure that personal circumstances remain confidential. These fictional attributes would obscure a truly scientific study, since data need to be objective. However, philosophical truth, and more specifically moral truth, can also be expressed through literary means, such as the fables of Aesop or Jean de la Fontaine. Fontaine, by choosing animals as characters for his satire, not only added humor to the situations he wanted to scorn but was also then able to describe them more effectively. I do not employ such drastic character transformations in my philosophical biographical narratives. The contents, insights, and ideas of the conversations I present reflect genuine experiences and philosophical truth; the details of personal histories and social surroundings are changed by eliminating or adding to the story. The moral of the story, however, remains the same.

The idea of a philosophical portrait as a philosophical biographical narrative falls within the ancient and modern tradition of confessional philosophy, which includes the philosophical confessions of Heraclitus, Marcus Aurelius, Augustine, Vico, Rousseau, and Barthes. The idea of creating a philosophical portrait has its paradigm in Rousseau's self-portrait, as found in the *Confessions of Jean Jacques Rousseau*. However, Donald Verene finds that the Platonic dialogues already present a philosophical portrait: Plato's writings are not so much a theory as "the figure of Socrates as the figure of philosophy itself." What is known of Socrates through Plato is "biographical 'autobiographical.'"[34] Today, any person making his or her philosophical self-portrait needs the courage to defy the commonly believed psychological cliches about self. Robert Nozick recently had the courage to create a philosophical self-portrait, about which he wrote, "Philosophical meditations about life present a portrait, not a theory. This portrait may be made up of theoretical pieces—questions, distinctions, explanations. . . . Yet the concatenation of these bits of theory constitutes a portrait nonetheless. . . . To live an examined life is to make a self-portrait."[35] Nozick's self-portrait is relevant for the philosophical counselor in that it sets forth a philosophical paradigm for self-analysis. In comparison with Nozick's "bits of theory [that] constitutes a portrait," my practice-oriented portraits do constitute bits of philosophical-counseling theory as well. Nozick's philosophical-autobiographical self-analysis has been succeeded with those of Stanley Cavell and Richard Shusterman.[36]

Besides describing the new phenomenon of philosophical practice, I invite my readers to widen their philosophical perspective to achieve a philosophical way of life. With this aim, this book can be considered an instance of philosophical practice. It is an invitation to begin or deepen an already begun philosophical dialogue with yourself or with a philosopher. It is not an invitation to develop, grow, change, or be cured. These are not the goals of philosophical counseling. It is only an invitation to philosophize, and this for its own sake; nevertheless, since philosophizing involves not only theoretical but also practical issues, changes in persons' lives resulting from philosophizing are welcome—in the same way that I would welcome a person who came along with a guest I had invited.

Elizabeth Wright analyzed structural psychoanalysis as "psyche as text," and poststructural psychoanalysis as "text as psyche."[37] Analogously, I call this book on philosophical practice and counseling "the questioning of psyche through text" and "text as a quest into psyche." By presenting this book as practice, I intend to provoke a wide range of questions within the reader about him or herself and about the search for general human knowledge and understanding. And in distinction from some postmodern assumptions that reading and/or writing a book is a psychoanalytic event, I do not assume that reading this text is philosophical counseling, since the text is a monologue, in spite of the inclusions of dialogue. Nevertheless, philosophical self-help and self-practice can often be as effective as a dialogue with a philosophy counselor. Philosophy as self-practice can also be seen as a way of preparing oneself for a philosophical dialogue with a philosopher and with others, but most of all it should be viewed as a way to prepare oneself for a philosophical lifestyle.

NOTES

1. Edmund L. Erde, *Philosophy and Psycholinguistics* (The Hague: Mouton, 1973), 59.

2. Stanley Cavell, *In Quest of the Ordinary* (Chicago: University of Chicago Press, 1988), 73–74.

3. Simon Blackburn, *The Oxford Dictionary of Philosophy* (Oxford: Oxford University Press, 1994), 286.

4. For a lucid description of the content and use of philosophy, see Robert Audi, *Philosophy: A Brief Guide for Undergraduates* (Newark: University of Delaware, 1981).

5. Nicholas Lobkowicz, *Theory and Practice: History of a Concept from Aristotle to Marx* (Notre Dame, Ind.: Notre Dame University Press, 1967); Richard J. Bernstein, *Praxis and Action* (Philadelphia: Duckworth, 1972); Richard Shusterman, *Practicing Philosophy: Pragmatism and the Philosophical Life* (New York: Routledge, 1997).

6. Thomas S. Szasz, *The Myth of Mental Illness* (New York: Harper & Row, 1974); Susan Sontag, *Illness as Metaphor* (New York: Farrar, Straus,

and Giroux, 1978); Susan Sontag, *AIDS and Its Metaphors* (New York: Farrar, Straus, and Giroux, 1988); David Cooper, "Metaphors We Live By," in *Philosophy and Practice*, ed. A. P. Griffiths (Cambridge: Cambridge University Press, 1985), 43–58; Ivan Illich, *Medical Nemesis* (New York: Random House, 1976).

7. Mordechai Rotenberg, *Damnation and Deviance* (New York: Free Press, 1978), 90.

8. David Rieff, "Victims, All?" in *The Best of American Essays 1992*, ed. S. Sontag and R. Atwan (New York: Ticknor & Fields, 1992), 254.

9. Victor E. Frankl, *Man's Search for Meaning* (Boston: Beacon, 1962), 117–118.

10. Irwin Edman, "Introduction," in *The Consolation of Philosophy*, ed. I. Edman (New York: The Modern Library, 1943), vii.

11. Ernesto Spinelli, *Demystifying Therapy* (London: Constable, 1994), 44.

12. Emmy van Deurzen-Smith, *Existential Counselling in Practice* (London: Sage, 1994), 21.

13. Emmy van Deurzen-Smith, *Everyday Mysteries: Existential Dimensions of Psychotherapy* (New York: Routledge, 1997), 170–173.

14. Judy Tame, "Psychotherapy: Philosophy, Not Medicine," in *Psychological Notes*, vol. 8 (London: Libertarian Alliance, 1992): 1, 6.

15. Ibid.

16. Thomas Szasz, *Insanity: The Idea and Its Consequences* (New York: John Wiley & Sons, 1987), 9–26.

17. Howard H. Goldman, *Review of General Psychiatry* (Los Altos, Calif.: Lange Medical Publications, 1984), 656.

18. A. N. Wear and D. Brahams, "To Treat or Not to Treat: The Legal, Ethical and Therapeutic Implications of Treatment Refusal," *Journal of Medical Ethics* 17 (1991): 131, 135.

19. William M. Walton, "The Philosopher and the Psychiatrist," *Philosophy and Psychiatry: Proceedings of the American Catholic Philosophical Association* 35 (1961): 11.

20. Bertrand Russell, *The Problems of Philosophy* (Oxford: Oxford University Press, 1977), 160.

21. Paul Tillich, *The Courage To Be* (New Haven, Conn.: Yale University Press, 1952).

22. Anthony Quinton, "Madness," in *Philosophy and Practice*, ed. A. P. Griffiths, 17–41; Szasz, *Myth of Mental Illness*; and Michel Foucault, David Cooper, Jean-Pierre Faye, Marie-Odile Faye, and Marine Zecca, "Confinement, Psychiatry, Prison," in Michel Foucault, *Politics, Philosophy, Culture*, ed. L. D. Kritzman (New York: Routledge, 1990), 178–210.

23. *The New Webster Comprehensive Dictionary of the English Language*, s.v. "diagnose."

24. See Shlomit C. Schuster, "On Philosophical Self-Diagnosis and Self-Help: A Clarification of the Non-Clinical Practice of Philosophical Counseling," *The International Journal of Applied Philosophy* 12, 1 (1998): 37–50.

25. Rita L. Atkinson and Ernest R. Hilgard, *Introduction to Psychology* (New York: Harcourt, 1983), 514.

26. Ronald D. Laing, *Knots* (New York: Vintage, 1972), 1.

27. Michael Zdrenka, "Eine Philosophische Praxis in Israel," *Information Philosophie* 2 (1997): 80–85.

28. Els Backx, "Filosofie schrikt veel mensen af," *Filosofische Praktijk* 9 (1992): 12–17; and Mieke Julien, "Veel mensen voelen zich pas gelukkig als ze nuttig zijn," *Filosofische Praktijk* 10 (1992): 6–11.

29. Oliver Sacks, *Awakenings* (Harmondsworth, England: Penguin, 1976).

30. Jeffrey M. Masson, *Against Therapy* (New York: Atheneum, 1988), 254.

31. Mary Bruce, "Befriending the Lonely," in *The Samaritans*, ed. C. Varah (London: Constable, 1965), 143–148.

32. Anthony Giddens, *Durkheim* (London: Fontana, 1987), 45; Emile Durkheim, *Suicide: A Study in Sociology* (London: Routledge and Kegan Paul, 1952).

33. Paul Goodman, *Nature Heals*, ed. Taylor Stoehr (New York: Free Life Editions, 1977).

34. Donald P. Verene, *The New Art of Autobiography* (Oxford: Clarendon, 1991), 79–80.

35. Robert Nozick, *The Examined Life: Philosophical Meditations* (New York: Simon and Schuster, 1989), 12.

36. Stanley Cavell, *A Pitch of Philosophy: Autobiographical Exercises* (Cambridge: Harvard University Press, 1994); Shusterman, *Practicing Philosophy*, 179–195.

37. Elizabeth Wright, *Psychoanalytic Criticism: Theory in Practice* (New York: Routledge, 1984), 107–156.

CHAPTER 2

Classic Instances of Philosophy as Practice

> We can determine the nature of philosophy only by actually experiencing it. Philosophy then becomes the realization of the living idea and the reflection upon this idea, action and discourse on action in one.
>
> Karl Jaspers, *Way to Wisdom*

Most philosophers through the ages did not philosophize purely for the pleasure of it. For people of ancient times philosophy was a necessity. Today, improving technology seems to be what people need most. Our technological age has smoothed the rough edges of physical existence, but it does not offer people solace in their search to understand themselves or their lives. Moreover, traditional philosophical areas of study, which emphasized reflection on oneself and one's way of life for the purpose of gaining philosophical self-knowledge, have been technologized; for example, research into the psyche has led to psychology, a discipline with scientific status.

The contribution of the human sciences such as psychology and sociology to the understanding of the intangible side of human life is to be appreciated and respected. Nonetheless, these "sciences," because of their scientific technological approach, are limited in their understanding of people. Could a philosophical approach—that is, philosophical psychology or philosophical anthropology—free the human sciences from their methodological constraints and thus

permit a more competent comprehension of people? Or do human beings need—now perhaps more than in other ages—pure philosophy in
their quest for understanding? If people are philosophical creatures,
as Friedrich Nietzsche understood them to be, then philosophers have
a concrete task of serving persons and the community—that is, facilitating the efforts of people to become who they are.

A philosopher may talk each session just with one individual, yet
the practice of philosophy will reach beyond the individual range;
it will have a wider, communal effect, and it will change the world.
Or a philosopher may not only work with individuals; groups may
ask for philosophical help in the field of social philosophy, such as
social justice, ethics in public matters, a discussion on a certain
subject, or a philosophical analysis of a group process.

Just as there are now psychiatrists, psychologists, and physicians
who recognize people's need for philosophy, so there are philosophers who recognize that they can use philosophy practice to help
themselves and others question, answer, or solve, or let be the existential, ethical, ontological, or metaphysical aspects of the problems life poses. This can be done on a purely theoretical level as
well as through personal interaction with others. Pierre Hadot in
Philosophy as a Way of Life and Richard Shusterman in *Practicing
Philosophy* clearly demonstrated that at the end of the twentieth
century, theorizing on philosophy as a way of life is alive and well.[1]
My description of philosophy practice accentuates how philosophers
can make philosophy available to a large public instead of only to
themselves, that is, to scholars and fellow philosophers.

When people's nutritional needs are not met, undernutrition or
starvation is the ultimate result. A deficiency in practical philosophical reasoning might have even greater catastrophic effects: If
one imagines a multitude of competent and healthy persons not
living rationally, morally, or philosophically in other senses, a lack
of vitamins, minerals, proteins, or carbohydrates would be preferable to the human hell these philosophy-starved individuals very
likely would be in.

HISTORICAL SKETCH

Socrates's philosophical examination of life was intended to make
human beings virtuous, thus directly influencing human action.
Though it is often thought that the practice of philosophy started
with Socrates telling the citizens of Athens that "the unexamined
life is not worth living," long before Socrates, the Pythagoreans had
a philosophy of life, or a praxis, that united them into a philosophical community.

We do not know when people began to perceive that wisdom—the original goal of philosophy—has a special bearing on life. In the Vedanta, one of the earliest extant scriptures, we find, as in later religious and mythological texts, the idea that wisdom and knowledge lead to liberation, bliss, goodness, and peace. In the eighth chapter of the Bhagavad-Gita, for example, Arjuna asks for philosophical guidance when he says, "What is the self? What are fruitive activities? What is this material manifestation?"

Johan Huizinga observed that, for the ancients, knowing was magical power; any knowing was directly related to the cosmic order itself. Riddle-solving competitions were one method of obtaining knowledge. It was accounted to be the highest wisdom to put forth a riddle which nobody could answer. To question was the sign of wisdom par excellence.[2] The great sage lead others to know the limit of their knowledge; accordingly, wisdom had a higher status than knowledge.

The history of Western philosophy is largely the development of the idea that contemplation and the intellectual search for wisdom and knowledge both improve human existence. This improvement may be within a personal or a communal level of perception; from a personal ethics to a social ethics; or from a personal metaphysics to a metaphysical understanding of the cosmos. Martha Nussbaum observes that the Hellenistic thinkers "insist that human flourishing cannot be achieved unless desire and thought, as they are usually constructed within society, are considerably reformed."[3]

Until the end of the classical period, reason and piety were the guiding ideals in life; these were the wise and healing principles lived and taught by the ancient philosophers. However, in that logos-centered world there were also dissident schools. Exceptions to the reason-oriented tradition were the Cynics, who taught that there was no need for reason because the wisdom that leads to virtue—the "natural" life—depends on an insight that makes the sage judge rightly what best serves for future happiness: self-sufficiency and asceticism. Sextus Empericus and other Skeptics realized that reason has its limits, but they still considered reason useful in life. The Skeptics sought mental tranquility by attempting to expel all inconsistencies from rational judgment. Unable to arrive at the ultimate rational truth, they withheld judgment. The Skeptics discovered that by suspending judgment, they arrived inadvertently at the goal of their unsuccessful rational search: clearness of mind and tranquility of soul and body.

The Stoics were perceived by some thinkers as "philosophical practitioners" par excellence. Voltaire, for instance, considered Cicero an exemplary advisor. Cicero certainly conveys the essential ethos of the classic praxis of philosophy in statements such as "every part of philosophy is fruitful and rewarding," or "if we clearly understand these [our duties], we have mastered the rules for leading a good and consistent life."[4]

Philo of Alexandria inaugurated the philosophy of religion, which was the dominant type of philosophy throughout the Middle Ages. Philo's synthesis of religion and reason combined the classic image of the praxis-oriented philosopher with that of the saint. In the scholastic tradition, wisdom obtained through dialogue and rational analysis was replaced by wisdom obtained through divine revelation, to which philosophy became the lowly handmaiden.

The Renaissance *libido sciendi* (passion for science) was not satisfied by the scholastic art of religious disputation, searching instead for an encounter of mind and world, as in ancient philosophy. Renaissance sages such as Desiderius Erasmus and Michel Montaigne revived ancient ideals of wisdom. In *The Praise of Folly*, Erasmus juxtaposed the concepts of wisdom and folly. His heroine Stultitia compares "Foolosophers" wisdom—a small candlelight-like wisdom, sufficient only for hermits living in the woods—with practical common-sense, which Stultitia names the great wisdom of Everyman. Though Everyman is a fool by nature, his wisdom consists in knowing how to make life pleasant through wit and foolishness. Montaigne's *Essays* have much in common with Stoic attempts to put life into harmony with universal reason.

The Renaissance humanists' faith in human intellectual powers led curiously enough to a Faustian vision in which people can (and did!) lose their humanity through applications of thought and science in a grandiose conquest of nature and nations. About fifty years after the gas chambers of Auschwitz, Mauthausen, and Treblinka, as well as the atomic horrors of Hiroshima and Nagasaki, can one possibly assume that intelligent human beings will never again employ their intellectual powers for wholesale destruction? Human intelligence without a morality that keeps destructive forces in control may ultimately lead to total destruction. With the fulfillment of the Faustian vision in the twentieth century, it became commonplace to mock claims of wisdom and understanding. Though this mocking attitude is understandable after all the moral disgraces and political disasters that people in this and other centuries have brought upon humanity, moral deficiency has not yet been proven as the dominant factor in human nature. Though cynics, pessimists, and skeptics may doubt it, persons might yet develop a higher morality and philosophy of life in the centuries to come.

From the seventeenth to the twentieth centuries there have been philosophers who lived philosophical lives and who elaborated on practical reasoning in their writings. In previous times it was mainly the aristocracy, the clergy, and the bourgeoisie who were interested in philosophy. With the beginning of the industrial and technological revolution, people became less interested in philosophy and its realization in daily life. This occurred to such an extent that Marx, for example, concluded that philosophers only interpret the world in various ways but have not perfected philosophy by developing a praxis grounded in philosophical theory—and a theory based on concepts developed through an encounter with life.[5]

Poverty of praxis appears to be the state of existence for modern philosophers, except for a few singular thinkers. The leading figures of modern philosophy, such as Kierkegaard, Nietzsche, Marx, James, Dewey, Russell, Wittgenstein, Sartre, and Foucault, all accentuated facets of philosophy as praxis or action, but this was not enough to make most of their followers into philosophical practitioners. Even their philosophical lives were not an adequate appeal to most of their students to become philosophers in daily life.

My sketch of historical philosophical practice focuses on presenting philosophy as it points toward action or practice. I do not consider the entire history of philosophy as a practice; rather, I follow the historical division between the concepts of theoretical and practical philosophy.[6] This in contradistinction to David W. Hamlyn's account in *Being a Philosopher*, in which philosophy in general is considered as a practice.[7] Hamlyn's history of philosophical practice is concerned with the social context in which philosophy developed and how it became the academic profession it is today. What is central to his account is not the direct bearing of philosophical thought on action, but the way in which philosophy has been discussed and examined: through arguments, dialogues, philosophical schools, publications in philosophical journals and books, teaching, associations of philosophers, and universities. Hamlyn's description of the institutionalization of philosophy—that is, its professionalization in the academic setting—is presented as an answer to the fashionable postmodern negation of the meaning of philosophy. Some late twentieth-century philosophers see philosophy as a discipline in crisis; the end of philosophy and its institutions has been announced and philosophers themselves aim at destroying philosophy.

Hamlyn's historical analysis of the practice of philosophy may help philosophers today rediscover some of the value of philosophy, although the final concept of *Being a Philosopher* confines philosophy practice to the following paradox: It is not desirable to replicate the classical ideals of the Renaissance and Enlightenment (all these seem to lack the essential academic professionalism!). Nevertheless, "the value of philosophy in the end lies in itself and what it does for human thought and life."[8]

The aim of philosophical practice and counseling is making philosophy valuable and relevant for concrete situations and questions of individuals or groups. Although I disagree with Hamlyn's pessimistic view concerning philosophical life outside the ivory tower, his analysis contributes to and shares the aim of philosophical counseling in that it provides a theoretical reevaluation of philosophy as a practice for the present and future age.

Albert W. Levi described the practice of philosophy as a social expression. His argument is not opposed to Karl Jaspers' assumption that philosophy has "a permanence of meaning outside of time," but he has a definite sympathy with the argument of contextualism, which "implies that the very nature of a philosophy as such is that to discuss it apart from its author and its age is to falsify and misunderstand it." Levi observed that philosophers following Quine, Carnap, or Wittgenstein usually ignored the historical rich sources of philosophy "as philosophy" and "placed [the history of philosophy] in the hands of historians—not as an act of violence, but as a permitted appropriation in the face of philosophic indifference and unconcern." What is valuable in Levi's research for the philosophical counselor is his demonstration that even though classic philosophies are responses to the needs of their particular times, they are still eternally relevant. He finds that philosophers like Plato, Descartes, Locke, Hume, and Kant "remain active philosophically because, although no one today can possibly be a complete Platonist, or Cartesian, or Kantian, yet the stages which they register in the philosophical tradition are critical, and their resonance remains such that the process of their adaptation and assimilation is endless."[9]

I illustrate Levi's claim with an example from my practice, which shows the relevance of the ideology of the seventeenth-century philosopher Spinoza for a particular Israeli man today. Although my client was not brought up in an Orthodox Jewish home, as he became older he sought a philosophical justification for being Jewish and secular. He had emigrated from the United States and had become an Israeli, but secular Zionism did not fit his metaphysical attitude to life. He found Spinoza's example of rejecting orthodox religion as superstition admirable, and a desirable example for some of the Orthodox Israelis. To his regret he did not have friends he could share his Spinozistic interests with: his friends regarded his philosophical interest as "weird." Talking about Spinoza in the setting of philosophical counseling sessions gave him self-confidence and helped him to deepen his secular Spinozistic philosophy of life.

For the last two decades, prominent philosophers have been writing about what had before become taboo subjects in philosophy departments, such as the meaning of suffering and death or the ethics of abortion, sex, lying, or madness.[10] Analytical philosophy sees the verification of concepts as a matter of "form" and of language, and not a matter of content. Accordingly, philosophy is only useful or "therapeutic" in that it clears up misconceptions and misunderstandings caused by language abuse.

The involvement of philosophers in public debates about nuclear weapons, bioengineering, and euthanasia indicates that at the present time there is now a movement from language-centered philosophy to a philosophy of public concern and care for people. There is much less contempt for philosophy that is not "purely" academic (i.e., theoretical). However, this new shift of some philosophy departments and other academic circles with the aim to apply philosophy to actual life problems—the so-called "applied philosophy"—still often remains a merely academical and theoretical exercise. The essential difference between applied philosophy and philosophical practice is that in the former, a philosopher applies philosophical theories to problematic situations, while in the latter the counselee does the philosophizing—with help from the philosopher—about the problematic circumstance or question.

Applied philosophy as an "ivory-tower" discipline judges issues, while philosophical counseling as a "grassroots" movement helps people think for themselves. Instead of offering a solution for an ethical dilemma, philosophical practitioners evoke educational processes in their clients. Such processes can lead to a solution of the current problem; they can also bring about changes in how one lives.

Although some applied philosophers only try to clarify and not resolve issues, it is nevertheless clear that the philosopher is the authority in the clarification. At present most books on applied philosophy are evidence of the preeminence of monologue over dialogue. I find the difference between applied philosophy and philosophy practice to be within the realm of tone and accent. Philosophical counseling is personal in tone. In applied philosophy, a philosopher clarifies a problem in a theoretical, objective context. The philosophical counselor, however, practices philosophy based on his or her experience with the question and discusses the problem with empathy. Praxis demands, as does psychoanalysis, a personal experience of the professed knowledge. As for accent, philosophical counseling accentuates practicing philosophy through dialogue—not through a written, academic dialogue, but through an actual conversation with an actual person. The counselor tries to evoke the hidden

philosopher within the counselee to clarify issues; the intention of
the dialogue is not so much in obtaining the results of this clarification, but in practicing philosophy.

   Philosophical counseling is a very promising alternative in those
areas where applied ethics has failed, such as bioethics, environ-
mental ethics, and legal and business ethics. Current criticism about
the devastating gap between the theoretical and the practical sides
of applied ethics has already generated alternatives: practical ethics (not to be equated with applied ethics); integrative ethics; and
narrative-found ethics.[11]

   It is possible to see the emergence of Gerd B. Achenbach's philosophical practice in the 1980s as the coming of a new Renaissance
and a return to the ancient ideal of wisdom, in the sense that philosophy is "lived" and philosophical living becomes a standard for
all. As modern people are different from their ancestors, philosophical practice also differs from former conceptions of wisdom and ways
of life. In the following section I describe philosophy practice by
showing how it has developed over the last few decades in Europe
and elsewhere. (It is regrettable that most of the important books
on philosophy practice I refer to still need to be translated into
English from the German, Dutch, or French.)

ACHENBACH'S OPEN-ENDED INQUIRY

   If it were possible to characterize Achenbach's philosophical innovation in one sentence, the following quotation from *Philosophische Praxis* might do the job: "The concrete image of philosophy is
the philosopher, and the philosopher, as philosophy institutional-
ized in one particular form, is the philosophical practice."[12]
Achenbach also describes philosophy practice negatively as not
therapy compared to the negative descriptions of God in theology.
Basically Achenbach finds any definitions of his practice problematic because such denotations would be too elementary. A definition of philosophy practice is definitely not the crux of Achenbach's
type of practice.[13] Though we may now have an abstract notion of
what philosophical practice is, we can only form a concrete image
of it through a detailed description of how it functions.

   Achenbach began his philosophical practice in 1981 by receiving
visitors for philosophical conversations in his consultation office.
There are many differences between these encounters and psychological or religious consultation practices. First, the practitioner is
an academically trained philosopher, philosophizing with a visitor
or counselee—not a patient—about questions or problems. Second,
the visitor's problematic situation is approached as a problem that

the practitioner can relate to through empathy. Empathy is needed for philosophizing itself; the knowledge of what Heidegger, for instance, thought about truth and death as theoretical knowledge is not sufficient. Such knowledge is not understood until the philosopher himself has experienced a need to question the meaning of truth and death. Achenbach maintains that philosophy is really understood only through its practice, through a personal empathic experience and intellectual cultivation of the subjects of thought.

Achenbach rejects the medical methodology used in most consultation practices, where the patient's problem are understood as symptoms, are diagnosed, and are treated in accordance with the diagnosis. Even though diagnostic methods are generally taught to therapists in training, quite a few therapists seem to be unaware of using these methods in their practice, and many even deny that diagnosis is part of their work. At least, this has been my experience with most of the therapists with whom I tried to discuss Achenbach's critique of diagnosis. There are indeed a few contemporary psychiatrists and psychologists who completely reject the medical model and its accompanying diagnostic treatment.[14] But in spite of this development, the medical model is still widely advocated and practiced.[15] The existence and wide usage of the prestigious *Diagnostic and Statistical Manual of Mental Disorders* (DSM-IV) seems to me enough evidence that people are diagnosed in accordance with medical psychotherapeutic and psychiatric practices. Those who want to verify the application of DSM terminology can do so by reading medical records written to describe patients' state of mental health. According to Achenbach, the "logic of all therapies" is that a symptom makes a person into a case to be treated. But this logic has created a growing resistance, expressed by people's search for other types of practice. Philosophical counseling is such an alternative practice: "It is not a new therapy, even more definitely, it is no therapy at all."[16]

What is significant in philosophy consultations is that instead of classifying the visitors' problematic situations as complexes or deviations, the consulting philosopher considers their situation unique, and for that reason not to be understood through generalizations or reduction. The philosophical practitioner accompanies his or her visitor in thinking through complex situations, which leads to the replacement of the problem by a philosophical understanding. After the visitor or counselee expresses his questions or troubles, the philosophical practitioner helps to rearrange the problematic issues in a philosophical framework.

What is meant by a philosophical framework? This I can best explain through an example from my practice. A client differed in opinions from her husband, and this led to intense conflicts and alienation. She could not understand his decisions, which seemed to her to be cold, rational decisions. She decided on issues mostly according to her feelings. The important decision that they had to make at that time concerned their son's schooling. What should they do? I placed this problem in a philosophical framework by questioning the rightness and the rationality of feelings, and from the opposite position I questioned the rightness of rationality. I asked questions such as "Is it always right to act on one's feelings?" or "Since foresight, or intuition might not be always 100 percent correct, isn't it better to decide about issues rationally?" which gave her a different perspective on the family conflict. She then realized that sometimes she did things that she knew were right, even though she didn't feel it that way, and even felt unhappy about certain unavoidable duties. This helped her to accept her spouse's choice of school for their son as right even though it did not agree with her feelings.

In a clinical framework therapists follow up their diagnosis with the appropriate treatment, while in Achenbach's approach the dialogue partners both try to understand the possible reasons or the nature of the problem. Where thinking is obscure it can be clarified. The suitability of solutions and the consequences of particular choices can be assessed. A manifold understanding can be created by the client explaining himself. Whether one or more interpretations or solutions (or even none) are found is not the essence, since it is the educational process of philosophizing that eventually may lead to the visitor's improvement. Even when one has found a satisfying understanding of an issue or solution to a problem, rethinking it may lead to a new, more satisfying perspective. Accordingly, philosophical activity should not come to a halt or be blocked by unequivocal conclusions or a final philosophy.

Instead of being inflexible discourses, the ways of philosophy have to be open to the new and unknown. In a dialogue with Peter Sloterdijk, Achenbach characterizes philosophical practice as opposing the positivist notion that it is necessary to have a method: "Philosophy does not use methods, it develops methods; it does not use theories, but develops theories."[17] Likewise, Sloterdijk views creativity in philosophical theorizing as an essential component of a vital philosophy. In the *Critique of Cynical Reason*, Sloterdijk analyzes the postmodern cultural climate.[18] He finds people cynical and paralyzed by a paranoid distrust, unable to break through to a real dialogue. Whereas ancient cynicism was liberating and revolutionary, modern cynicism is repressive because it does not care about morality. In dialogue with Achenbach, Sloterdijk adds that modern philosophy is sick with methods; only by doing away with all the predefined ways can health be found again. In contrast to philosophy as a methodology—the "way" from A to Z—philosophizing as wayfaring was already practiced by Socrates.

Socrates, as known through Xenophon and Plato, assisted the young and old in reflecting on their way of life. The examination of a person's past, present, and future created a self-consciousness in Socrates's discussion partners. Instead of "being carried away" by an "unknown" self, people became self-conscious and self-determining beings. Socrates guided the young in the art of living by giving meaning to the burdens of life. The attempt to understand oneself made the difficult life bearable. This coming into a new life or "coming to birth" through philosophizing is encouraged by Achenbach; outside the philosophy practice, coming to new understandings is often discouraged. Though it seems that the goal of most psychotherapy is likewise to create new understandings in patients, here the new understandings are usually the values implicit in the therapy, which the patient adopts without being aware of it.

In daily life, people are generally advised not to think about difficult or complex issues of life, or even better, not to think at all. Whenever people are discouraged from thinking profoundly about philosophical issues that confront them in life, philosophy becomes a suppressed and "fearsome" activity. Consequently, when people are troubled with existential questions such as the meaning of suffering, being, death, or evil, they go to see a psychotherapist. Generally, these mental-health workers attempt to help people by showing their search for meaning as symptoms or rationalizations and suggest they better start working on the emotional mess they are in. Another way out of the dangers of thinking is to enjoy oneself with the material aspects of life; to work; or to lose oneself in an addiction or a dogma; all this to forget these "depressing" subjects.

Rather than abort these authentic human questions, Achenbach, as a modern Socratic "midwife," encourages his visitors to "give birth" to philosophical insights into the problematic and complex issues of life. Socrates as a philosophical midwife and as philosophical practitioner are themes which constantly recur in the literature of philosophical practice. Ekkehard Martens considers that the three sources of information about Socrates—Xenophon, Plato, and Aristophanes' caricature of the sophist Socrates in *The Clouds*—present three different images of Socrates: the sophist, the moralist, and the skeptic. Only an amalgam of these three images is a good model for the philosophical practitioner today. Martens presents a list of ten characteristics of Socratic discourse that are relevant for Achenbach's type of philosophy practice.[19] Some of these are as follows:

- The axis of practice is not a theoretical but a practical knowledge.
- Both counselee and counselor are philosophical practitioners.
- The efficiency of the counselor exists in a profound insight and experience in the process of self-knowledge.
- This is a communal process, and during the counseling sessions, both the practitioners develop self-knowledge.

If the concrete instantiation of philosophy is the philosopher, philosophical practice instantiates hermeneutics. Sloterdijk, in dialogue with Achenbach, describes Socrates as practicing a "hermeneutics of burdensome [or complex] life."[20] For Achenbach, hermeneutics or interpretation is not the discovery of underlying truths (*Unterlegen*) behind communication. In philosophical practice, there is a dialectical process (*Auslegen*) in which the practitioner becomes united with the problem, not by imparting his own understanding of it, but by giving the visitor a fresh, self-explicatory impulse.

Accordingly, an unpredictable interpretation of the question comes into being: Philosophical practice is a hermeneutical happening. This is in contradistinction to most psychotherapists and "pretense" philosophers—these practitioners are accused by Achenbach "of creating additional realities, 'second' illusive realities"—who interpret questions, complaints, or problems exclusively in terms of a specific theory, such as Freud's sexual-dynamic interpretation of the psyche. I find the way Achenbach uses the notion of "pretense" philosophers to be a reminder of Socrates's request to the Athenians concerning his sons: "I would have you to trouble them, as I have troubled you, if they seem to care about riches, or anything, more then about virtue; or if they *pretend* to be something when they are really nothing."[21]

Achenbach's approach "is a skeptical and critical approach."[22] He designates his type of hermeneutics as *hermeneutische Eros*, which I translate as the "erotics of understanding," analogous to Sontag's conception of an "erotics of art." Much of Sontag's criticism of art criticism in "our hermeneutical age" parallels Achenbach's criticism of interpretation in the human sciences and humanities. Sontag writes that "the effusion of interpretations of art [cf. pretense philosophy] today poisons our sensibilities. . . . To interpret is to impoverish, to deplete the world—in order to set up a shadow world of 'meanings' [cf. 'second' reality]. Our task is to cut back content so that we can see the thing at all" (cf. the return to *die Sachen selbst*, i.e., a direct, fresh understanding of people's concerns).[23]

A much-discussed aspect of Achenbach's practice is that it is "beyond method." In answer to puzzled methodologists, Achenbach drafted a "protocol for a conversation."[24] This ironic and witty article, entitled "Scheherazade, Philosophical Practitioner," seems like a parody of Bruno Bettelheim's psychoanalytic interpretation of the tales. Scheherazade, in conversation with her sister Dinazade, explains how reflections of the "self" in and through narration affect the king radically. The philosophical practitioner of *The Thousand and One Nights* mirrors the king's homicidal compulsions in her fairy tales. Scheherazade's "method" changes every night. Her pluralistic interpretations of life help the king forget his murderous passions at crucial moments—that is, night after night. Achenbach claims that philosophical practice is at the same time psychoanalysis and the critique of psychotherapy. In Achenbach's practice, Freud's exclusive sexual-dynamic interpretation of people is turned into open-ended self-explanation and understanding in the setting of the dialectical relation between practitioner and counselee.

Achenbach's dialectical "beyond-method" method can be compared with the psychologist Lev Vygotsky's "tool-and-result" approach as it is used in social therapy, versus the "tool-for-result" method as it is applied in most therapies. In the tool-and-result approach, the "toolmaker must create the totality tool-and-result just as the poet must create meanings as she/he creates the poem. Unlike the user of hardware store tools who is defined and predetermined by the particular behavior of using those tools . . . the toolmaker is neither defined nor predetermined."[25]

Achenbach's visitors mostly have ordinary problems and questions, but visitors can also be on the borderline of "normality." People in the last group often find a philosophical equilibrium through Achenbach's practice. The aim of philosophical practice is not to heal visitors, but to have them come to a satisfactory self-explanation and clarification. Nevertheless, authentic dialogue and self-narration can have therapeutic effects. The visitors helped through philosophical talks usually have not previously thought about and talked through the crucial events of their lives. These events remain "undigested" and need to be integrated through the empathetic questioning of the reasons for and the meanings and phenomenology of these events. Mostly, Achenbach finds that visitors have more than one or two questions or problems; moreover, it is often not clear to counselees what the problem is. Philosophical analysis, then, has to involve self-analysis.

There is no set time limit in which a philosophy of life is worked out. Sessions can take place one or more times a week. The sessions become especially interesting and fruitful when carried on for a few years, though a few consultation hours can be effective too. Generally, once pressing problems and questions are talked through, addressing the "permanent burden of life" begins.

The Society for Philosophical Practice, founded by Achenbach in 1982, after one-and-a-half decades numbered more than one hundred and seventy members, including a considerable number of scholars in various academic disciplines. In 1997 this society became the International Society for Philosophy Practice (IGPP). The interdisciplinary interest in Achenbach is evidence against the unfortunate idea that philosophical practice is an antiacademic, "New Age" alternative healing practice. That Achenbach is apprehensive of being categorized as a part of the popular "healing" and "guru" culture can be concluded from his negative description of this modern sensibility in "Oedipus Bewitched." It was Schopenhauer who recognized in the pre-Freudian image of Oedipus the critical image of the philosopher: "Those who have the courage not to leave any question hidden have the power to philosophize."[26] The bewitched Oedipus is the person who does not question, but accepts without doubt the dicta of specialists, traditions, religion, science, or pseudoscience (e.g., astrology and palmistry). Critical thinking—as Achenbach conceives it—could make the conceptual world of all these "knowers" much more interesting and could generate a self-correcting impulse: To believe that one has not found the final answer or solution may keep a person open-minded enough to reconsider what he or she believes to be true. Achenbach finds it appropriate to raise the question of wisdom in his practice, but considers this a "very personal" and existential question. Philosophical counseling wisdom is the quest for answers which have to prove their wisdom "ever anew in any singular, particular case."[27]

In the context of philosophy practice, Achenbach organizes public seminars with lectures on various subjects. *ZPP* (*Agora* before 1994), the journal of the IGPP, informs its readers of new developments and literature in the field. Achenbach's theoretical writings make his practice professionally interesting and valuable. I consider the study of his theoretical reflections on philosophical practice a prerequisite for any responsible practice of philosophical counseling. In an article in the *Historisches Wörterbuch der Philosophie*, Odo Marquard mentions Ekkehard Martens and Hans Krämer as coworkers with Achenbach on the development of the theory of philosophical practice in Germany.[28] Within ten years of their publication, Achenbach's ideas have found a response in many countries of Europe and even beyond the continental borders: There is evidence of philosophical practices having been opened in such diverse parts of the world as Australia, Canada, Israel, Japan, South Africa, Taiwan, and the United States.[29] It is difficult to find out how many philosophers are at present doing philosophy practice worldwide, where they are located, and how they practice philosophy, but they seem to be propagating rapidly all over the world. Philosophy practice organizations flourish in Germany (IGPP and DGP), Canada (ASPP), The Netherlands (VFP), Israel (ISPPI), Britain (SCP), Norway (NPP), the United States (APCA, SPI, PG, and ASPCP), and in Australia (AAPCP). Most of these organizations consider an M.A. in philosophy the prerequisite for obtaining membership as a philosophical practitioner, but their membership lists also include people that are not professional practitioners. These organizations organize, on an annual or once every two years basis, international conferences in different parts of the world.

In Germany philosophers have the option of studying the new profession of philosophical counseling with Achenbach or his colleague Thomas Macho in a *Lehr-Praxis*. The importance of the *Lehr-Praxis* is that the would-be philosophy practitioner thinks through the socialization of philosophy in his or her life. This seems to me to be appropriate additional training for the philosopher, since the philosophical counselor must facilitate philosophical self-knowledge and philosophical knowledge of the human subject in general. A philosophical counselor who does not or cannot *relate* (the expression I use for being in touch with oneself, or having self-knowledge) to himself or others cannot facilitate philosophical self-knowledge in others.

At least twelve members of the International Society for Philosophical Practice were inscribed as philosophical practitioners who trained with Achenbach or Macho. Achenbach evaluates the quality of the philosophical dialogue in its beneficence; such is his criterion for distinguishing between competent and incompetent counselors.[30]

A comprehensive critical account of the first ten years of the development of philosophical counseling in Germany can be found in Melanie Berg's *Philosophische Praxen im deutschsprachigen Raum.* Her overview presents several philosophical practitioners who work with a different theoretical basis from that of Achenbach: Steffen Graefe, Joachim Koch, Alexander Dill, and Günter Witzany.[31] Berg considers philosophical counseling as a variant of a series of philosophy activities, such as the summer philosophy school, philosophy weekends, public lectures, and discussion groups. A significant section of the book is dedicated to a comparison of Achenbach's approach with Victor Frankl's logotherapy. She finds substantial parallels between these two approaches and wonders why philosophical practitioners are not inclined to integrate Frankl's concepts more in their work. Berg also mentions however Achenbach's reservation for Frankl's project because of its "missionary ambition disguised as a pseudo-philosophy."[32]

Michael Zdrenka's *Konzeptionen und Probleme der Philosoph-ischen Praxis* contains much well-informed documentation about practices in Germany as well as about practitioners elsewhere. It contains, for example, a list that locates eighty practitioners in Germany, Austria, and Switzerland and another list locating forty practitioners in the rest of the world.[33] Zdrenka discusses criticisms and difficulties on a theoretical and organizational level. He de-scribes and compares Achenbach's practice with that of Günther Witzany in Austria and my own practice in Israel. He also presents a listing of applications of philosophy practice to specializations such as homeopathy, pathognostic, schamanism, psychology, femi-nism, and management. Most of these various practitioners relate in their work to Achenbach's way of practicing philosophy. I only will discuss here the philosophy–homeopathy practice of Martina Winkler-Calaminus. She argues in her article on Vonessen's book, *Was krank macht, ist auch heilsam*, that the homeopathic essence of philosophical practice has been revealed. The ancient Greeks considered excessive self-love, or *hubris*, to be the origin of all suf-fering. Its homeopathic antidote is found in diluted love for the self: empathy.[34] In an interview with Zdrenka, Winkler-Calaminus points out that the strict individual approach of homeopathy has much in common with Achenbach's approach.[35] Both types of prac-titioners try to understand the idiosyncratic characteristics of each person; likewise, the approaches are both alternatives to the medi-cal paradigm. Winkler-Calaminus and others are to be praised for making it clear that their own type of practice has elements of philo-sophical practice as well. Thus, they create a new type of practice without losing their own initial identities.

DILL'S MYSTIC–PHILOSOPHICAL PRACTICE

Alexander Dill's book *Philosophische Praxis* appeared in July 1990.[36] Dill, an occupational therapist and sociologist, started his philosophi-cal practice in Berlin in 1984. Dill's practice is "anti-Socratic" in that it rejects the logical verification of thought as an instrument of power. In his view, Socratic dialogue is not an authentic dialogue because Socrates insisted on getting particular answers to particular ques-tions. Instead of a logical philosophical investigation, Dill offers a strat-egy of thinking while trying not to think, the aim being to arrive at the silence of those who know. Dill's philosophical practice can be inter-preted as "a therapy for the search for truth." Zen masters are domi-nant images in Dill's practice. He tries to answer the question "What is philosophical practice?" in the mode of Wei-Kuan. When the sage was asked, "What is Zen?" his reply was, "Something like a beautiful mountain." Dill compares his practice with a revolving door placed in an open field. Few who travel past it notice it. Generally, these observant few do not consider it a necessary item. Only curious travelers, or those who like to play, enter Dr. Dill's revolving door.

In Dill's view, "to question why" obscures thinking; following the stream of thought without these interruptions leads to an inner silence. Not Socrates, but children, teach authentic philosophical discourse. Children ask not only because they want to know, they also ask because they want to do away with knowledge. Children especially want to destroy that knowledge which has become an instrument of repression in the hands of adults. In a sincere dialogue, the dialogue partners want to say something; they are not particularly looking for any answers.

The basic intentions of Dill's practice are paradoxical: the negation of negations. Dill considers the notions of self, self-realization, and self-definition to be facets of the Western "cult of identity"— that is, the "I" or self-centeredness in most psychological theories. Dill considers the ancient Chinese and mystical understanding, "It is better not to be a self," as having pragmatic implications for modern people. Lao-Tse showed the self to be an imaginary entity which becomes a source of evil. If there is "no person," there is no source of evil, nor anybody to experience evil. According to Dill this imaginary view of the self has parallels with avant-garde and poststructuralist ambitions of overcoming the subject. He quotes Gilles Deleuze in his quest for inner pluralism: "People in themselves should not be one or many, but manifold." Such paradoxical self-distance is justified and functional, according to Dill.

In contrast to most chapters of Dill's book, the theme of the chapter on "Political Existence, The Political Animal" is surprisingly common-sensical: Kant's practical reason teaches us how to be good citizens. After being immersed in Dill's mystique, one wonders if this sudden turn to reason is a last chance to escape an ominous apocalyptic future.

Dill's book evoked considerable criticism from members of the IGPP. For example, Martens sees Dill's philosophical practice as lacking in philosophical content.[37]

Dill's practice gives expression to Kantian, existentialist, poststructuralist, and mystical philosophical ideas. Dill's motivation for his practice is his "love of talking," and thus he keeps the philosophical discourse going. This type of discourse is interesting as a postmodern cultivation of arguments, but it is highly questionable whether Dill relates thought to action. Even Dill himself finds his practice aimless. It has no significance for the activities of daily life, other than political life.

VON MORSTEIN'S APEIRON PRACTICE
OF PHILOSOPHY

Petra von Morstein, professor emeritus of philosophy at the University of Calgary, Canada, comes to terms with the questions and problems of everyday life in her private philosophical practice. In 1987 von Morstein founded the Apeiron Society for the Practice of Philosophy (ASPP). The members of this nonprofit society numbered more than sixty after its first few years of existence. Von Morstein as president of the ASPP has organized seminars on topics such as the rationality of sensations and feelings; self-realization; philosophical ideas for leading one's life; Wittgenstein and psychoanalysis; and absolute and relative ethics. Though von Morstein has published on a variety of subjects, her writings on philosophical practice proper consist so far of only a couple of short texts and her lectures.[38] Besides organizing seminars, the ASPP encourages the practice of philosophy in individual philosophical counseling.

Von Morstein describes her practical philosophical activity as follows: "Philosophical expertise consists in scholarly knowledge of methods of thought, in their critical comprehension, in skills and techniques of wielding them. Although to be human is of necessity to think and to think about thinking, most of us lack philosophical expertise." Like most philosophical counselors, von Morstein rejects any claims that her consultations are cures. Although she finds philosophical counseling therapeutic in its aim to enliven and empower its clients, this does not mean that von Morstein employs medical methods to give a philosophical diagnosis or that she uses therapeutic means to cure philosophical diseases. The indefinite and limitless are for von Morstein principles of the practice of philosophy that facilitate the understanding of life in its complexity. "To make sense of human experiences is not just to explain and describe them, but to make sense of them in their particular actuality." Accordingly, "philosophical counsel cannot proceed according to an underlying theory.... In this respect, philosophical counselling is essentially different from most forms of psychological counselling." She is willing to consider the possibility of cooperation with mental-health workers, but she cautions that "the professional philosopher is not necessarily called upon to make things better or to help eliminate problems, but rather to help make them comprehensible in their complexity, so that the other can live with them rather than against or in spite of them." The philosophical counselor accompanies the other in the development of self-expression. Problems are transformed rather than eliminated; the visitor becomes "free and fully alive with her or his problem." Von Morstein considers philosophical writings rich resources for people to use to devise or improve their own ways of living. New ways of thinking on how to lead one's life can be developed through studying these sources of thought in the public and the individual counseling practice of philosophy.

Philosophers, as artists of deliberation, may help their clients find ways of thinking that clarify confused or confusing feelings, showing the rationality of such feelings without rationalizing them away. Philosophical ideas and methods are considered tools for comprehending our experience. Von Morstein's rejection of the medical method and the practice of diagnosis in philosophical consultation is influenced by Wittgenstein: "Methods if fixed are illnesses. Rather, philosophical methods are to be considered as curative practices. Thus they must be grounded in concrete lived experiences of what Wittgenstein calls "illness: being captivated by a picture, stuck with a sentence." Such thought captivation may lead, for example, to depression, anxiety, uncertainty and lack of motivation. Nevertheless, the aim of the philosophical counselor is not to cure those suffering from symptoms of this sort, but to cure them of "fixity, stasis, and induce process and movement. Philosophical methods and ideas are then invoked as potentially effective sources of renewed liveliness."

According to von Morstein, Wittgenstein's therapeutic conception of philosophy has methodological features in common with psychoanalysis: the emphasis on immediate lived experiences, description as a symbolic process, the revelatory force of "explanations" as descriptions, and the continuous process of reassembling what is remembered.

Von Morstein does not accept therapeutic success in philosophical practice as an experimental vindication of the method used, the way psychoanalysis does in its practice. From her point of view, "evidence" for the appropriateness of a counselor's method of philosophical practice should be found in problems made comprehensible in their complexity and not so much in therapeutic effects or changes achieved.

An important characteristic of von Morstein's practice is the idea that self-understanding might be impossible to achieve without discussing the basic questions of such issues as ethics, philosophy of mind, and philosophy of religion. Questions and problems that von Morstein welcomes for clarification and transformation are ethical dilemmas, illnesses, problematic relations, conflicts from one's past, professional crises, and crises of confidence, as well as less definite states of mind such as depression, anxiety, and despair. In addition, consultation may focus on basic issues such as the meaning of life.

In contrast to other philosophers at work in North America, von Morstein's practice is not a mixture of psychotherapeutic and philosophical methods, but philosophical practice proper. In the United States, for example, philosophers have been working in diverse professional situations, such as social work, education, medicine, business, psychotherapy, parapsychology, religion, mysticism, and politics.[39] Although these philosophers may do an excellent job as counselors in their particular field such as educational, marriage, or pastoral counseling (the mixture of philosophy with psychotherapy, educational, and religious practices), their practices are very different from the profession of philosophical counseling, as it was defined by Achenbach in 1981. Although I have no objections to pluralism in philosophical counseling, I find it praiseworthy of Elliot D. Cohen that he makes it very clear where the origins of his approach lie: Philosophical counseling is a modified version of rational–emotive therapy, combined with insights from other therapies and existentialism. From his cognitive and interdisciplinary perspective, he claims that philosophical counselors should have the authority to correct irrational thinking in clients. He applies a deductive logical model to counseling, in which the rules of logic define the didactic and evaluative roles of the therapist or counselor.[40]

Then and now, Achenbach's conception of the philosophical counselor does not include mixtures of philosophy with therapy or psychological counseling. It would contribute to clarity if one would confine the use of the term "philosophical counseling" to types of Achenbachian philosophical consultations, and invent other names for the hybrid types of counseling that make clear the compounds of the type of consultation, such as interdisciplinary counseling. Von Morstein as a North American practitioner is exemplary among others, especially among some of the practitioners in the United States, in that she does not seek legislation for philosophy practice. The political power games of a handful of academic philosophers in the United States—who so far have failed to monopolize and dominate philosophy practice by offering some university courses and a certificate that represents them—are far remote from the Canadian ASPP and most European practitioner organizations. (There are also in the United States several practitioners organizations that actively oppose turning philosophizing into an economical and political power structure.)

For Achenbach, Nicholas of Cusa's "learned ignorance" is the humble distinction with which a philosophical practitioner may perfect his professional aims and knowledge: "The philosophical practitioner has no relation with the specialist, doesn't compare himself with these experts, he has the pretence of a layman. His standard is to be in his way the best conceivable layman."[41]

The professionalism of twentieth-century philosophy seems to have greatly contributed in making philosophy into a technical issue that is devoid of meaning for the majority of people. Furthering the academic professionalization of philosophy practice will very likely deplete it from its revolutionary ethos and turn it into a highly professional discourse that actually contributes little. Needed is not the professionalization but the humanization of philosophy and its practice.

PHILOSOPHY PRACTICE IN THE NETHERLANDS

Whereas in Germany the initiative of one person grew into a society for philosophical practice, in The Netherlands philosophical practice was a group effort from the beginning.[42] In the late 1970s, several students of the Central Interfaculty of the University of Amsterdam were concerned about discrepancies between academic philosophy and their own motivations for philosophizing. They solved this problem by studying with those lecturers who understood their objections; they were allowed to philosophize about matters of personal significance. When the news of Achenbach's practice reached Amsterdam, it encouraged these students to develop a philosophy with practical implications. In 1984, five of these students who had by then graduated, organized the Amsterdam Work Group for Philosophical Practice. This work group has been active in self-training discussion skills and theoretical reflections on practical philosophy. After two years of preparation, Ad Hoogendijk was the first to start a private practice in The Netherlands. Interviews and lectures aroused increased interest in philosophical practice, and soon there were additional practitioners such as Eite Veening. The Amsterdam work group became a center of contact for interested philosophers throughout the Dutch provinces. In 1989 a society called the *Vereniging Filosofische Praktijk* was founded to replace the former organization. The Hoogendijk and Veening practices can be thought of as representative of individual philosophical practice in The Netherlands, while Jos Kessels and Gert de Boer's Socratic project is representative of group philosophical practice. My selection of these and other practitioners was on the basis of theoretical accounts of their practice. It is obvious that one practitioner may appeal to a reader or client more than another. To conclude that one practitioner is better than another on the basis of these theoretical accounts might be too hasty an inference. However, future research in the area of how clients experience the usefulness of philosophical counseling with different practitioners might provide some helpful information.

HOOGENDIJK'S PLURALISM OF DIALOGUES

In 1988, after a year of practice, Hoogendijk published his first book on philosophical practice, *Spreekuur bij een filosoof* (Consultation hour with a philosopher).[43] My description of his practice is primarily based on this book and a more recent book of his, as well as interviews in 1987, 1989, 1992, and 1995.

Hoogendijk distinguishes between "philosophism," a technical or encyclopedic knowledge of philosophy, and philosophy proper. In philosophical practice one is not concerned so much with philosophism as with philosophical skills and attitudes, that is, what I would call "intellectual posture." One philosophical attitude is "relaxed concentration," a free and detached listening-in-depth where openness is crucial. Hoogendijk finds that openness is dependent on a loving, humane heart and mind; love makes a person tolerant and respectful of other people's thought. Until the Renaissance, love was a condition for knowing reality; since the Enlightenment, such a prerequisite is to be found only in a few minor philosophies.

Fascination is another philosophical attitude the counselor needs to develop. Fascination begins when the self-evidence of a situation is taken away. Self-evidence is visualized as a circle that leads to nothing but more of the same; nothing new can occur. Through fascination, breaches are continually made in the closed circle of self-evidence. The philosophical practitioner who sees fascination as the origin, the foundation, and the inner perpetual motive of philosophy, will thereby experience each philosophical consultation hour as unique.

The practitioner also has to find out which type of conversation or combination of discourses is best for each visitor. A conversation can have the qualities of the Socratic "maieutic"—Socrates's so-called "midwife" technique of making the other conscious of his or her thinking habits as well as helping to evaluate the counselee's conceptions critically. A conversation can also have a dialectical style: One argues in favor of one point of view and against another. Eventually new conceptions are achieved by each of the debating sides. Hoogendijk uses also Buber's ideas in his dialogues. In a Buberian dialogue, the practitioner has to step out of his or her own mental world. Through a relaxed concentration on the other, and the "active inclusion" of the other—without losing oneself in the other—the other becomes known to the counselor. Nonetheless, the counselee remains to a certain degree a perpetual mystery. I add here that Buber's philosophy of dialogue and its addressing of the other as "other" restores the other to authentic selfhood.[44] To Buber all authentic living means encounter and dialogue—which in turn promotes healing. It seems to me essential to distinguish between the meaning of the words "therapy" and "healing." Healing can be a consequence of therapy, but it is not in itself therapy. The success of therapy depends greatly on vital personal forces, which one may call the personal or natural healing gifts. Opinions differ concerning the factors or sources for such vitality. It cannot be proven if these healing gifts or vital forces depend on personal willpower, positive imagination, paranormal gifts, a divine touch, or something else. Healing is definitely not only resulting from medical treatment; neither can its source be reduced to any other domain. It is a mysterious influence that some persons seem to possess in a greater measure than others, such as great healers like the prophets Elijah and Moses. I find that Buber's "I–Thou" relation touches this mysterious healing influence; this may explain its beneficial influence on counselees.

Hoogendijk considers the following characteristics essential for a philosophical practitioner: a critical capacity, an awareness of cognitive blind spots (collective as well as personal), and an ability to discover prejudice. Often prejudice is the basis for arguments. Moreover, prejudice can take the form of "scientific" theories or myths, such as the claim that IQ tests are reliable in selecting people or the controversial assertion that social backgrounds affect educational development. I find that at present, only radical skeptics accept that one knows very little about what another person knows or can know. How could one possibly assess another person's intellectual potential? How does one compare educational progress and results among people working in so-called comparable situations?

According to Hoogendijk philosophical practitioners do not want to conceal reality with interpretations based on preconceived notions of reality. They want to clarify the "truth" through an openness, which can be attained through honest self-knowledge and love. Hoogendijk's method in his practice is presented as follows. In the first instance he asks questions, which not only make clear what the person's problem is, but also the philosophical worldview which is, as it were, the intellectual background of the problem.[45] An example of the types of questions a practitioner may ask is from my own practice. A male client admits that he is living a double life: He is an Orthodox Jew and a teacher at a Yeshiva (religious school), yet his favorite pastime is dressing up as a woman, which is forbidden by Jewish law. Moreover, he says he has a justification for it in his religious belief. Nevertheless he suffers from the fear that one day he might be identified as a cross-dresser. In this case it was relevant to question the client's religious belief: Did it differ from the ordinary, that is, from other persons' religious beliefs? Did he start to justify his behavior through his faith, or did his behavior originate in it? The general questions also had to be asked: What is religion? Can one have a private religion? Had he ever discussed his belief with a Rabbi? (These questions are summoned by the client's situation and answers; there are no stock questionnaires or interview forms for the counselees.)

Clarification of a problem may cause the original issue to be seen in different proportions or may lead to a change in interpretation. Special attention is paid to presuppositions, attitudes, and ideas taken for granted by the visitor. The philosopher is sensitive to inconsequent, uncritical, or culture-bound thinking. When the counselor refuses to avoid sensitive issues such as class, sex, education, and race, but rather discusses them in a wider social and philosophical context, the client may begin to perceive him or herself differently. Hoogendijk often found that inconsistencies in the visitors' "philosophical dimension" (e.g., presuppositions, views, self-image, or human image) create problems in their lives. Such inconsistencies are further analyzed by questioning the client about the concepts involved in the inconsistent beliefs.

This I illustrate with an example from my own practice. A person claims that he is born free, yet "everywhere in chains." Is this contradiction in terms an inconsistent belief? Is the reason he says it that way is that he is quoting Rousseau? What does the concept of freedom mean to this person? Why does he adopts Rousseau's way of looking at it? How many types of freedom can one think of?

Hoogendijk finds that this sort of analysis (or thematization, as he calls it) can make situations seem even more problematic, which may disturb the client. On the other hand, the practitioner's philosophical attitude and skills should be absorbed and mastered by the visitor during the conversations. For example, the practitioner's tranquility will have a calming influence on the client. Similarly, I find that one can learn from Nietzsche's enthusiasm for life under all conditions to dance over the abyss of life: "That you would learn my wisdom from me: even the worst thing has two good reverse sides—even the worst thing has good dancing legs; that you would learn, you higher men, to put yourselves on your right legs!"[46] All great "living" philosophers may have their own sort of balancing and enlivening influence on practitioners and clients.

Hoogendijk's studies led him to realize that there are no philosophical certainties. When people are confronted with uncertainties, they often become anxious. The practitioner's questions about how they think about the relationship between being and becoming can create a new openness and calm. I find that the person who chooses continuous becoming might find in Heraclitus's philosophy some intellectual comfort. Heraclitus's conception that everything is in flux led him to say that one can cross the same river only once. Crossing the river of life in the "company" of a great thinker or together with a philosophical counselor seems to bring relief from anxiety.

Another significant feature of philosophical dialogue is that the roles maintained by the visitor and the practitioner and the presuppositions of the conversation can be subjects of discussion. Among Hoogendijk's visitors are also people just attracted to philosophy, who want to consult him, for example, about research projects or theoretical philosophical problems. In addition a philosophical practitioner may be chosen because he or she is considered an unprejudiced partner in conversations.

People are generally stirred by concrete situations to philosophize. Possible questions for Hoogendijk's practice are, Should I finish my studies? What do I want in the future? Should I view my life as wasted? Is it all right to divorce? Am I the only egoistic person, or are all people like that? Is life after death a possibility? What is reality?

I have been puzzled by the naive, optimistic faith practitioners seem to have in the practice of philosophy. When I met Hoogendijk in 1987, I wanted to find out what gave him and others this confidence in their profession. Rather than founding their praxis on a metaphysics or ontology, they base their philosophical faith on experience. Hoogendijk claims that philosophy is a considerable help in his personal existence. Moreover, it was through study for a degree in philosophy and not merely by reading some existentialist writers that he became an authentic human being.

Additional support for an experiential basis as evidence for the effectiveness of philosophical counseling comes from Dries Boele. He wrote an article, based on self-observation, about his experiences as a client in a philosophical practice. According to Boele— now a philosophical practitioner himself—he attained new insights through the critical questions and remarks of the practitioner, which led him to an awareness of a dilemma based on several inconsistencies in his "philosophical dimension." "On one side, there was in me the pedantic will to control my life and to organize it as I wanted . . .; on the other side there was the longing to trust in the wisdom of life itself. . . . The explicit knowledge of this contrast in my personality was an important influence in my further self-realization."[47]

As Hoogendijk explained to me, philosophical practice is a "way of life," and is not based on dogma, although there are statements that one can accept as true. Philosophical practice can be compared to wisdom philosophies, such as those practiced by the Stoics, Montaigne, and Ludwig Klages.[48] Hoogendijk's book includes a chapter about "The Wisdom of Life," in which he writes about Zanussi's movie *Imperative* as an illustrative example of a tragic search for modern wisdom: "This beautiful movie of Zanussi shows the philosophical lacunae in our society: a lack of knowledge of our philosophical inheritance, and above all a lack in the capability to be fascinated, and a lack in philosophical openness. To what extent is there a taboo on philosophical questions? A philosophical question may seem out of place in our society."[49]

Nevertheless, there are chances to obtain wisdom in life, when the experience of life motivates people to a philosophical search and a longing for wisdom. Hoogendijk believes that people (although, I must add, probably not all) victimized by sexual or racial discrimination may come to question what discrimination is: what conditions underlie it, what it means, what its purposes are, and how to justify or condemn it. Such an intellectual search will guide the questioning person into philosophic domains, where one may find or create wisdom for one's life. Hoogendijk's choice to understand racism, sexism, or other kinds of discrimination and repression as issues for discussion in philosophical counseling is of paramount importance. Philosophers such as John Stuart Mill, Albert Camus, Simone de Beauvoir, Jean-Paul Sartre, and others have found these subjects philosophical enough to devote their energies to analyzing them. But not only philosophers have been or should be concerned with these matters—specialists from other disciplines are as well. The psychiatrist Frantz Fanon's analysis of colonialism is exemplary for an interdisciplinary ethical and political concern.[50]

Hoogendijk has expressed skepticism about the assumption made by Aristotle and Augustine, and in more modern times by Russell, that living life wisely brings happiness. However, he does not doubt the necessity for a philosophical search for wisdom as the foundation for a stable existence.

Hoogendijk regrets that philosophical counselors are so often compared to psychotherapists. Philosophical practice should be understood as arising out of the philosophical tradition. He finds that the "pathology metaphor," the description and labeling of oneself, others, or situations as sick and in need of therapy, is in fact wishful thinking. Medicine now knows how to cure many illnesses. Generally speaking, most sick people can remain hopeful; for almost every illness there is a painkiller or a therapy or a medicine. A combination of certain drugs now even seems to be useful in HIV treatment.

Hoogendijk obviously does not recommend tranquilizers as the answer for existential questions and problems; nevertheless his criticism of the mental-health field is mild; it is practically an affirmation. He believes that problems can be looked at from a theological, medical, or psychotherapeutic perspective, and accordingly the problems take on different contours. People with "problems" can be called sinful, sick, confused, problematic, or abnormal. However, the philosophical practitioner sees problems as the focus of philosophical life. Consequently, philosophical practice is not an alternative therapy, but an alternative *to* therapy, a supplement to psychotherapy, or a way of preventing psychological problems. Moreover, Hoogendijk believes that psychotherapy may effect changes in the patients' "philosophical dimension." However, from my point of view, it seems very unlikely that psychotherapy—with the exclusion of the work of the exceptional psychotherapist—could positively affect philosophical consciousness. Antipsychiatrists such as Laing, Cooper, and Szasz have shown that most psychotherapeutic practice drastically deprives problems of their social, political, economical, historical, and philosophical contexts and roots. When problems are based not on the "emotional development" of clients but on objective situations and cultural contexts, psychotherapeutic awareness tends to obscure the factual causes of distress and discontent. In Susan Sontag's words, "If . . . discontent isn't channeled off to be repaired by the kind of psychotherapeutic awareness which robs it of social and political, of historical, dimension, the wide prevalence of unfocused unhappiness . . . could be the beginning of *real* knowledge . . . that would lead to a new version of human nature. . . ."[51]

Hoogendijk's second book, *Filosofie voor managers*, was inspired by his increasing number of clients with problems connected to their work, such as career planning, change of profession, conflicts or stress at work, the need for reflection on leadership and management, or unemployment.[52] Consequently, in 1990 Hoogendijk changed his field of interest from private counseling to counseling companies and organizations.

What is new in his treatment of the subject of philosophy and management is that Hoogendijk now places his philosophical practice in a postmodernist setting. He distinguishes between modern and postmodern thinking and culture as two opposing trends and lifestyles. In his cultural and philosophical analysis of the late twentieth century, various influences are shown as leading to a postmodern attitude. A growing secularization, the welfare state, the Holocaust, the end of ideologies, the increase in higher education, "unlimited" communication and transport options, and a multicultural society are likely causes for widespread relativism and of the shift of morality and culture from the public to the private domain.

Though Hoogendijk appreciates postmodernism, he considers it problematic when it leads to an absolute relativism, apathy, and disorientation. Nevertheless, a reflective form of postmodernism can prevent chaos and totalitarianism from destroying people in the postmodern age. Philosophical practice par excellence invites and encourages such reflection. It enables people—especially those who have to take on weighty responsibilities in their work—to modify or adapt value systems in spite of, or because of, the postmodern trend.

Hoogendijk views descriptive business ethics as a means for establishing reasonable and responsible relations among management, personnel, clientele, society, and environment. In his description of the work of the Philips Corporation's philosopher, Rademaker, Hoogendijk identifies three patterns in the philosophy of management:

1. Business philosophy: the nature of a company, analyzed according to its characteristic collection of presuppositions.
2. The philosophy of business: a specification of social, political, and cultural philosophy. It considers more general themes like "the place of a company in our social organization or the specific features of modern management."
3. Philosophy and business: what a philosopher can do for a company. Some examples are
   a. Fundamental research on the company's concepts, values, and decision-making processes. A philosophical (not psychological or sociological) analysis of the relations between the company and its society, market, clientele and milieu. I add here that a philosophical counselor in management advising may take his inspiration for analysis from the works of Adams Smith, David Ricardo, Karl Marx, John Maynard Keynes, and so many other "worldly" philosophers.[53]
   b. Helping the manager reflect and being a critical sounding-board.
   c. Suggesting alternative ideas for management.[54]

Hoogendijk's reflections on the meaning of labor and its history—mostly based on Hannah Arendt's *The Human Condition* and the writings of Hans Achterhuis—reveal that work is one of the major domains in human life.[55] Consequently, in this wider perspective, Hoogendijk relates the three questions, "Who am I?" "What can I do?" and "What do I want?" to the domain of work. This leads to the idea of life design, something that is also in fashion in ordinary business counseling. A person brings desires and dreams for the future, and afterward discusses the possibility of realizing this ideal life design. Considering one's life design can bring clarity to the conception of a person's future and cause changes in one's self-image, mood, and skills in communicating. When these newfound data are discussed philosophically in the workplace, both managers and employees can derive meaning, motivation, and new prospects for their labor.

VEENING'S METALOQUE

The philosophical practitioner Eite Veening looks at thinking as something one can and should think about. He calls himself a "tradesman in thinking tools." In daily activities, care often prevents calamities; in the same sense, careful and proper thinking about life situations can be a rewarding activity. In contrast to Achenbach and Hoogendijk's Frankfurt-school orientation, Veening mostly models his thinking on analytic and poststructuralist philosophy. Though philosophical practitioners are not missionaries for their personal philosophy and convictions, nevertheless the differences found in the practices of, for example, Achenbach, Dill, Hoogendijk, Veening, Kessels, and de Boer, show that the practitioner's individual orientation has a creative influence on his or her praxis. Individual attitudes have already created a diversity of "methods" in this new profession.

Veening does not share the "positivist idealistic illusion" that proper thinking would change the world into a paradise, but he believes that it can improve life. Veening distinguishes between people with emotional problems and people with conceptual puzzles. Only the last group are welcome in his practice. Veening, a professional philosopher and social worker, makes a sharp distinction between the clientele of mental-health workers and that of the philosophical practitioner. For Veening someone with "emotional problems" had best see an old-fashioned therapist. Those who still believe in the privileged understanding of the psychologist in the area of the emotions can now be impressed with Veening's double loyalties: to philosophy and to social work. Veening finds that his clientele consists of people who have to make important life decisions, such as divorce or adoption, and those involved in complicated situations who need a good conversational partner. Existential and ethical questions also fit into Veening's practice.

Veening's theory of practice is related to Karl Popper's theory of interactionism, in which the objective contents of thought can influence states of consciousness and the material world, and vice versa. Popper pictures a threefold world: world one, the material world of physical objects and situations; world two, the field of consciousness, mental states, and behavioral dispositions to act; and world three, the ideal world of the objective contents of thought.[56] Veening often found his visitors to be confused travelers in Popper's trichotomous world, lacking the intellectual tools to distinguish between the domains and to orient themselves within them. In his philosophical practice, Veening "travels" with his visitors through the three worlds and visualizes the visitor's intellectual "landscape, direction, and travel manners." The question is the philosopher's ship; the metaphor, its compass.

Another characteristic of Veening's practice is "metalogue": "Distance in thinking, and once more, thinking about thinking." The notion of metalogue had been invented by Gregory Bateson, who presents a theory of schizophrenia based on communication analysis and on Whitehead and Russell's philosophy. Bateson's hypothesis is that patients acquire mental habits characteristic of schizophrenic communication through specific sequences of events, which he calls "double bind" situations. People in these situations are faced with paradoxes and contradictions which they are unable to analyze or understand, so that they end up feeling confused. A Zen-Enlightenment method provided Bateson with an example of such a double bind: The Zen master holds a stick over the pupil's head and threatens to beat him with the stick if he says that the stick is real or that it is not real, or if he doesn't say anything at all. Through metalogue one may reach an awareness of the double bind situation and then transcend it.

Unlike therapists, Veening is not in search of "pathogenic backgrounds" or of a way of placing his visitors into a "therapeutic double bind." On the contrary, he engages in a metalogue with his visitors. Bateson defines the metalogue as follows: "A conversation about a problematic subject in such a way that the participants not only discuss the subject but also the structure of the conversation, which is seen as predominantly relevant to the subject."[57] Metalogue, translated into philosophical practice, examines thinking patterns and demystifies confusion by questioning thought structures that lead to an illusory "no exit."

Thinking about thought structures is illustrated by Veening through the following event. During one of Veening's teaching hours (some philosophical practitioners organize seminars on philosophical practice or teach philosophy at universities, social academies, or colleges, or at other institutes of higher education), a student asked a question that had been troubling him for some time. The young man, who worked in a psychiatric hospital, had been against electroshock therapy in principle. As a member of an action group against this form of therapy, he was clear in his mind about his reasons for his unconventional opinion. The student became confused about his objections to electroshock therapy when he found himself willing to give it to a patient. He asked himself, "Did I abandon my principle that easily? Did it mean so little to me?" Veening suggested that instead of looking at the problem as a matter of principle versus no principle, it could be interpreted as a competition among principles or as a combination of principles. A different principle could at a different time rise to the top of the student's hierarchical structure of norms. This reduced the young man's confusion, and after a short time, his problem was resolved by understanding that in that specific situation it was not a matter of *either* electroshock treatment, *or* having principles.[58] Another characteristic of Veening's practice is reflection on the use of language, which Veening considers interwoven with power and regulation.

Veening also aids "problematic people" (the persons he classifies as suffering from emotional problems) indirectly, by improving the thinking habits of those who traditionally have the authority to provide care. He does this by giving courses for doctors, pastors, social workers, and therapists. A high quality of work, says Veening, is determined by a high quality of thinking about work. Chaotic, badly argued, or undisciplined "thinking-work" can be improved by philosophical skills acquired through exercises in philosophical thought. Thinking-work is also the English translation of the title of a book by Veening, *Denkwerk*, a book that contains material for thought, written to help professional helpers think through their professional activities.[59] *Denkwerk* is free from professional jargon and accessible to anyone interested in philosophy and well-being. *Denkwerk* bridges the gap between Veening's two loyalties—philosophy and social work—to some extent in that it offers thinking tools to the established helping professions as well as to others. *Denkwerk* would be uselessly old-fashioned if Veening had introduced philosophical tools (such as analytical, existential, or phenomenological ones) as counseling tools. To aid therapists, social workers, nurses, and others in their oft neglected thinking-work, Veening introduces philosophy as the discipline of thought and describes Popper's "three worlds" as a grand puzzle. To solve this puzzle, and the puzzles within the puzzle, we can use the Veening-designed thinking tools. First, Veening distinguishes among knowledge puzzles, evaluation puzzles, and practical puzzles. Second, he distinguishes personal, scientific, and philosophical narratives. The various puzzles and narratives form a matrix that the professional helper can fill out for clients or for him or herself.

In addition to the theoretical explanations of how the puzzles and narratives fit together, every chapter is followed by thought exercises and a lucid monologue from "Mam," a client. The anecdotal, humorous, but also sensitive story of "Mam" supplies common-sense feedback on what Veening has to say. For a kleptomanic, alcoholic, gambling, debt-ridden, desperate, forty-one-year-old, divorced mother of two, Mam is exemplarily rational in her personal commentary on the reflective guidelines for her helpers. Veening solves knowledge or epistemological puzzles using criteria based on correspondence, coherence, pragmatics, existentialism, and communication. Correspondence criteria are verifiable through empirical observations, while coherence criteria are judged by logical argumentation. Or, as Mam's commentary puts it: "If my helper cannot see or measure the mess I'm in, and if he or she wants to explain how it all comes together, then he or she ought to use his or her head logically" (my translation).[60] As a consequence of the particular criteria chosen for solving a puzzle, different solutions emerge. This explains why the existence of different solutions of the same puzzle does not instantly imply a wrong observation or faulty argument. Evaluation puzzles can be solved with ethical or aesthetic criteria. For example, with these two criteria in mind, a firefighter might no longer remain paralyzed with indecision when he has to decide between saving a Rembrandt or a cat from a fire.

Veening considers that the choice of specific knowledge criteria has its effect on evaluation puzzles and practical puzzles; the different types of puzzles are layered one on another. For practical puzzles Veening subscribes to a preference criterion: "The preference for an act is the product of the likelihood of a certain effect and the value of that effect."[61] Though it is impossible to predict with certainty the effect or value of certain acts, it seems that even if the preference criterion only has value as a theoretical account, it may help persons to rationally evaluate decisions that have to be made. Professional helpers aware of Veening's conceptual matrix, puzzles, and thinking tools may perceive more nuances in their clients' or patients' stories. And Veening's reflections can widen the range of intelligent, justifiable choices for counselor and counselee.

SOCRATIC DISCOURSE

With the growing popularity of individual philosophical consultation, another form of philosophical practice—one which originated with Leonard Nelson and goes back to the Germany of the early 1920s—has gained interest in The Netherlands through lectures and seminars organized by Jos Kessels, Gert de Boer, Dries Boele, Jos Delnoy, and others.[62] Philosophical group discussions under the name *Socratic discourse* or *Socratic dialogue* are organized by these philosophers at universities, recreation centers, and other public places. In Germany and Britain practitioners of the Socratic method had gained some ground before the arrival of the philosophical practice and counseling movement and had founded their own organizations, respectively the Philosophisch-Politische Akademie and the Society for the Furtherance of Critical Philosophy.[63] In The Netherlands, and increasingly also in Britain and the United States, philosophical counselors and the Socratic practitioners work in one organizational structure, in spite of the essential difference between their ways of philosophy practice.

Before presenting an account of how Socratic discourse is actually practiced today, I would like to dedicate some paragraphs to Leonard Nelson. Unlike most of the practitoners discussed so far, some of Nelson's books have been translated into English.[64] In the introduction to Nelson's *Socratic Method and Critical Philosophy* and a *System of Ethics*, Julius Kraft describes the life of the exceptional philosopher, mathematician, educator, and political theorist. He finds that Nelson's philosophy needs to be rediscovered as the unofficial European philosophy of the beginning of the twentieth century. Nelson's antirelativism, antimysticism, and ethics of practical reason had been a major scandal for the official European philosophy of that era. On the other hand, Nelson "had always contended that the rejection of rational philosophical truth by his contemporaries could only result in subjection to an invented irrational 'truth.'" Whether one agrees with Nelson's philosophy or not, the academy he founded realized its aim of raising responsible political leaders since "out of this Academy and the youth groups connected with it, came a number of heroic men and women who fought against the National Socialist regime."[65] Would the methodology of the contemporary practitioners of Nelson's concept have a comparable wholesome effect in situations where human rights were downtrodden?

A change of method seems to have occurred over the years, and the Socratic creed professes now the need for reaching a group consensus. However, the aim of Nelson's method still is to teach people to philosophize. The following quotations let Nelson speak for himself on how his method is accomplished: "[The teacher] can do no more than show his students how to undertake, each for himself, the laborious regress that alone affords insight into basic principles. If there is such a thing at all as instruction in philosophy, it can only be instruction in doing one's own thinking." Nelson's method is not a *Weltanschauung* but criticism: "Criticism is the concept of

a *method* and not of a philosophical system. Whoever adheres to
this method is a criticist, no matter what conclusions he [or she]
may reach with it; and whoever does not adhere to it and wants to
establish philosophical knowledge as true through an objective verification, be it proof or comparison with the objects, is a dogmatist."[66]

Kelley L. Ross of the Los Angeles Valley College is an outstand-
ing U.S. scholar on Nelson, but is not active as a Socratic group-
discourse facilitator. In an illuminating article titled "The
Foundations of Value," he traces Nelson's thoughts through the
ideas of Plato, Aristotle, Hume, Kant, and Fries, concerning the
justification of first principles (Aristotle's concept of propositions
that need not be proven).[67] It seems to me that the practice of the
Socratic method would much benefit from a greater orientation to
and foundation in its theoretical origins.

In Germany, Socratic Weeks are organized about three times a
year. This description of a Socratic Week in Willebadessen, Germany, should give the reader a notion of how Socratic discourse is
performed.[68] About forty participants of various ages and educational levels (though the majority are students and academics) meet
to discuss philosophical and mathematical subjects three times a
day for a week. The participants are divided into four groups. Each
group chooses a subject for discussion. The philosophical issues
chosen include such topics as "power and violence" and "truthful
living." In the morning sessions each group discusses its own subject, and in the afternoon session the morning's discussion is recon-
sidered in a metadiscussion. After dinner the participants choose a
particular subject as a theme to discuss. These so-called "theme-
evenings" generally turn into political discussions. One evening is
reserved as the Socratic evening, during which the participants
discuss the usefulness of the conversations for their private life.
Some results of the Socratic discourse mentioned by participants
are greater ability to formulate their thoughts; greater sensitivity
in listening to others; better insight into the structure of arguments;
and greater realism or practicality in thinking. The present mentor of the Socratic Weeks in Germany is Gustav Heckmann, who
continued and developed the thinking of his teacher Nelson. Kessels
describes Nelson's and Heckmann's thought as follows.[69]

Nelson, a neo-Kantian, believed in the direct evidence of truth;
"the self-confidence of reason" should be a basic philosophical attitude. Philosophy is understood as a science, and its aim is to create
a worldview explained by rational arguments. The method used in
Socratic discourse is "regressive abstraction": inquiry into people's
concrete and abstract conceptions by exposing the basis of the more
general truths upon which these conceptions are founded. Method-

ological reflection should allow all truth to become clear, since philosophical truth is found in people. Through Socratic discourse, the philosophical knowledge that exists in members of the discussion group is openly discussed and criticized; this educational process consolidates the formerly "unknown" truths into the philosophers' magic stone: "the truth." Plato's *Meno* is the prototype of Socratic discourse; the Kantian "a priori" is understood by Nelson as the true idea underlying Plato's philosophy.

The Socratic image emulated in the method practiced by the "followers of Nelson" differs essentially from Achenbach's conception of Socratic dialogue. Whereas in Achenbach's practice Socratic questions can be answered in various manners, in the neo-Socratic group sessions, there is one right answer that participants should disclose through honest self-exploration in dialogue with each other.

Kessels admits that Plato's theory of remembering truth is not acceptable to most people today. He claims, however, in defense of Nelson's and Heckmann's thought, that philosophers such as Descartes, Leibniz, Locke, Hume, Kant, Wittgenstein, and Polanyi were all concerned with the transformation of obscure and confused knowledge into clear and distinct concepts. In a recently published book, *Socrates op de markt* (Socrates on the Market), Jos Kessels directs the Socratic dialogue to the management and enterprise world.[70] He finds the ability to engage in dialogue crucial in methodological learning processes in organizations, but observes a lack of available techniques to teach dialogue skills. Our dominantly scientific orientation is blamed for this lack: "These techniques were for ages, in the form of dialectic, an important instrument for investigation, until they were replaced by the formation of scientific theories. But several fundamental organizational problems cannot be solved by scientific knowledge."[71] Although Peter Senge recognized the importance of dialogue in learning organization, Kessels finds that Senge's suggestions for such dialogues are not sufficient assistance to people in setting up productive talks. In addition classical methods such as those developed by Socrates and Aristotle seem appropriate in learning organization processes. Some examples of technics are delimitating an investigation to its core questions; defining concepts by giving examples; distinguishing between different levels of dialogue (on the content, strategic, and emotional level); and dissociation of concepts.[72]

I found another example of the Socratic method described in an interview Molly McQuade had with Susan Sontag. Sontag tells that in her student days at the University of Chicago, she studied with Joseph Schwab, "the best embodiment of Chicago's version of the Socratic method": "Schwab taught several sections of Observation,

Interpretation, Integration ('OII'). This was the master course, the philosophy course. In the second year, I audited the whole course with him again. I still think with tools I learned from Schwab."[73] The Socratic Chicago style of teaching did instruct students not only in reading and reasoning, but also in debating and experiencing "a constant dialogue of texts." Although Harvard University also has been a component in Sontag's education, she finds her exposure to the Socratic method in Chicago to have been a persitant influence in her writing. I conclude then that the Socratic method seems to have countless appearances and may include university instruction and the literary essay as well.

PUBLIC PHILOSOPHY: PHILOSOPHICAL CAFÉS, SALONS, AND PHILOSOPHY AT THE SHOPPING MALL

The French philosopher Marc Sautet began in a "systematic manner," that is in a regular and consistence manner and backed up by philosophical arguments, what has become known as the cafés-philos or philosophical cafés movement.[74] Inspired by Achenbach's private philosophy practice, Sautet began a Cabinet de Philosophie in 1992. However, the little interest he encountered for his newly opened cabinet gave him the idea to take philosophy practice to the favored abode of the French: the café. He situated the first café-philo in the Paris Café des Phares. Since then philosophical cafés have become popular worldwide. Sautet founded an organization called the Association Les Amis du Cabinet de Philosophie and the society's journal *Philos*.[75] It is most unfortunate that Sautet only saw the beginning of his international success. In March 1998 he died at the age of fifty-one from a brain tumor.

Though cafés and salons are a seventeenth-century bourgeois invention and have little to do with Socrates, public debates and wine were essential to Socrates's lifestyle. Sautet's interpretation of Socrates's style of dialogue is similar to that of Achenbach's: No techniques are presented on how the dialogue has to unfold, but there are a few guidelines. The philosopher asks the café visitors which topics they would like to discuss, and from these topics the public may select one or more. The discussion begins without dictating any preconceived aims, methods, or discussion goals. The philosopher may contribute to the discussion by asking questions or giving a philosophical interpretation, but basically his or her task is that of a facilitator. Since philosophical cafés became fashionable, other variants of the Sautet cafés began to develop:

1. A philosopher presents a lecture followed with a discussion.

2. A philosopher presents a number of topics from which the public chooses which one to discuss.

3. A philosopher presents a discussion topic and guides the group discussion with the intention of attaining consensus about the particular topic.

In Minneapolis, the popular magazine *Utne Reader* published in its April 1991 issue a group of eight articles titled "Salons: How to Revive the Endangered Art of Conversation and Start a Revolution in Your Neighborhood."[76] Apparently many people had enough of gathering around the T.V., and consequently the article received an overwhelming response. The *Utne Reader* reports that within a year about 20,000 people joined their Neighborhood Salon Association. Accompanying the surprising success of the Minneapolis salons is *The Joy of Conversation: The Complete Guide to Salons.*[77] Although the "big talk" advocated by the Minneapolis movement may only by coincidence be philosophical in content and degree, the philosophical–literary salon is doubtless quite similar to the Minneapolis salon. The philosophical–literary salon in which a lecture is presented or philosophical books and topics are discussed have been events organized by philosophical practitioners—for example, by Achenbach, Ida Jongsma, and myself.

Another public philosophy novelty is the shopping mall and public park philosopher Peter March of Saint Mary's University, Halifax, Canada. For about a decade March has been investigating sympathetically the philosophies of people he meets in public places, with the aim to understand how philosophy influences their lives. In a lecture titled "Vernacular Philosophy," presented at an ASPP seminar on 28 September 1993, March argued: "A new view of philosophy would encourage young philosophers to think with the Jesuits but walk with the Franciscans: They must carry the seeds of their subject, so long dormant, out of the safe stores of academe." A new type of philosopher is needed for developing vernacular philosophy: Academic harshness in debate has to be left behind. Only gentle philosophers can facilitate people in giving birth to their thoughts.

CONCLUSION

It may be too soon to come to more than a temporary conclusion about the practices described here. Achenbach has already pointed out that philosophical practice is still in its infancy and that timely reflections on it are likely to be changed by lessons learned through further experience.

Nevertheless, it can be said that the unifying and possibly enduring characteristic of the various philosophical practices described here is their educational value. A counselee learns from meetings with the philosophical practitioner to question, think about, and comprehend the self and its problems in various philosophical ways. The consultation sessions and group meetings are philosophical exercises concerning subjective states of mind, emotions, and other issues connected to the counselee's life. To relate one's subjectively bound consciousness to an objective, analytic, phenomenological or synthetic awareness, requires the exercise of new ways of thinking. Philosophical practice offers, at least potentially, what philosophy itself is supposed to offer: freedom from the preconceived, the ill-conceived, the prejudiced, and the hubris of knowing it all.

NOTES

1. Pierre Hadot, *Philosophy as a Way of Life* (Oxford: Blackwell, 1995); Richard Shusterman, *Practicing Philosophy: Pragmatism and the Philosophical Life* (New York: Routledge, 1997).

2. Johan Huizinga, *Homo Ludens* (Boston: Beacon, 1955), 112.

3. Martha C. Nussbaum, *The Therapy of Desire: Theory and Practice in Hellenistic Ethics* (Princeton, N.J.: Princeton University Press, 1994), 11.

4. Cicero, *Selected Works*, ed. E. Rieu, B. Radice, and R. Baldic (Harmondsworth, England: Penguin, 1965), 157, 160.

5. Karl Marx, *Selected Writings*, ed. D. McLellan (Oxford: Oxford University Press, 1977), 158.

6. Nicholas Lobkowicz, *Theory and Practice: History of a Concept from Aristotle to Marx* (Notre Dame, Ind.: Notre Dame University Press, 1967); Richard J. Bernstein, *Praxis and Action* (Philadelphia: Duckworth, 1972).

7. David W. Hamlyn, *Being a Philosopher: The History of a Practice* (London: Routledge, 1992).

8. Ibid., 173.

9. Albert W. Levi, *Philosophy as Social Expression* (Chicago: University of Chicago Press, 1974), 1, 12–13, 316.

10. Robert Baker and Frederick Elliston, *Philosophy and Sex* (New York: Prometheus, 1984); Sissela Bok, *Lying* (New York: Vintage, 1979); A. Phillips Griffiths, ed., *Philosophy and Practice* (Cambridge: Cambridge University Press, 1985); Oswald Hanfling, *The Quest for Meaning* (New York: Blackwell, 1987); Peter Singer, ed., *A Companion to Ethics* (Oxford: Blackwell, 1993).

11. Barry Hoffmaster, "The Theory and Practice of Applied Ethics," *Dialogue* 30, 3 (1991): 213–234; Hans Krämer, *Integrative Ethik* (Frankfurt: Suhrkamp, 1992); Hans Krämer, "New Paths in Philosophical Ethics," *Universitas* 27, 3 (1985): 209–220; Peter T. Kemp, "Toward a Narrative on Ethics: A Bridge between Ethics and the Narrative Reflection of Ricoeur," *Philosophy and Social Criticism* 14, 2 (1988): 179–201.

12. Gerd B. Achenbach, *Philosophische Praxis* (Cologne: Jürgen Dinter, 1987), 14.

13. Gerd B. Achenbach, "About the Center of Philosophical Practice," in *Perspectives in Philosophical Practice: The Proceedings of the Second International Congress on Philosophical Practice*, ed. W. van der Vlist (Doorwerth, The Netherlands: The Dutch Society for Philosophy Practice, 1997), 7–15.

14. Herbert Goldenberg, *Contemporary Clinical Psychology* (Los Angeles: California State University, 1973), 108, 114; Stephen Murgatroyd, *Counseling and Helping* (London: The British Psychological Society, 1988), 42.

15. Goldenberg, *Contemporary Clinical Psychology*, 32–37; Jeffrey M. Masson, *Against Therapy* (New York: Atheneum, 1988).

16. Achenbach, *Philosophische Praxis*, 29.

17. Gerd B. Achenbach and Peter Sloterdijk, "Gespräch über die Lebenskunst, zur Welt zu kommen," *Agora: Zeitschrift für Philosophische Praxis* 4 (1988): 1–3.

18. Peter Sloterdijk, *Critique of Cynical Reason*, trans. M. Eldred (Minneapolis: University of Minnesota Press, 1987); Merold Westphal, "Briefer Book Reviews," *The International Philosophical Quarterly* 39, 4 (1989): 479–480. See also Peter Sloterdijk, *Der Zauberbaum: Die Entstehung der Psychoanalyse im Jahr 1785* (Frankfurt: Suhrkamp, 1995).

19. Ekkehard Martens, "Sokrates als philosophischer Praktiker," in *Philosophische Praxis*, ed. Gerd B. Achenbach (Cologne: Jürgen Dinter, 1984), 143.

20. Achenbach and Sloterdijk, "Gespräch über die Lebenskunst," 2.

21. B. Jowett, *The Dialogues of Plato*, vol. 1 (New York: Random House, 1937), 423.

22. Gerd B. Achenbach and Thomas H. Macho, *Das Prinzip Heilung* (Cologne: Jürgen Dinter, 1985), 7.

23. Susan Sontag, *Against Interpretation* (New York: Farrar, Straus and Giroux, 1966), 17, 23.

24. Achenbach and Macho, *Das Prinzip Heilung*, 49–81.

25. Fred Newman and Lois Holzman, *Lev Vygotsky, Revolutionary Scientist* (New York: Routledge, 1993), 47. See also Fred Newman and Lois Holzman, *The End of Knowing: A New Developmental Way of Learning* (New York: Routledge, 1997); Fred Newman, *The Myth of Psychology* (New York: Castillo, 1991).

26. Achenbach and Macho, *Das Prinzip Heilung*, 86–126.

27. Gerd B. Achenbach, "On Wisdom in Philosophical Practice," *Inquiry: Critical Thinking across the Disciplines*, 17, 3 (1998): 5–20.

28. Odo Marquard, "Philosophische Praxis," in *Historisches Wörterbuch der Philosophie*, vol. 7 (Basel, Switzerland: Verlag Schwabe, 1989), 1307; Odo Marquard, *Tranzendentaler Idealismus, Romantische Naturphilosophie, Psychoanalysis* (Cologne: Jürgen Dinter, 1987).

29. Regular updated information on philosophical practitioners and their organizations worldwide, including addresses and/or links to their homepages can be found on the Philosophical Counseling Website: http://www.geocieties.com/Athens/Forum/5914.

30. Gerd Achenbach and Odo Marquard, "'Diese Biene ist ein Lügner': Der Philosoph als Berater," *ZPP: Zeitschrift für Philosophische Praxis* 2 (1994): 4.

31. Steffen Graefe, *Was heisst Philosophiche Praxis?* (Hamburg, Germany: Privatdruck, 1989); Günther Witzany, *Philosophieren in einer bedrohten Welt* (Essen, Germany: Die Blaue Eule, 1989) and *Zur Theorie der Philosophischen Praxis* (Essen, Germany: Die Blaue Eule, 1991).

32. Melanie Berg, *Philosophische Praxen im deutschsprachigen Raum: Eine kritische Bestandsaufnahme* (Essen, Germany: Die Blaue Eule, 1992), 165, 175; Achenbach, *Philosopische Praxis*, 53.

33. Michael Zdrenka, *Konzeptionen und Probleme der Philosophischen Praxis* (Cologne: Jürgen Dinter, 1997), 179–189.

34. Martina Winkler-Calaminus, "Similia similibus curantur," *Agora: Zeitschrift für Philosophische Praxis* 5–6 (1989): 13–14; Franz Vonessen, *Was krank macht, ist auch heilsam: Mythisches Gleichheitsdenken, Aristoteles' Katharsis-Lehre und die Idee der homöopathischen Heilkunst* (Heidelberg, Germany: Haug, 1980).

35. Zdrenka, *Konzeptionen und Probleme der Philosophischen Praxis*, 66–70.

36. Alexander Dill, *Philosophische Praxis* (Frankfurt: Fischer Taschenbuch Verlag, 1990).

37. Ekkehard Martens, "Philosophische Praxis ohne Philosophie," *Agora: Zeitschrift für Philosophische Praxis* 8–9 (1990): 17–18.

38. Information on von Morstein's practice is taken from the following sources: personal correspondence with von Morstein; Petra von Morstein, "Breath Life into Philosophy, Professor Urges," *Calgary Herald*, 11 September 1987, F14; and summaries from lectures by von Morstein at the ASPP seminars. All quotations are from the newspaper article, "Breath Life into Philosophy, Professor Urges," with the exception of the quotations from von Morstein's paper, "Wittgenstein on Philosophical Methods as Therapies," *ZPP: Zeitschrift für Philosophische Praxis* 2 (1994): 13–19.

39. Elliot D. Cohen, *Philosophers at Work* (New York: Holt, Rinehart and Winston, 1988).

40. Elliot D. Cohen, "Logic, Rationality and Counseling," *The International Journal of Applied Philosophy* 5, 1 (1990): 43–49. See also on philosophical counseling as rational emotive therapy: Roger Paden, "Defining Philosophical Counseling," *The International Journal of Applied Philosophy* 12 (1998): 1–17; Warren Shibles, "Philosophical Counseling, Philosophical Education and Emotion," *The International Journal of Applied Philosophy* 12 (1998): 18–36.

41. Gerd B. Achenbach, "What Does It Mean to Say: Philosophical Practice Is No Psychotherapy," in *Perspectives in Philosophical Practice: The Proceedings of the Second International Congress on Philosophical Practice*, ed. W. van der Vlist (Doorwerth, The Netherlands: The Dutch Society for Philosophy Practice, 1997), 19. The Norway-based philosophical practitioner Anders Lindseth likewise subscribes to the concept of the philosophical practitioner as lay-helper; see Anders Lindseth, "Was ist Philosophische Praxis?" *Agora: Zeitschrift für Philosophische Praxis*, 8–9 (1990): 13.

42. Ida Jongsma, "Ontstaans geschiedenis van de filosofische praktijk in Amsterdam," *Filosofische Praktijk* 1 (1987): 17.

43. Ad Hoogendijk, *Spreekuur bij een filosoof* (Utrecht, The Netherlands: Veen, 1988).

44. Martin Buber, *Pointing the Way* (New York: Harper & Row, 1963).

45. Mariette Huisjes, "Mensen hebben ideeën nodig," *Cimedart*, Faculteitsblad van de Centrale Interfaculteit, Universiteit van Amsterdam (1987): 7–9; Hoogendijk, *Spreekuur bij een filosoof*, 78–91.

46. Friedriech Nietzsche, "Thus Spoke Zarathustra," in *The Portable Nietzsche*, ed. W. Kaufman (New York: Viking, 1954), 407.

47. Dries Boele, "In Dialoog met het gewetene," *Filosofische Praktijk* 2 (1987): 7–18.

48. Hoogendijk, *Spreekuur bij een filosoof*, 128.

49. Ibid., 53.

50. Franz Fanon, *The Wretches of the Earth* (New York: Grove Weidenfeld, 1963).

51. Susan Sontag, *Trip to Hanoi* (New York: Farrar, Straus, and Giroux, 1968), 89.

52. Ad Hoogendijk, *Filosofie voor managers* (Amsterdam: Veen, 1991).

53. Robert L. Heilbroner, *The Worldly Philosophers* (New York: Simon and Schuster, 1972).

54. P. Rademaker, "Filosofie en bedrijfsleven," *Wijsgerig Perspectief* 29 (1988–1989): 132–136.

55. Hans Achterhuis, *Arbeid, een eigenaardige medicijn* (Baarn, The Netherlands: Amboboeken, 1984); Hans Achterhuis, *De markt van welzijn en geluk* (Baarn, The Netherlands: Amboboeken, 1988); Hannah Arendt, *The Human Condition* (New York: Doubleday, 1958).

56. Eite P. Veening, *Over de werkelijkheid van drie werelden* (Groningen, The Netherlands: E. P. Veening, 1998). Ph.D. diss., "An attempt to present a coherent and relevant reconstruction, expansion and revision of Karl Popper's Tree-World Theory." Chapters 10 and 11 demonstrate the potential usefulness of Popper's theory in philosophy practice.

57. Gregory Bateson, *Steps to an Ecology of Mind* (San Francisco: Chandler, 1972), 201.

58. Eite Veening, "Monoloog, dialoog en metaloog," *Filosofische Praktijk*, 2 (1987): 19–25.

59. Eite P. Veening, *Denkwerk* (Culemborg, The Netherlands: Phaedon, 1994).

60. Ibid., 75.

61. Ibid., 114.

62. Leonard Nelson, *Vom Selbstvertrauen der Vernunft* (Hamburg, Germany: Felix Meiner, 1975); Jos Kessels, "The Socratic Dialogue as a Method of Organizational Learning," in *Perspectives in Philosophical Practice: The Proceedings of the Second International Congress on Philosophical Practice*, ed. W. van der Vlist (Doorwerth, The Netherlands: The Dutch Society for Philosophy Practice, 1997), 45–60; Dries Boele, "The 'Benefits' of a Socratic Dialogue," *Inquiry: Critical Thinking across the Disciplines* 17, 3 (1998): 48–70.

63. A contact person for the Philosophisch–Politische Akademie e.V. is Nora Walter in Ronnenberg, Germany. Rene Saran is an experienced instructor in the field of the Socratic method in Britain and belongs to the Society for the Furtherance of Critical Thinking. Similar to the organizational developments in The Netherlands, the British Society for Consultant Philosophers, under the presidency of Karin Murris, has taken up the practice of Socratic discourse as well. See Rene Saran, "How to Prepare a Socratic Dialogue," in *Perspectives in Philosophical Practice: The Proceedings of the Second International Congress on Philosophical Practice*, ed. W. van der Vlist (Doorwerth, The Netherlands: The Dutch Society for Philosophy Practice, 1997), 293–314; and Karin Murris, "The Baby and the Bath Water," in *Perspectives in Philosophical Practice: The Proceedings of the Second International Congress on Philosophical Practice*, ed. W. van der Vlist (Doorwerth, The Netherlands: The Dutch Society for Philosophy Practice, 1997), 117–134.

64. Leonard Nelson, *Socratic Method and Critical Philosophy*, trans. T. K. Brown III (New York: Dover, 1949); Leonard Nelson, *System of Ethics*, trans. N. Guterman (New Haven, Conn.: Yale University Press, 1956). According to Julius Kraft's introduction to the last mentioned book, manuscript translations of the first volume of Nelson's *Critique of Practical Reason* are available on microcards at leading libraries.

65. Nelson, *Socratic Method and Critical Philosophy*, ix, x.

66. Ibid., 11, 130.

67. Kelley L. Ross, "The Foundations of Value," in *The Proceedings of the Friesian School*, parts 1 and 2, http://www.friesian.com/founda-1.htm and http://www.friesian.com/founda-2.htm (last accessed 18 August 1998).

68. Gert de Boer, "Socrates in Willebadessen," *Filosofische Praktijk* 6 (1989): 21–23.

69. Jos Kessels, "Korte karakteristiek van het Socratisch gesprek volgens Nelson en Heckmann," and "Een repliek aan Eite Veening," in *Filosofische Praktijk* 6 (1989): 5–12, 16–20.

70. Jos Kessels, *Socrates op de markt: Filosofie in bedrijf* (Amsterdam: Boom, 1997); Loes de Jong and Wim van der Vlist, "Socrates op de markt: Interview met Jos Kessels," *Filosofie* 8, 1 (1998): 37–42.

71. Jos Kessels, "The Socratic Dialogue as a Method of Organizational Learning," in *Perspectives in Philosophical Practice: The Proceedings of the Second International Congress on Philosophical Practice*, ed. W. van der Vlist (Doorwerth, The Netherlands: The Dutch Society for Philosophy Practice, 1997), 45.

72. Ibid., 48–49; Peter Senge, ed., *The Fifth Discipline Fieldbook: Strategies and Tools for Building a Learning Organization* (London: Nicholas Brealey, 1994).

73. Molly McQuade, "A Gluttonous Reader: Susan Sontag," in *Conversations with Susan Sontag*, ed. L. Poague (Jackson: University Press of Mississippi, 1995), 274.

74. Marc Sautet, *Un café pour Socrate* (Paris: Robert Laffont, 1995). *Un café pour Socrate* has been translated into German and Japanese. Forthcoming are translations in English, Italian, and Portuguese. For articles

in English on philosophical cafés see Jeremy Iggers, "Pensées au lait: France's Latest Culteral Invention—the Philosophical Café—Has Arrived," *Utne Reader* 82 (1997): 12–13, Internet publication: http://www.utne.com/lens/act/82culturecafe.html (last accessed 11 March 1999); Debra Galant, "Cream and Sugar? Philosophical Discourse?" *The New York Times*, 1 June 1997, sec. 13; Peter B. Raabe, "Philosophy in Public," *Elenchus* 2, 1 (1997): 6–8; Joseph Chandler, "Ceci n'est-pas un philosophe," *The Philosophers Magazine* 2 (1998): 10–11; Joseph Chandler, "The Philosophers' Paris: A Walk Through *La Rive Gauche*," *The Philosophers Magazine* 3 (1998): 12–13.

75. Association Les Amis du Cabinet de Philosophie, 15 rue de Sevigne 75004, Paris. The association has a listing of philosophical cafés worldwide.

76. Gareth Branwyn, Stephanie Mills, John Berendt, David Bohm, Cary D. Wintz, Jack Zimmerman, Virginia Coyle, Christopher Lasch, and Beth Lapides, "Salons: How to Revive the Endangered Art of Conversation and Start a Revolution in Your Neighborhood," *Utne Reader* 44 (1991): 66–88, Internet publication: http://www.utne.com/cafe/caferesources.html (last accessed 11 March 1999).

77. Jaida n'ha Sandra, *The Joy of Conversation: The Complete Guide to Salons* (Minneapolis, Minn.: Utne Reader Publications, 1998).

CHAPTER 3

Philosophical Care

> If philosophy would become therapeutic, it would really come
> into its own.
>
> Herbert Marcuse, *One-Dimensional Man*

This chapter consist of an introduction, a historical sketch of the
use of philosophy to take care of the soul, and a section on modern
philosophical care. The term "philosophical care" includes the concepts of what is therapeutic and transtherapeutic. The term
"transtherapeutic" describes philosophies that, in spite of their
therapeutic effects, were not considered therapy by their inven-
tors. Among the instances where philosophy has been perceived as
therapy, Plato's thought stands out, in that it has been compared
with both psychoanalysis and antipsychiatry.

The section on modern philosophical care, as embodied in my
own philosophical practice, includes: (a) philosophical criticism of
psychotherapy and the adoption of this criticism in philosophical
counseling (accentuating questions about truth and reality); and
(b) philosophical influences on psychotherapy and how these influences are used in philosophical counseling (accentuating questions
about friendship and love).

INTRODUCTION

Unlike modern philosophical counselors, philosophers who have cared for people in the past often believed their philosophy to be therapy. The first philosophical therapist might have been the Sophist Antiphon. Pedro Lain Entralogo quotes from the Pseudo-Plutarch (Vit. X orat., I, 18) that Antiphon "founded an art to cure griefs, analogous to that one which among physicians serves as a basis for the treatment of diseases; in Corinth, near the agora, he arranged a place with a sign, in which he announced himself as able to treat the grief-stricken by means of discourses." Antiphon also had a reputation as a rhetorician—he was well known for his performances of "soothing" and "consoling recitations"—and as an interpreter of portents and dreams.[1] Lain Entralogo showed that there were quite a few philosophers like Antiphon in classical antiquity.

Research on the relationship between psychology and philosophy has shown that until the mid-nineteenth century, the history of the philosophy of mind was identical with the history of psychology.[2] Psychology became emancipated from philosophy when psychologists claimed the status of empirical biological scientists. Nevertheless, philosophers continued to give their own new interpretations for concepts like soul, mind, self, and ego. Bertrand Russell, for example, proposed an overall theory that stated that the substance from which the universe is composed is neutral, not mental or physical. In "What is Soul?" he writes, "Matter has become altogether too ghostly to be used as an adequate stick with which to beat the mind."[3] Organized in one way, Russell's "neutral stuff" yields the laws of physics; organized in another way, it results in the laws of psychology. Such an account of nature can provide philosophers and psychologists with a new basis for collaboration. In addition, the Kantian dictum that human action cannot be the subject of science—because action originates in reason, deliberation, and choice—is a historical justification of philosophical care for modern people.

A modern voice that rejects—as Kant would have—the identification of scientific observations with human experiences and behavior is Norman Malcolm. Malcolm argues that though brain stimulations can trigger psychological and physical reactions in persons, this is no empirical evidence or indication of one-to-one correlations between mental and brain states. While Malcolm presents conceptual arguments against identifying mind states with brain states, he also makes use of Elliot Valenstein's scientific research, because of its philosophical significance: "Valenstein's research shows that there is no evidence of any one-to-one correlations between neural circuits on the one hand and, on the other hand, any emotions or moods, such as fear, anger, or anxiety, or even any behavioral sequences, let alone any particular thoughts, desires, or memories."[4]

In spite of this difficulty in constructing a behavioral or cognitive science, there is an increasing affiliation between psychology and philosophy in psychologists' awareness of the philosophical roots of psychology and the inherent value systems in psychotherapy. Nathaniel Pallone quotes Orvill Walters, who finds every psychotherapist a kind of philosopher, because of the value systems operating in psychotherapy.[5]

Psychologists Lawrence Brammer and Everett Shostrom consider that a philosophy of life has therapeutic value. Their research shows that there is a "need for each person to work out a philosophy to fit the times and circumstances. If he or she does not have such a philosophy, he or she generally suffers from feelings of drifting, pessimism, loneliness, disillusionment, and possibly even disintegration. Having a satisfying philosophy appears to build personal strength."[6] Brammer and Shostrom's way of helping patients to find a satisfying philosophy is as follows: After the therapist's introductory clarification of the patient's latent philosophy of life, patients who are considered ready for philosophical help are advised to see a theologian for "philosophical talks" or are directed by the therapist to read philosophical literature. Hopefully in a future edition of *Therapeutic Psychology: Fundamentals of Counseling and Psychotherapy*, Brammer and Shostrom will add to their list of references philosophical counselors for philosophical talks.

This seems to me preferable to choosing a theologian for philosophical talks, since pastoral care in both the Christian and the Jewish traditions (and possibly in other religions as well) have become closely interrelated with forms of psychotherapy in the twentieth century. Whereas in former times, theologians relied on the source of their faith or on philosophy in caring for their flock, at present most theological seminars teach pastoral psychology for use in spiritual guidance. *The Clinical Handbook of Pastoral Counseling* states, "Pastoral counseling as defined as the interdisciplinary use of theology and psychology for the task of mediating care is an important new movement within the church. But it is also a synthesis of two important cultural resources—the Judeo–Christian tradition and the modern psychologies."[7] The role of the spiritual director has become rather like that of the therapist, to such an extant that complaints are heard about spiritual directors who are not able to hear people's theological or philosophical questions because these were interpreted as psychological questions: "For many psychology had become a new religion."⁸ Among the voices raising a theological critique of the "new pastoral care" is that of the theologian Dietrich Bonhoeffer. He considers psychotherapy a secular offshoot of the religious confession; however, it "did not leave the person to him or herself but came as a form of bondage."⁹ The philosopher–theologian Paul Tillich presents a rather mild critique, but a vibrant alternative. He finds that pathological anxiety cannot be doctored away by medication or psychotherapy: "Existential anxiety has an ontological character and cannot be removed but must be taken into the courage to be. Pathological anxiety is the consequence of the failure of the self to take the anxiety upon itself."¹⁰ Tillich presents in *The Courage to Be* examples taken from the history of philosophy and theology that can help people to make a courageous self-affirmation in the face of despair and anxiety.

Rabbi Earl A. Grollman states, "[The clergyman] is most effective when he acts as a pastor, not as an amateur psychiatrist. He should not forsake his own traditional resources and spiritual functions."¹¹ Grollman backs up his insight with quoting Paul Moore, Suffragan Bishop of Washington, reminding his priests to refrain from becoming "clinical therapists" with the title "Reverend" in front of their name. Additional to the objections of Rabbi Grollman, Bishop Moore, Bonhoeffer, and Tillich against the psychologization of pastoral care, there are critical fundamentalist–evangelical voices as well, such as Gary Almy, a professor of psychiatry at Loyola Medical School in Chicago. Almy initiated the Biblical Counseling Center "in hope of raising a standard for truth in the morass of psychotherapy passing as 'Christian counseling.'"¹²

Research in the history of the philosophy of mind, with the aim of making explicit its therapeutic and transtherapeutic usefulness is new, but not without predecessors: The philosopher Stephen Clark claims, from a Neoplatonic Christian perspective, that philosophy "began as the pursuit of wisdom, the care of the soul, and has not wholly lost that office. When we have travelled down the many circles of our madness and insecurity, we may follow our great guide up through the cranny and so see again the stars."¹³ Likewise, William James and Michel Foucault described philosophy as care for the soul or the self. In *The Discovery of the Unconscious*, Henri Ellenberger writes about philosophical psychotherapy in the ancient world. He finds that philosophical psychotherapy was not generally practiced on an individual basis; rather, it took place as "collective education, discipline, and mental training that they [the philosophers] taught on a collective level."¹⁴ Becoming a member of a specific philosophical school is compared with a kind of philosophical conversion or being initiated into a certain mode of living.

Ellenberger demonstrates the effects of this collective therapy on an individual level as well: Galen's methods of individual therapy and his treatise *On the Passions of the Soul* were inspired by the ancient philosophical–psychotherapeutic culture and must be understood in this context.

Another historical account of therapy that considers the relevance of philosophy is Jan Ehrenwald's anthology on the ancient-to-modern combat against mental illness. Ehrenwald describes the development from magic to religious and scientific healing methods, the last of which he considers as having developed out of philosophy. Ehrenwald's treatment of the subject is marked by his accentuation of common aspects of the different methods: The psychotherapist in relation to his patients "may find himself in much the same predicament as the primitive medicine man seeking to control, to change or to foretell the weather."[15] The interrelatedness of the magical, religious, philosophical, and scientific healing methods made it conceivable for Ehrenwald to predict a return to former methods. It was about twenty-five years after Ehrenwald's prediction that philosophy proper, as a valuable and suitable alternative for psychotherapy, was again implemented in Achenbach's practice.

HISTORICAL PHILOSOPHY OF CARE

Some classical philosophies in their therapeutic or transtherapeutic capacities will now be examined. From each of these philosophies, central "caring" ideas will be highlighted. Finally, Plato's thought in depth as a paradigm for psychoanalysis, psychotherapy, antipsychiatry, and philosophical counseling will be considered.

Aristotle's ethics, in which virtue inheres in the mean, is an attempt to teach people "the good life" through moderation. "Any excessive state, whether of folly, of cowardice, of self-indulgence, or bad temper" is considered distressing for the human soul *Nichomachean Ethics*, bk. 7, ch. 5, 1149a.5).[16] Aristotle recommended that the state provide private supervisors—with a general knowledge of virtue—to guide people to the ideal of moderation; the Golden Rule, the way of moderation, could be taught through philosophy. Practical wisdom is the cure for the soul's extreme states, since this type of wisdom causes a person to take the right means. Practical wisdom is concerned with things just, noble, and good for people; it teaches the virtues of life. Although separate from philosophical wisdom, practical wisdom provides for its coming into being. Aristotle believed that, although virtues are innate, people must cultivate them. Students of practical wisdom have an affiliation for virtue and for what is noble. If the association with virtue is lack-

ing, punishments and penalties are initially used to change the
ways of people governed by immoderate passions.

The Stoics rejected Aristotle's notion of a nonrational (innate)
disposition of the soul that could be taught and corrected through
force. Chrysippus and other Stoics compared the deficiency of character at the root of moral errors with bodily diseases. The illnesses
of the soul corresponded to the soul's passions caused by emotional
disharmony. Impulses and passions were seen as produced by the
default of reason. Accordingly, the Stoics thought that people could
be improved or cured through the education of their reason. To the
Stoics, mental health is attained by a rational conception of matters, thus transforming inconsistent and hesitant opinions into a
knowledge of the good, which serves as the basis of inner harmony.[17]
The fourth book of Chrysippus's treatise on passions is called the
"therapeutic book" because it provides cures for life's maladies.
Bertrand Russell considered Stoic self-discipline more appropriate
than many twentieth-century psychotherapeutic methods. He characterized the Stoic attitude as the "acceptance of the unavoidable
with fortitude."[18]

Another example of philosophical care is Epicurus's *Letter to
Menoeceus*, in which the study of philosophy is explicitly called the
care for the well-being of the soul. Martha Nussbaum's impressive
book, *The Therapy of Desire*, investigates the "therapeutic argument" as a philosophical argument in the Epicurean, Stoic, and
Skeptic traditions. The analogy between philosophy and medicine
is more than a metaphor for these philosophers, yet philosophy is
above all the art of living. "All three schools, in short, could accept
the Epicurean definition of philosophy: 'Philosophy is an activity
that secures the flourishing . . . life by arguments and reasonings.'"
Nussbaum describes the analysis of the emotions in these ancient
texts as superior to any other work on emotions in the history of
Western philosophy. These classics, which were rich sources of inspiration for Descartes, Spinoza, and Adam Smith, have been ignored, in her opinion, by contemporary writers on the emotions,
"which therefore have to reinvent laboriously (and usually fall short
of) what was clear there."[19]

The ancient way of curing the soul with philosophy is also used
in the religious philosophies of Augustine, Philo of Alexandria, and
Maimonides. Augustine perceives philosophy as a port that can be
reached through a course founded on rational thought and individual will. From this port, "indeed a person can proceed to the
region and field of a happy life," which Augustine located in a
Neoplatonian type of Catholicism.[20] Philo and Maimonides likewise
synthesized Greek and Judaic ways of thinking, and both write

explicitly about philosophy as a cure. The synthesis of Greek philosophy with the Judaic and Christian religions created a new understanding of thinking and action in relation to physical and mental well-being. For the Hellenistic mind, there were direct links among proper thinking, right action, and well-being. In the Judeo–Christian worldview, the concept of "health" now became indirectly related to thinking and action, since God's volition had to remain the ultimate source of well-being.

A similar distinction can be found in contemporary therapeutic methods. Most human-centered and cognitive therapies are modeled on the Hellenistic pattern, while therapies focused on the unconscious correspond to the Judeo–Christian view of health. In the therapies previously mentioned, the therapist functions as a priest, guiding the afflicted into the healing domain of the decrees of the unknown God, "the Unconscious." If the mysteries of the unconscious are interpreted and obeyed, the patient may expect to become healthy, but when—if ever—this will occur cannot be predicted.

Philo was influenced by Plato. In *The Therapeutae*, Philo describes a Jewish philosophical community. Apparently these philosophers practiced an art of healing better than that of the doctors in the cities, "for the latter cures only the body, while theirs treats also souls mastered by grievous and virtually incurable diseases, inflicted by pleasures and lusts, mental pains and fears, by acts of greed, folly, and injustice, and the endless multitude of the other disturbances and vices."[21]

Maimonides writes in his *Eight Chapters on Ethics* that the soul, like the body, can be in good or ill health. The improvement of moral discipline is the appropriate therapy for the soul. The key to this sort of discipline is the Nicomachean middle way, which Maimonides compares to the ethical norms of the Jewish law. David Bakan explains in *Maimonides on Prophecy* that, in Maimonides's view, not only moral development but also intellectual cultivation is essential for well-being. Wrongdoing causes intrinsic injury to the intellect, while study promises relief for the confused mind and soul. Maimonides, following the teachings of the Talmudic sages, considered instruction—on a one-to-one basis—in "the Account of Creation" (*Maaseh Bereshith*) and "the Vision of Ezekiel" (*Maaseh Merkavah*) of special therapeutic value. Maimonides finds these treatises similar to Aristotle's *Physics* and *Metaphysics*, which he recommends for study.[22]

The modern philosopher who reintroduced the word and concept of "care" in philosophy is Martin Heidegger; he discusses care (*Sorge*) ontologically and existentially. He finds that Being-in-the-world is essentially care. "Care, as a primordial structural totality, lies 'before' ['vor'] every factical 'attitude' and 'situation' of Dasein, and it does so existentially *a priori*; this means that it always lies in them." Care means not only "cares of life," "worry," and "grief," but also "devotedness" and a commitment to personal perfection: "Man's *perfectio*— his transformation into that which he can be in Being-free for his ownmost possibilities (projection)—is 'accomplished' by 'care.'"[23] The psychiatrist Ludwig Binswanger interpreted in his theory on existential analysis existence as care and love, and in his definition of care, he incorporates much of Heidegger's understanding of care.[24]

Although Plato's philosophical care temporally preceded the other concepts discussed here, I have left it for last because I want to discuss it in greater detail. I have chosen Plato's thought because of its alleged similarity to psychoanalysis. In comparing it with various psychotherapeutic concepts, Plato's ideas are actually much closer to criticisms of psychotherapy and psychiatry and contain elements of antipsychiatry. In the case studies of "Daniel" and "Simone," presented in the second part of this book, I show how Plato's philosophical care is not only an inspiration for mental-health professionals but can also be useful in philosophical counseling by discussing the Platonian concepts of well-being, that is, justice and goodness.

Plato's thought is an inspiring paradigm for philosophical counseling in finding and thinking through concepts that induce well-being. Achenbach's understanding of philosophical practice as working *on* rather than *with* theories has considerable implications for presenting any paradigm: The theoretical paradigm is only a vague conception that has to be worked on—not with![25] In my presentation I identify concepts of care in Plato's thought, discuss these ideas in the context of contemporary psychology, and offer examples of how they can be practiced in life situations.

For Plato, goodness and justice were the essential ingredients of human well-being, though few therapists nowadays would claim that these features are *the* essential characteristics of the healthy personality. Mental health is often taken to mean normality; that is, a person's mental health depends on not behaving in opposition to the norms of society. If one maintains the accepted norms of the common world, one may be regarded as mentally healthy without having any respect or love for ideas such as being "good" or "just."

Though there are therapists with a critical sensibility towards commonly accepted norms of society, the norms of the so-called moral and materialistic majority still are the primary influence on most therapists' attitudes towards, for example, homosexuality, transvestism, and fetishism. An illustration of this is Betty Cannon's description of the so-called normal development of heterosexuality in Lacan's metatheory: "Lacan regards the phallus as the first pure signifier because it sets up the first set of 'binary oppositions' which the child, at the stage of entry into language, learns. One must locate oneself with respect to the phallus in order to enter the social order."[26] To Lacan, entering the social order is the proof of (heterosexual) mental health and maturity. How Lacan's theory, and likewise so many other psychological theories, comply to the standards of the DSM is another question. The latest version of this diagnostic manual only still recognizes some particular types of homosexuality as disorders. While homosexuals might have a moral stature similar to saints, transvestites to heroes, and fetishists to angels, they have not an equal part in a social order that declares its members as normal on grounds of a heterosexual preference.

Simone Weil properly asked how modern people "should be expected to learn to admire the good," since education and the development of talent apparently have no connection with morality.[27] Scientists and savants now enjoy the prestige once reserved for saints and sages. According to Weil, the Western genius used to be characterized by the love of truth and virtue, but this has been replaced by the love of power. Though it can be argued that the genius of Rome was building roads and waging war, one cannot deny that equally important aspects of its culture were art, religion, philosophy, and law.

Weil finds that in recent centuries the contradiction between science and humanism has not been recognized by most intellectuals, a contradiction that has undermined the vitality of Western culture. In the twentieth century, literary figures and even a few scientists have sounded alarms on this issue; an example is Sir Charles Snow in *The Two Cultures and the Scientific Revolution*.[28]

People became more aware of the chasm between the two cultures of science and humanism and it even seems to have had an impact on rejoining the estranged cultures: Susan Sontag, for example, observed that there has been a move toward one culture that unites the contradictory sides of the sciences and the arts. "This new sensibility is rooted, as it must be, in our experience, experiences which are new in the history of humanity."[29]

Weil's observations affirm some important ideas of Plato's *Republic*: Vitality and health are related to justice and truth. In Plato's *Republic*, the ideal state is founded in three stages. The "healthy city" is the first stage. It does not need laws or government. It is just (i.e., healthful) by nature, but lacks virtue and excellence. In the second stage, the city decays. In the third stage, the philosopher-king and the guardians restore and improve the city's former condition through moral education and rational rule. A rule of law and insight into its precepts was the care Plato prescribed for the city-state and its population.[30]

According to Anthony Kenny, the concept of mental health was Plato's invention. In Plato's *Dialogues*, physical therapy is used as a metaphor for therapy of the soul: Medicine and gymnastics are compared with justice and virtue. Judges were, for Plato, doctors of the soul. Though medical doctors, even if they themselves are sick, may nevertheless cure others, conversely, doctors of souls need themselves to have been "cured" of vice. A sound (healing) judgment is for Plato nothing but "the rule of soul by soul."[31]

A modern analogy to Plato's ethical therapy is found in the works of the critical psychiatrist Thomas Szasz. He interprets human behavior as dependent on "moral or social rule-games"; a person's survival depends on adapting to the social rules or changing them to suit one's needs. Szasz experienced that therapeutic attempts to alter human behavior without considering ethical issues are disappointing and ultimately fail; consequently he argues for the explicit introduction of ethical considerations into the mental-health professions. Freud's implicit ethical ideals (such as paternalism) are criticized by Szasz, whereas Alfred Adler is lauded for having made explicit the moral values inherent in Adlerian psychotherapy. Szasz recognizes the human need for rules as well as the desire to reject rules. His solution to this fundamental human paradox is in the realm of philosophy: "One of the most useful methods for resolving this dilemma is our capacity for abstraction which makes it possible to construct progressively higher levels of symbolization; these constructs, in turn, lead to a lessening of the feeling of compulsion attached to rules explicitly understood as rules."[32]

Similarities and differences between Plato's philosophy and Freud's psychology have been pointed out (among others) by Richard Norman and Bennett Simon.[33] Richard Norman views Freud's conception of the ego and the id as corresponding to Plato's conception of reason and desire. The superego approximates Plato's "spiritedness" in that it assists the ego by giving it emotional force to keep the id in check. Justice and virtue are identified with mental health, while compulsive and obsessive actions are considered insane and unjust. For the proper inner harmony to be achieved, reason in alliance with spirit must exercise strict control, inhibiting some desires and eliminating others. Freud sees a moderate repression of desires as desirable and inescapable, but excessive repression becomes harmful and self-defeating and may lead to mental illness. One can visualize this as a circular movement: Excessive repression causes the ego structure to break down and return to the chaotic "child-life" of the id.

Bennett Simon, a professor of psychiatry at Harvard, notes several differences between the conflict models created by Plato and by Freud. Plato envisioned that conflicting aspects in a person are likely to be harmonically ordered through philosophically attained truth. In contrast, Freud considered inner conflict inevitable because of prevailing infantile wishes. Simon believes that the idea of therapeutic catharsis, as found in Freud's early writings, was influenced by the idea of catharsis in the Greek tragedies. However, the healing charms of tragedy were rejected by Plato; a countercharm of dialogue and dialectics, uncovering and discovering truth, was to be the new way of purifying and healing the soul. Although both psychoanalytic discourse and philosophical dialectic discourse are concerned with the search for truth, they have different ideas about how it is to be found. The knowledge obtained through psychoanalysis comes from the analyst's interpretation of symbols (i.e., the "factual" understanding of personal myths). In Platonic discourse, in contrast, an inner search directed by logic causes people to remember the truth they already possess.

Simon claims that Freud should be understood in a wider philosophical framework, one beyond Plato. Indeed, it could be concluded from some of Freud's writings that he equates his hypothesis of the pleasure principle to the adoption of a philosophical system. For example, Freud considered belief in God—like philosophy—an illusion, but he thought that scientific intellectual activity shares the aims of religion: "This being so, we may tell ourselves that our antagonism is only a temporary one and not irreconcilable. . . . Our God, Logos, will fulfil whichever of these wishes nature outside us allows, but he will do it gradually, only in the unforeseeable future, for a new generation of man."[34] Nevertheless, Freud's attitude to philosophy is biased and ambiguous because of his supposition that philosophical and religious questions are, in fact, masks for repressed sexuality. Jung's observation that one of Freud's major faults was "to turn his back on philosophy" may explain the inconsistencies and ambiguities in Freud's conceptions, as well as his attitude to Plato's thought and philosophy in general.[35]

According to Rollo May, Freud and some of his followers supposed "the Eros of the divine Plato" to coincide exactly with the love force and the libido in psychoanalysis.[36] However, contrary to Freud's repressive sublimation of sexuality, Plato's sublimation of Eros is nonrepressive. Freud's Eros is turned back by a perpetual struggle with Thanatos, the death instinct, whereas Plato's Eros may ultimately lead to the love of wisdom and the good. Plato described Diotima, a wise woman of Mantinea—possibly a prophetess and psychic healer—from whom Socrates learned about love. The dialogue between Diotima and Socrates (Symposium 206) includes the following passage: "'Then love,' she said, 'may be described generally as the love of the everlasting possession of the good?' Socrates: 'That is most true.'"[37] This makes John M. Heaton, a member of the Philadelphia Association founded by R. D. Laing, conclude that Plato is Freud turned upside down: "Socrates understands sexual desire as a blind groping for the wisdom of philosophy. Sexual desire, rightly understood, leads to philosophy."[38]

I can agree with Heaton's understanding of Eros as the expression of a desire for wisdom and the good, but it is not to be identified with what Plato considered true or the right kind of love, wisdom, and the ultimate truth. Eros may lead to true love, but this a different kind of love. It is the love of beauty and order, temperance and harmony, not erotic sensual pleasure which distracts the human faculties just as pain does (Republic III, 403).[39]

Plato perceived not only Eros as beneficial, but also certain types of madness: for example, prophetic, ritual, poetic, or divine erotic madness. Eros, especially in its aspect of divine erotic madness, is a means a person can use to obtain self-knowledge and self-control. Plato was not the only philosopher in antiquity with a positive attitude towards some benign kinds of madness. In general ancient philosophers affirmed the concept of madness as divine and purposeful.[40] For example, in *On Tranquility*, Seneca summarized the classic affirmation of madness in the following words: "It (the mind) cannot attain anything sublime and lofty so long as it is sane."[41] R. D. Laing's antipsychiatric understanding of madness is comparable to the affirmation of madness by the ancient philosophers. Laing seeks "mad liberation."[42]

Norman wants to retain Plato's concept of goodness as significant for modern persons. Not goodness as a utopian, mystical concept, but "goodness as psychic health, and . . . the analysis of this health as a harmony between the parts of the personality."[43] Contrary to Norman, I maintain that the utopian vision of goodness can likewise be a source of mental health. The deficiency of justice in society, unethical behavior, and the apparent evil nature of life, are often in reality grounded complaints of those diagnosed as neurotics. I have found that these so-called neurotics often envision life as lacking any goodness because they have not developed an ethical understanding that purports the existence of good, that can define the concepts of good and evil, or that can think beyond good and evil. An ethical conception of life leads to a more realistic and balanced conception of the presumed malice in a person's life and world. Questioning why things are experienced as good or evil can serve as a basis for constructing an ethical worldview, which in turn may restore shattered hopes for goodness in emotionally injured people— or, one might more accurately say, ethically injured people.

Another invention of Plato with therapeutic and transtherapeutic consequences is the notion of soul or self. According to Alfred Taylor, the word "psyche" did not have the same meaning in the Homeric age as it has had throughout the rest of the history of Western civilization. The ancient meaning of the word was that of an "impersonal ghost." Plato's Socrates conceived of the soul as "that within us," causing a person's actions to be wise or foolish, good or bad.[44] The Socratic examination of the self was more than an improvement in understanding the conceptual and active realms of life: "This reflection, by creating the integration of one's system of opinions (and actions), also creates, in itself, the integration of the soul."[45] From this point of view, the soul is preexisting and born into a body. During the soul's stay in the body, the soul can rise or descend in purity. Nevertheless, vice cannot destroy the soul. After death, the souls of the righteous will not be reincarnated on earth, but in their purified state the immortal and indestructible souls will return to their celestial home.

In the twentieth century the concept of soul has almost vanished and has been replaced by the Freudian concept of ego. Simultaneously feelings of alienation and personal disintegration appear to have become more threatening and frequent. People envisioned with souls, as in Plato's definition, are like ships with anchors; they can let down their etherial anchors in a mystical haven if they wish. Without this anchor of soul, individuals may find themselves forever drifting and without a specific identity. When a clear identity is considered a prerequisite for peace of mind and well-being, a Platonian interpretation of self—in which the self is an inalienable but unfolding unity in a person—may provide some fundamental principles for identifying the self. However, other theoretical understandings of the self may likewise create tranquility—for example, the self as a Buddhist no-self.[46] The articulation of the notion of self can be beneficial. Whereas William James considered "self as the principle of being and operation in the psychic sphere," in contemporary counseling and psychotherapy it is only nondirective therapies—like the Rogerian ones—that regard the concept of the self as important.[47]

What is relevant for philosophical counselors and their counselees is not the rightness or wrongness of Plato's thought; nor is it to convince the counselee of the "need" to be healthy, to be in love, to be good and just, or that a person must have an indestructible soul. What is relevant is the Socratic–Platonic practice of dialogue and its dialogue subjects.

Thinking about and discussing these questions is useful for many but is probably not for everybody. Plato's thoughts might be considered especially appropriate for specific clients—for instance, when the notions of goodness, justice, love, or the definition of an inner world are a problem in a client's conceptional world or have never been reflected upon. A philosophical counselor may motivate his or her client to think these concepts through by showing how Plato and other thinkers found these concepts significant. After presenting the way Plato or others envisioned these elementary ideas of care, the philosophical practitioner may invite the client to take an independent view of these matters. When a client concludes that there is a causal relation between justice and well-being, it becomes possible to question how these two concepts are combined in his or her life. If a client finds it difficult to connect the "story" of his or her life to abstract notions, the practitioner may show through literature how the concrete and the abstract can be combined.[48]

Plato's philosophy remains a source of inspiration for many, even in this postmodern, anti-Platonian area. Pierre Grimes, for example, developed a method based on Platonian dialogue and concepts named philosophical midwifery. Central in Grimes's method is the "pathologos," a false belief blocking the inner development and achievement of a person. Through a systematic analysis of the origin, content, and elements of the pathologos, Grimes aspires in eight stages to resolve—or in midwife terminology, abort—such blocks. Unlike other philosophers or therapists using Socratic or Platonian dialogue methods, philosophical midwifery is fused with the goal inherent in Plato's conceptional vision: "The pathologos follows the same logic as the general description of the theory of participation in the Ideas. . . . [We] draw our comparison from Proclus, rather than Plato or Plotinus, for his thought most fully articulates the metaphysical dimension of Platonic thought."[49] The ultimate concern of Grimes's method is helping people achieve a spiritual destiny through development of consciousness as described in Plato's Republic, book six. Perhaps, on these grounds, Grimes considers philosophical midwifery a mode of philosophical counseling (obviously quite different from Achenbach's beyond-method approach); nevertheless it seems to me much more a faithful epitome of Platonian therapy. However, Grimes finds his method a mode of psychotherapy as well.

MODERN PHILOSOPHICAL CARE

Philosophical Criticism of Psychotherapy and the Adoption of This Criticism in Philosophical Counseling: Truth and Reality

"The need to re-examine the problem of mental illness is both timely and pressing. There is confusion, dissatisfaction and tension in our society concerning psychiatric, psychological and social issues," writes Thomas Szasz in the introduction to his book *The*

Myth of Mental Illness.[50] Many philosophical works are expressions of this dissatisfaction. One aspect of the criticism involves reality and truth in the therapeutic situation.

Jean-Paul Sartre published an essay called "Psychoanalytic Dialogue," which is supposed to be a transcription of tape-recorded psychoanalytic sessions made by patient "Mr. A." (Often therapists record or make videos of their sessions with patients.) But is it perhaps a Sartrean parody of a therapeutic session? Sartre asks in the introduction of the text, "Who is this man A . . . speaking? Is he no more than a blind psychological process, or is he the transcendence of this process by an act?"[51]

Several times during the psychoanalytic session, "Dr. X." accuses his patient Mr. A. of dangerous behavior caused by A.'s inability to cope with reality. Mr. A. responds to this accusation by asking what reality actually is. Mr. A. believes that it involves definitions that people have to agree on. He then continues with a sarcastic explanation of "the" therapeutic reality: "I know one thing, from the point of view of your reality, and that is that you're very angry . . . you're getting yourself in a state and that helps no one. I've got nothing against you, you've got no reason to be angry. I'm not your father!"[52] In another part of the dialogue, the patient expresses the philosophical view that time does not exist, to which Dr. X. responds from the perspective of his mechanically ordered world: Time always brings the therapeutic session to a sharp end. Though the analyst may believe that time does not exist in his patient's unconscious, discussing the different conceptions of time in psychoanalytic theory would not be appropriate in most psychoanalytic sessions.

Sartre's ideal of truth is the remaining illumination of all of being. On the other hand, Sartre finds that "it must be understood that *truth* is a kind of recovery of the In-itself by itself. . . . Being always reveals itself to a point of view and we are tempted to turn this point of view into subjectivity. But this is not so. Subjectivity is only *the illumination.*"[53]

Questions about reality and truth are not only important elements in the philosophical criticisms, but also in the practice of psychotherapy. Freud presented his theory as a scientific truth. Like Freud, many persons today still believe in the objectivity and truth of scientific, empirical findings, as if the day after tomorrow may not deliver different "objective" evidence.

Freud took psychoanalytic success as a proof of its truth, although his results could not be checked conclusively. Freud insisted that his method was scientific, in spite of his awareness that the patient is influenced by the therapist's suggestions because of the special relationship between them, which detracts from the evidential value of analysis. Accordingly, Popper, Ricoeur, and Habermas criticized Freud's theory as unscientific.[54] However, in "Criteria for a Psychoanalytic Interpretation," B. A. Farrel contends that science was not Freud's prime aspiration. Farrel demonstrates this claim by showing that the essence of psychoanalysis is not to give a scientific explanation of the patient but to cause him or her to change.[55]

In contradistinction to the many therapies that claim a monopoly on reality and truth, Maurice Friedman in *The Healing Dialogue in Psychotherapy* implies no prior definition of reality.[56] The therapist begins by honoring each person's unique relationship to reality. So-called "sick" people are not outside reality, but they need to be brought into dialogue with the aspects of reality held by others. Friedman calls contemporary society sick and sick making, because it does not recognize confirmation of otherness. An either–or orientation makes it necessary for each person to share in the reality of a community of affinity and to be one with it; otherwise, a person is considered different, one who disturbs the community's harmony or like-mindedness. In the latter case the community of affinity will label the other as "sick." In contrast a dialogical orientation could lead to a genuinely pluralistic and vital society. Friedman's approach and philosophical counseling in general are radically different from many forms of existentialist psychotherapy in the aspect of commitment to truth and reality. For example, one of the "glimmer" books, written by Emmy van Deurzen-Smith, of the London-based School for Existential Analysis states, "Existential therapists are required to be disciplined enough to pursue truth rather than the client's imagination, although coming to terms with the imaginative side of one's existence is of course part of the truth." Some of the basic truths of the van Deurzen-Smith's type of existential analysis are

1. People do not come to existential psychotherapy to catalogue themselves, but to change—to reorder their selves.
2. There must be hidden facets to the life of a counselee.
3. The therapist will face reluctance (the existential analysis term for resistance)—that is, the all-too-human habit of evasion.
4. Human nature is egocentric.
5. Value and self-esteem are crucial. Value is found in communal exchanges, not in one-sided self-assertion and self-justification.
6. The clients have to gain emotional awareness.[57]

In philosophical counseling the neutral and open attitude of the counselor toward the counselee's experience and understanding of reality and truth is of paramount importance. The philosophical attitude of wonder allows for an authentic interest and respect for the other's perspectives on truth and reality. The other's reality can be what most psychotherapists would diagnose as schizophrenic. For instance, a seventeen-year-old girl who came for several consultations with me had a problem with hearing "voices." I did not consider this as symptomatic of some illness, but something curious that would be interesting to understand. I asked the girl if she had an explanation for her experience. She said that she had entered her voice world by reading books on mind control that belonged to her parents. She had tried mind control exercises and believed that she could control her environment with her thoughts, but she also believed that her environment could order her to do various things. When she first entered the voice world, she heard her parents' voices; but after awhile the voices changed, and she could not identify them, which frightened her. The voices seemed so real to her that questioning their reality would have obviously raised a communication barrier between us. I thought it best to approach the issue from a pragmatic point. All she asked for was help coping with these voices.

I accepted her explanation for what it was, but questioned the morality behind the so-called "brain control system": Is it right to take a person's free choice away by controlling his or her mind? Maybe a person has powers of free choice in all situations, and it would be possible to resist such distant control? I suggested that if she would stop speaking to minds or voices, they might stop speaking to her. In addition, I suggested that it was more important to identify what the voices say—the morality of their demands—than why they were and who they were. I told her (and her family) about a study done on ordinary people who had had experiences with auditory hallucinations, explaining how these people had by themselves found ways of coping with the voices without clinical intervention.[58]

Another interesting alternative, though clinical, approach is described by Simon Du Plock. He finds a "careful application of the phenomenological method, though, may serve to disclose, if not the meaning of the hallucination . . . then its crucial significance in the context of the client's way of being in the world."[59] He disagrees with the usual applications of the diagnostic system that fixes the person into a category of illness and causes the unique experience of the individual not to be the object of close attention. Du Plock considers self-libeling, in addition to the clinical professionalist's libeling, to be unhelpful; his method is one of helping clients consider their lived reality as experientially valid. Another philosophical psychotherapist, Carl Rogers, likewise felt that not only

maladjusted individuals could be helped by his approach, characterized by congruence, empathy, and unconditional positive regard,
but also those persons labelled as chronically schizophrenic.[60]

I find it important to remember that Socrates seems to have had
experiences with auditory hallucinations. Apparently, the great philosopher had had to learn to live with an inner voice; he first began to
hear his "sign," a mysterious, forbidding voice, when he was a child
(Apology, 31).[61] In his time hearing voices and seeing visions were
acknowledged as valid human and divine experiences. However, this
fascinating aspect of Socrates' inner life seems not to have contributed much to averting his tragic, but nevertheless heroic death.

The philosophical counselor's knowledge of many philosophical
understandings of reality and truth allows him or her to further
articulate others' concepts. Whereas the counselee might have regarded his or her own deep thoughts and experiences as weird, the
philosopher tries to find a community of affinity for the counselee
by relating these thoughts and experiences to those of a philosopher or a philosophical school. The counselor can present a wide
perspective of truths and realities. By examining various concepts
of truth and value systems, the counselor challenges dogmatic
worldviews that would like to exclude any other philosophical perspectives. The counselor can also support the counselee's opinions
by articulating and questioning opposing views. Through a philosophical dialogue about truth and reality, the counselee may not
only become interested in philosophy and philosophers, but may
find a community of affinity among persons with a similar philosophical inclination.

Philosophical Influences on Psychotherapy
and How These Influences Are Used in
Philosophical Counseling: Friendship and Love

There have been noteworthy philosophical influences on various
psychotherapies. I consider it an advantage for psychotherapists
to use ideas created or developed by philosophers, although the
eclecticism found in most philosophical psychotherapies frequently
leads to unrecognized contradictions between philosophical ideas
and therapeutic methodology. Van Deurzen-Smith's comprehensive and interesting book, *Everyday Mysteries: Existential Dimensions of Psychotherapy*, presents an interesting overview about
twelve philosophers used for establishing the underpinnings of
existential psychotherapy. In addition, she describes a diverse group
of psychotherapists and psychiatrists who sought philosophical–
psychological alternatives to conventional methods of treatment

(e.g., Jacques Lacan, Ludwig Binswanger, Rollo May, and Irvin Yalom). Three pages are dedicated to Achenbach and Hoogendijk, although van Deurzen-Smith acknowledges that philosophical counselors or consultants are not therapists. She believes philosophical practitioners may learn much from therapists, and vice versa. To me, however, philosophy practitioners, like anyone else, rather must try to rid themselves of the burden of therapeutic consciousness. A "learned ignorance" concerning therapy, in spite of knowing what goes on in the world of therapy, is ideal for the philosophical practitioner. Learning from therapists seems to me only justified in the way Socrates learned from his dialogue partners. (Also, as an aside, van Deurzen-Smith's description of Hoogendijk made me wonder about her source. She refers to a 1983 text, which might be a mistaken reference, since this text does not appear in the bibliography of her book. In addition, to my knowledge, Hoogendijk started practicing philosophy only in 1987 and did not publish on the topic before that date. Hoogendijk's practice is described as one where "the philosophical issues that come to the fore in the client's discourse are always part of a polarity, for this is how [he understands that] the human condition is arranged."[62] However, I have not been able to find a trace of this polarized human condition as the essence of philosophical counseling dialogue in any of my conversations with Hoogendijk or in any of his writings.)

Van Deurzen-Smith's chapter on the general rules and additional instructions concerning existential work (i.e., outlining the entire existential approach) is further evidence that an indiscriminating eclecticism turns methodology into a mysterious venture: for example, "multiple consciousness" becomes a little diluted Freud, a bit of Gestalt, some Heidegger and Sartre, and a tiny bit of Jaspers and Foucault. Arguments pro or con regarding Freudian, Sartrean, or other types of consciousness are from van Deurzen-Smith's viewpoint "red-herring" debates. But is philosophical thinking and speaking not precisely about differences between red or other shades of colors, no matter if these colors are metaphorical adjectives for herrings, submarines, books, or philosophical debates? After Wittgenstein's *Remarks on Colours*, philosophical wonder and articulation of viewpoint about pigmentation is more than justified. The philosophers van Deurzen-Smith mentions are not material for dialogue talks with clients in therapeutic sessions, because the intent of van Deurzen-Smith is to provide through these philosophers underlying guidelines and principles for therapy methodology. The one-page appendix, "Four Dimensions of Existence," reveals the existential therapist's directions and shows in the blink of an eye that DSM-IV terminology is also used in existential therapy for diagnosing (or "describing," the less-loaded word van Deurzen-Smith prefers to conceal the therapeutic reality).

In contrast to this full-blown existential approach, the more modest existential–phenomenological framework proposed by Hans W. Cohn is to revive "the creative confrontation with Freud which characterizes the works of Binswanger and Boss." Cohn's attitude of confrontation seems to me to be philosophically coherent and an example of the wholesome type of eclecticism in psychotherapy. But even such coherent use of philosophy does not transform a psychotherapist into a philosophical counselor.

In a paper I gave at the Second International Conference for Philosophical Practice, I pointed out that apart from Achenbach, only Karl Jaspers and Michel Foucault present a radical and consistent change in practice paradigm; a change from a psychological to a philosophical methodology and way of life. Jaspers and Foucault both underwent a philosophical conversion by which they separated themselves from contemporary psychiatry and psychology, including many of the confused theories of existential psychotherapy.[64]

There are only a few therapies that use philosophical ideas consistently in their theories, or at least with the awareness that consistency is desirable. Examples are Laing's antipsychiatry, Buberian philosophical therapy, and Sartrean clinical practice. I will describe some of the philosophical influences of these psychotherapies and will show how these particular ideas that advocate friendship and Platonian love relationships find expression in my practice of philosophy.

Laing's Antipsychiatry

Whereas often humanistic and other untraditional therapists can hardly be understood (as their random eclecticism engenders the wildest paradoxes and contradictions), R. D. Laing's antipsychiatry has a clarity that belongs to philosophy proper. Basic in Laing's approach is that theory has its beginning in experience.[65] Experience is not only essential for theory, but for well-being in general. Human beings become alienated and mystified about themselves through the lack of the experience of reality, and this can lead to violence. Since "any experience of reality is indescribable," the interaction between therapist and patient is not an intellectual exchange, but "a matter of communicating experience" directly.[66] For example, the immediate experience by DSM standards diagnosed of a particular schizophrenic teaches Laing that the person is scared stiff. Laing does not know why this is the case, but he knows he must let the person experience that there is no need to be afraid: He walks around the room or reads a book, or might even fall asleep in front of the patient. In Laing's thought, philosophy is not the icing on the cake; it is an essential ingredient of the cake, which is the therapy itself. In his foreword to Laing's and Cooper's book *Reason and Violence,* Sartre discussed similarities between his own view and the antipsychiatrist approach: Human beings have to be understood from the inside, and not from "outside the illness as lived and experienced."[67]

In an interview with Max Charlesworth, Laing described Sartre's influence on his work as including (1) Sartre's concept of the dialectic; (2) the idea of human interaction placed within the context of social systems in which people are embedded; and (3) the distinction Sartre made between "process" and "praxis," or the distinction between "conceiving of events as simply happening without the mediation of any human agent, and as the result of human action."[68] Laing rejected a master–disciple relationship; instead, Sartre's work offered him ideas and categories to use in interpreting his own. However, Douglas Kirsner finds Laing to be a follower of Sartre, although most do not specifically recognize him as such.[69] Cohn confirms this last statement: "I find it difficult to discern a consistent philosophical framework in the work of R. D. Laing, and it was probably not his intention to provide one."[70]

Laing's concept of therapy as grounded in praxis is analogous to Sartre's *Critique of Dialectical Reason* as the de-mystification of psychological, sociological, and philosophical riddles. In Laing's antipsychiatry, Wilhelm Dilthey's "Verstehen" is a determining issue. Laing sees in psychotic and schizophrenic expressions "hieroglyphic" speech and action, rather than a distortion of logical thought processes. In the same way as Dilthey characterizes the relation between author and reader as the determining factor for the comprehension of a text, the relation between therapist and patient is essential for the therapist understanding the patient. Even if the therapist could know everything possible about the various disorders of cognition (e.g., thought, language, logic, memory, or perception), this would be no guarantee for understanding the patient. Understanding for Laing is not an intellectual process; it is a relation between therapist and patient. "For understanding one may say love is necessary."[71]

Relationships of love and friendship are in general unacceptable goals in therapy sessions, not to mention sexual relationships. Although avoiding the last type of relationship as helpful in general might be justified, the taboo on love and friendship seems unnecessary. Not only Laing, but others as well, have discovered that friendship and love can be extremely helpful for the therapist as well as the client. Susan Baur's research discloses that most therapists are unable to handle the intimate relationships they spontaneously come to experience with their patients and accordingly abandon feelings of love.[72] In Baur's view, this is regrettable. The neo-Jungian Adolf Guggenbühl-Craig advocates friendship as necessary for the therapist, but after working hours and away from his or her office and clientele; these friendships with colleagues and family members seem to help the therapist to cultivate the Jungian ideal of individuation.[73] If friendship is conceived as having such a benevolent effect for Jungian therapists, it seems to me that only the therapeutic role-play in the relationship between therapists and their clientele make friendships seem like an impossible mission. Also, as I pointed out in Chapter 2, Hoogendijk finds, just as the ancient philosophers and the philosophers of the Middle Ages did, that love is a condition for knowing reality, and that the alienation from love as an instrument of knowledge seems to have occurred during the Enlightenment. In spite of the negative overtones accompanying the idea of love in our age, Hoogendijk's attitude in his practice includes love, in the sense of openness as a criteria for meeting others.[74] The Socratic practitioner Leonard Nelson considers friendship the highest form of community. Nelson accepts Kant's definition of friendship, in which two persons are united in friendship through reciprocal respect and love. He considers two forms of love, fondness and benevolence: "Fondness expresses sensitiveness to another person's value; benevolence implies a desire to enhance his value, to bring him nearer to perfection."[75] This implies that friendship, as a mutual, active relationship, has as a purpose the realization of common ideals.

Other philosophical practitioners that estimate love and friendship are Stephen Palmquist, Warren Shibles, and Martina Winkler-Calaminus. Palmquist quotes Ivan Illich's *Tools of Conviviality* as a radical critique of the friendship destroying tendencies in modern culture. Illich predicts that there would be less need for psychotherapists if one could restore autonomous and creative relationships among persons. This will enable people to establish friendships with others in their working situation. At present, most economical and political structures are considered major interferences to creating friendship and healthy work situations. Palmquist sees friendship as therapeutic, not only for people, but also for philosophy: "*Friendship-in-conversation* is actually the essence of good philosophy. This, and not merely the logical rigor of his reasoning, is the primary lesson to be learned from the profound influence of Socrates on Western thought."[76] Shibles provides a philosophical analysis of love, as well as a short bibliography of philosophical and psychological literature on this topic. In contradistinction to a behavioral–cognitive (psychological) approach, Shibles maintains that rational love is love that involves specific cognition and actions; it cannot be the result of commands or rewards: "Rational love is not a passive thing but must be deliberate. . . . A passive love is not love at all. Love does not just come from the outside, and if it does it will not long remain. We must consciously attempt to make others happy."[77] Martina Winkler-Calaminus accentuated the importance of friendship relationships by saying a philosophical practitioner has to be a friend to another person, not just a friend to wisdom.[78]

My way of describing the ideal relation between philosophical counselor and counselee is as intellectual love and friendship, in the sense of a philosophical idea to practice, rather than a feeling or concept. Friendship, not as a word out of an ideology, but as an art—an Aristotelian praxis—is an idea that is rarely found in the philosophical or psychological textbooks of today.

However, the power of friendship as a method for relief has been proven successful in the activities of the suicide-prevention telephone hot line organization, the Samaritans. The idea of "A friend in need is a friend indeed" needed to be made anew, since in our time, people prefer to believe that one should not and cannot be friends with people in need. The task of being a good neighbor (or Samaritan) is happily removed from the individual, and is ascribed to professional caregivers only. Chad Varah, the founder of the Samaritans, discovered that it was not so much the advice given to people as the friendship offered that was effective.[79] This observation made "befriending" the main element in the Samaritans' contact with desperate people. Richard Fox's research on the effectiveness of the Samaritans shows a "remarkable decline in recorded suicide by about a third during the period following 1963 to the lowest British rate ever."[80] In the first-aid philosophical hot line I operate, I combine the ideas of Achenbach with those of Varah.

In the postmodern world, classical ideals of friendship do occasionally resonate in the hearts of people. Up until the fifteenth century, ancient ideals of friendship were practiced, but urbanization and the breakdown of small communities caused a change in human relations, and people became pessimistic about friendship.[81] An important characteristic of contemporary friendship is the "sharing of selves." It is likely that the strain of modern society has caused people to experience dehumanization and depersonalization; human contact has become superficial, while sincere friendship has become seclusive. For C. S. Lewis, "Every real friendship is a sort of secession, even a rebellion."[82] When a philosophical practitioner chooses friendship as an important characteristic in his or her practice—mainly because love and friendship make understanding and living a possiblilty—it is a friendship of which many forms are conceivable. Drawing near to "selves," with a loving attitude, is parallel to the attitude of the philosophical practitioner in general. In this way, loving wisdom and drawing near to it is generalized to include loving all beings.

In the ancient world, philosophers sharing the same philosophy were friends; the ideas they held in common were practiced in a communal life. In Aristotelian ethics friendship is considered *the* human form of conduct for the city-state. Friendship guaranteed "right" conduct among people; it preceded justice. The hierarchical model of friendship—leading up from friendship with the aim of mutual advantage to friendship for the sake of pleasure and virtue—would eventually bring about an intellectual community of friends, in which people shared activities, discussion, and thought. Plutarch gives some good advice on how to distinguish between true and false friends. The latter ones are described as flatterers, with no outspoken opinion of their own: "A friend is always ready to counsel and promote the better, like a physician who preserves and enlarges what is sound; but the flatterer supports the passionate and irrational part, which he tickles. . . . He devises disreputable pleasures for it to set it against the rational part." However, sincere outspokenness "needs to be carefully compounded and the proper juncture for administering it carefully observed."[83]

The Aristotelian model of friendship can be taken as an ethical paradigm for transactions between philosophical practitioner and client. Initially the relation is one of friendship with mutual advantage: Both client and practitioner profit by practicing philosophy. The practitioner who receives money for his or her philosophizing is not applying inconsistently the ideals of love and friendship as the regulators for the relationship between practitioner and visitor. The philosopher is not paid for love and friendship, but for thinking; the counseling relationship is not an emotional but an ethical relationship that facilitates freedom of thought and understanding. This can be compared with the relationship between psychoanalyst and analysand, where transference has to occur for successful treatment. That emotional and ethical ties can exist between people, even though they give and receive money for a specific service, is obvious. If the visitor is penniless, the acceptance of money by the philosopher cannot be to their mutual advantage. It would be ideal if every client gave freely according to ability. Since such a utopian approach is not very realistic in the late twentieth century, it is advisable that practitioners have fixed prices. Philosophical practitioners could give reductions, and short- or long-term credit, or even may counsel for free, clients that seem worthy of such generosity. Philosophical counselors should take care that financial gain is not the main purpose of their job, and that their practice does not become a practice only for the rich and affluent or for enriching monetarily the philosophical practitioner.

After the first stage, when the client's need to philosophize has been satisfied, the practitioner and client may continue philosophizing just for the sake of the pleasure of philosophy. Eventually, philosophy and its praxis become "a way of being" for the client, just as it already is for the philosophical practitioner. Clients sharing such philosophical virtue with the philosophical counselor then create a community of philosophical friends.

Buberian Philosophical Therapy

Martin Buber's concept of the I–Thou relationship is comparable to a love relationship: "Love does not cling to an I, as if the You were merely its 'content' or object; it is between I and You. . . . Love is responsibility of an I for a You: in this consists what cannot consist in any feeling—the equality of all lovers." Love happens as the I–Thou relationship happens; it is comparable to a cosmic force. Buber considers that love and the I–Thou relationship can endure only in the alternation of actuality and latency relationships between people; he envisions a person's relationship to God in a similar fashion. But in this all-embracing relationship, even latency is actuality.[84] In certain aspects Buber (as well as Carl Rogers) anticipated Achenbach's philosophical practice. This is in contradistinction to other therapies, such as logotherapy and existential analysis, which have no common features with Achenbach's ideas, except for the use of specific philosophical ideas. It has to be stressed that I am referring to *similarities* among Buber, Rogers, and Achenbach, rather than identical aspects, and that I am not discussing the many differences, whether obvious or subtle, between Achenbach and the therapies under consideration. The differences and similarities between the ideas of Buber and Rogers on therapy were pointed out by Friedman: Though Rogers acknowledged Buber's I–Thou relation, the purpose Rogers envisioned for this relation is not identical to that of Buber.[85]

A Comparison of Achenbach with Rogers, and Buber with Respect to the Characteristics of Philosophical Practice

The following comparison of Achenbach with Buber and Rogers does not equate Buberian and Rogerian therapy. Accordingly I describe *separately* the characteristics of philosophical counseling in

Buber and Rogers, and then discuss Achenbach's ideas, comparing them with those of Buber and Rogers. The following four characteristics of philosophical practice resemble features of Buberian and Rogerian therapy.

1. *The sincere communication in philosophical practice, based on a free, spontaneous developing conversation for which no method can exist.*

For Buber, the I–Thou relation is what makes an encounter genuine. Human reflection continually ascends and descends from the I–It world of objects to the I–Thou world of subjects. These two worlds do coexist, but in Buber's understanding they oppose one another. Nevertheless, therapeutic or other professionalisms are not a Buberian ideal since "the improvement of the ability to experience and use generally involves a decrease in man's power to relate."[86] In philosophical counseling, as in the therapies inspired by Buber, the genuineness of the encounter and the quality of people relating to each other is of paramount importance.[87] Buber finds that the patient asks the therapist to step out of his or her security that has been achieved through professional training and understanding. The patient desires to meet the therapist in an "elementary situation between one who calls and one who is called." There self is exposed to self. The meeting of self-with-self, the encounter with the dark domain of the therapist's passions, anxieties and so forth—this abyss is in the control of the therapist through his or her wrestling with these forces, and this strengthens the patient. Thus Buber concludes in his essay "Healing through Meeting": "In the immediacy of one human standing over against another, the encapsulation must and can be broken through, and a transformed, healed relationship must and can be opened to the person who is sick in his relations to otherness."[88] There is no knowledge or method for genuine encounter in the Buberian dialogue; it happens, it is given. Friedman noted that for Buber the I–Thou relation is not of instrumental value but is rather a value in itself: "We become whole in order to go out to the meeting with the Thou."[89]

Rogers described the essence of person-centered therapy in "Persons or Science?: A Philosophical Question."[90] He wrote this essay as a personal clarification of his "double life," while he was inwardly divided between the subjective and the objective understanding of life. Rogers came to a resolution of the dilemma of being an objective scientist and a subjective therapist. He envisioned science and therapy—as well as all other aspects of living—as flowing from personal subjective experience.[91] Both the reflective and the nonreflective aspects of living have their origin in the I–Thou relation. In person-centered therapy the I–Thou relation occurs when there is unity between client and counselor. In his dialogue with Buber, Rogers called the I–Thou relation a transparent relationship in which nothing is hidden. In this type of relation he found himself an effective counselor. Not the objective knowledge of science, but the knowledge the counselor acquires through the other's sharing of his or her inner world, causes healing. The transparent relationship excludes the experience of the client or the counselor as something objective. A measurable "objective knowledge" of an outside reality has for Rogers "nothing to do with the relationship that produces therapy."[92]

In Achenbach's practice, visitors' problematic situations are not diagnosed as "objective," empirically established complexes or deviations. The client's situation is considered unique, and for that reason not to be understood through generalization or reduction. The philosophical practitioner thinks through complex situations with the visitor. Whether one or more interpretations (or even none) are found is not the essence, since it is the educational philosophical process that accounts for the visitor's improvement. Achenbach rejects the positivist requirement of a method. Instead of working with a priori methods and scientific knowledge, the philosophical practitioner works together with the client on knowledge of the self and life.

In the views of Buber, Rogers, and Achenbach, dialogue itself is, respectively, the criterion for authentic existence, genuine therapy, and vital philosophy. Or in Mikhail Bakhtin's words, "When dialogue ends, everything ends."[93]

2. *The importance of dialogue as enlivening and as flowing from being.*

For Buber, thinking and speech were to be understood in the context of living. In the "beginning" language was communication; it needed to be addressed to another person to be meaningful. Personal existence, expression, and meaning are interwoven. Monologue came into existence where dialogue broke off or broke down.[94] Buber finds that modern philosophy has lost much of its former influence on society because it does not consider existence the origin or aim of philosophical thought. The unity between thought and existence, as indicated by Buber, can be rediscovered through dialogue.

Rogers sees the profession of the person-centered counselor as a way of being; the counselor has to *be* a dependable, trustworthy, and authentic person. The counselor's truthfulness to him or herself invites the client into a relationship that is felt as one where permission is received to grow into what one really is. Becoming a different person depends as much on what is said by the client and counselor as on how the counselor is as a person. Rogers defined the transformation of his early "client-centered therapy" into the "person-centered approach" as follows. He no longer wanted to talk "simply about psychotherapy, but about a point of view, a philosophy, an approach to life, a way of being, which fits any situation in which growth—of a person, a group, or a community—is part of the goal."[95]

Achenbach believes that the philosopher has to be a practitioner—that is, his or her philosophy must be lived personally. Achenbach accuses "pretense philosophers" of creating additional, metaphysical realities; what shows that they are merely pretending is that they do not apply their pure theories to their own existence. The dialogue with life is necessary for the formation and development of philosophy. Without the encounter with life, philosophy is an obstacle, rather than a way to life.

3. Auslegen *(looking for explanations) in which the practitioner becomes united with the problem, not by imparting his own understanding of it, but by giving the visitor a fresh impulse to explain him or herself.*

Friedman's analysis of Buber's education of character distinguishes between "propaganda" and "legitimate influence."[96]

Buber's "propaganda" can be compared with Achenbach's *Unterlegen* (the discovery of underlying psychological or other truths), whereas *Auslegen* can be compared with "legitimate influence." The last is an open dialogic relationship in which one participant finds and supports in the other's soul "what one has recognized in oneself as the right . . . as a possibility among possibilities, a potentiality which only needs to be unlocked—unlocked not through instruction but through meeting, through the existential communication between one who has found direction and one who is finding it."[97] Propaganda in educational and other relationships proceeds from an authoritarian height as the truth, in which the authority is not necessarily an authentic person.

Rogers's empathic understanding is not to be confused with Buber's concept of inclusion, though both concepts correspond to Achenbach's ideas about *Auslegen.*[98] Person-centered counselors do not interpret the client's problem out of their own understanding of the problem. Instead these problems are comprehended through the client's experience and understanding. However, the counselor must be unambiguous in communicating as an authentic person. Empathetic listening and understanding is a policy of noninterference. Rogers cites Buber to explain this issue better: Buber saw the perfected person as somebody who does not interfere in the life of beings, who does not impose him or herself on others, but rather, in the words of Lao-tse, "helps all beings to their freedom."[99]

For Achenbach, interpretation is not the discovery of presumed underlying truths behind communication. Although some philosophers view philosophy as science, in Achenbach's practice philosophy is a search for conceptual arguments and not for scientific truth. However, this does not exclude explanations on a basis of causal or logical connections from the domain of philosophical practice; the philosopher is not limited to the phenomenological and hermeneutical tools of description and interpretation. Achenbach and von Morstein consistently highlight the free and unlimited ways of inquiry and understanding in philosophical practice.[100] The philosophical practitioner can present the visitor with his or her understanding of the question or solution to the problem. However, the practitioner's personal philosophy is only an example of his or her understanding and not a suggestion to be accepted or followed by the counselee. Just as Nietzsche's Zarathustra renounces "followers," the philosophical practitioner asks visitors to respond to his or her ideas with critical assent or rejection, thus facilitating authentic self-understanding.

4. *The innovative component of dialogue—the element of critical wonder in philosophical practice—which does not allow for fixed viewpoints, standard attitudes, or permanent solutions.*

Buber compared the surprise aspect of dialogue with the surprise factor in a game of chess.[101] The players enjoy the game because they cannot know what the next move in the game will be. Likewise authentic dialogue produces the element of surprise.

In Rogers's description of the "helping relationship," surprise and the wonder of innovation are recognized in the "process of becoming." In this process a person is not understood as bound by his or her past. On the contrary, what Rogers does is to reinforce "*all* that he is, the person that he is with all his existent potentialities."[102] When a counselor expects innovative, creative, inner development throughout the sessions, people tend, accordingly, to respond to such a "prophecy." I compare this with the idea of "wonder" in philosophical practice.

In Achenbach's "Protocol for a Conversation," the practitioner's paradigm is *The Thousand and One Nights*.[103] Scheherazade (possibly, together with King Solomon, one of the first Oriental philosophical practitioners) interprets the king's compulsions in her fairy tales, each night in a different manner. The originality of these pluralistic clarifications of life's situations helped the king to forget and to overcome his murderous passions.

In addition to the therapies that were inspired by Buber's philosophy, an educational project based on Buber's dialogical principles can be compared to Nelson's project of group philosophy practice, the Socratic dialogue groups. The Buberian dialogue groups had as their aim, in a metaphorical sense, to heal the sick relationships between Jews and Arabs. Under the direction of Dr. Haim Gordon, this project for Peace Education took place at the Ben Gurion University in Israel from 1979 to 1982.[104] During these three years, approximately two hundred participants took part, in large or small dialogue groups studying the works of existentialist philosophers and writers such as Buber, Sartre, Nietzsche, Kafka, Kierkegaard, and Naguib Mahfouz. Gordon expected that, through dialogue based upon existentialist themes, the participants would be able to illuminate hidden aspects of themselves. The dialogically attained self-knowledge was expected to change the participants and allow the creation of a degree of peaceful coexistence in Israeli society.

In contradistinction to Achenbach's free dialogue, Gordon organized the philosophical dialogue groups with the specific aim of creating mutual understanding and cooperation between Jews and Arabs. At the root of this project was Gordon's analysis of the Middle East conflict as being one based on mutual existential distrust, which could be transformed into existential trust through genuine dialogue. According to the research done on this project, a significant number of the participants did in fact undergo an inner transformation. Though Gordon finds it hard to put the results of his complex educational project into percentages, an analysis at the end of one year of participation in the Buberian learning group shows that existential mistrust towards other participants in the group diminished by 65 percent, and that 50 percent of the participants became interested in self-education and dialogue in their daily life.[105]

The influence of Buber's philosophy on my practice may be seen in my discussions of his thought with clients, and in awaiting the arrival of an I–Thou relationship in these contacts. The following is a summary of seven basic characteristics of the I–Thou encounter as listed by William E. Kaufman, which are also characteristics of the way I work.

1. The I–Thou involves a person's whole being (i.e., no divided mind).
2. The relationship is exclusive, in that I am grasped by the encounter.
3. There is a direct relationship; I do not pretend or try to impress.
4. The relationship is effortless not an act of will: "The Thou meets me through grace; it is not found by seeking."
5. The relationship is in the present. A present relationship is not a fictional relationship, as is the transference relationship in psychodynamically oriented therapies.

6. The relationship takes place between people, and is an organic process—the "whole is more than the sum of its parts."

7. The relationship is reciprocal: "As I become I, I say Thou."[106]

Sartrean Clinical Practice

As Nietzsche is known by a majority of people for advising fellow men to take along a whip when visiting the opposite sex, Sartre is famous for seeing others as damned souls in hell. This gloomy fame is mainly based on a few sentences written in his play, *No Exit*. On the basis of such distorted knowledge, it is impossible to recognize Sartre as the man who had a passion to understand people and did so for most of his life with much empathy.

It is one of Cannon's achievements in *Sartre and Psychoanalysis* to have referred repeatedly to Sartre's views of positive reciprocity and authentic love. She offers a definition of Sartrean authentic love: "Authentic love involves giving up the idea of using the other person to create substantive freedom."[107] In my practice Sartre's ideas on positive reciprocity and authentic love are highly relevant. The influence of Sartre in my counseling may further be seen in my adoption of ideas from his existential psychoanalysis, which I transformed in my work into philosophical psychoanalysis and self-analysis. This transformation of terminology is significant to illustrate the differences between me, Sartre, and therapists who claim to have integrated the existentialist thought of Kierkegaard, Heidegger, Sartre, and others into psychotherapy and usually call these therapeutic approaches existential psychotherapy or existential analysis. Essential differences between these approaches and Sartre's philosophy proper are found in the following examples.

Ludwig Binswanger compares psychoanalysis and existential analysis: "Since existential analysis undertakes to work out being-human in all its existential forms and their worlds . . . whereas psychoanalysis does so only in respect to the last of these [i.e., thrown-ness], it is clear that existential analysis is able to widen and deepen the basic concepts and understandings of psychoanalysis."[108]

The utilization of existentialist thought is in most cases of existential psychotherapy only an additional dimension—a widening and deepening—of psychoanalysis. Most therapists seem not to realize that the actual meanings and intentions of existentialism are subverted through psychoanalysis and psychotherapy. I detected such "repressive tolerance"—Herbert Marcuse's notion of using tolerance as a tool to make the opponent powerless—in Amedeo Giorgi's article on "Sartre's Systematic Psychology": "Sartrean metapsychology is a corrective to traditional psychology because it provides a sharper understanding of what man is. The resulting clarification of 'the human reality' does not so much cancel out traditional psychology as complement it."[109] Giorgi tolerates Sartre's critique of psychoanalysis, something which occurs frequently among existential and other philosophical psychotherapists.

Another example of what I consider an unhappy marriage between philosophy and psychology is Peter Koestenbaum's method. The tendency to combine philosophy with psychotherapy without accepting philosophy's critique of psychotherapy, and without using philosophy to modify psychotherapy, is evident in his clinical philosophy. He believes that a mixture of phenomenology, existentialism, and ideas from Eastern philosophies are helpful in realizing the dreams and longings of philosophers for "a systematic theory of the person with highly specific and testable applications." As a psychotherapist, he has observed that many patients suffer from philosophical conditions and are in need of philosophical help. Koestenbaum detects the need for philosophy in psychotherapy, but, as in Binswanger's approach, philosophy is merely one more aspect: Koestenbaum's philosophy "in therapy" is really philosophy "in addition to therapy." Koestenbaum advocates training in the use of philosophy as a healing art, but insists that "philosophy exists *in addition* to therapy, not *in lieu of* treatment. Philosophy deepens therapy; it does not replace it."

His new image of people in psychotherapy, or "clinical philosophy," is presumably based on a nonmedical model of the person. Koestenbaum finds that the "medical model is already a form of cultural psychopathology. The philosophic 'cure,' as it were, is to overturn the model itself on which the putative cures of conventional therapy have heretofore been based." But, if philosophy does not replace therapy, and instead "cures" it to create a better therapy, is this not in contradiction to Koestenbaum's rejection of the medical model? Moreover his conception of modern philosophy as a "well-grounded world philosophy"—that is, Western science, theology, and the humanities flowing together with Eastern philosophy—has little to do with what most professional philosophers would consider a solid background in academic philosophy, though Koestenbaum finds it a prerequisite for clinical philosophy.[110]

Koestenbaum claims that the philosophical conditions people suffer from are at a layer deeper than psychological conditions. What are his criteria for establishing philosophical psychopathology? It seems to me that his diagnoses are based on so-called "philosophical facts": The phenomenological model of being is constructed out of philosophical fundamentals that "are not ancillary observations;

on the contrary, they make up the core and heart of what is anguished and what is hopeful in the human experience."[111]

Koestenbaum's philosophical diagnosis or classification of mental conditions ranges from the "Natural and Authentic Conscious" to the "Crippled, Collapsed, and Deconstituted Conscious." Symptoms such as impotence, a stiff neck, or a tight throat are expressions of underlying philosophical conditions, but these symptoms are treated with standard therapeutic methods. The task of the clinical philosopher is to invent a unique *psychology* for each client.[112]

Out of respect for genuine dialogue between different academic disciplines, philosophical and psychological dialogue partners should not avoid confrontation when they actually oppose one another. Only if essential differences in analysis are acknowledged can dialogue be worthwhile. Sartrean "psychology"—like Achenbach's practice of philosophy—is a philosophical critique of psychoanalysis; it contradicts basic assumptions made by "scientists of the soul."[113] I will discuss the essential differences between the clinical use of Sartre's thought and Sartre's philosophy proper after considering Betty Cannon's interesting attempt to unite Sartre's philosophy with psychoanalysis and psychotherapy.

Cannon's impressive research, in which she compares Sartre to Freud and to post-Freudian drive and relational theorists, as well as Lacan's psychoanalytic theory, acknowledges the difficulty of uniting Sartre's philosophy and psychoanalysis. Cannon claims that Sartre's philosophy is used very little in psychotherapy due to popular misconceptions of Sartre's thought. However, according to Cannon's own experience as an existential therapist, Sartre's philosophy is extremely useful in therapy. Although Cannon recognizes an ambivalence in Sartre's conception of psychoanalysis, she does propose the Sartrean understanding as a *foundation* for a reinterpretation of psychoanalysis. Unlike other existential therapists, Cannon points out "a compatibility–incompatibility between Sartrean existential psychoanalysis and traditional Freudian and post-Freudian psychoanalysis." In a section of Chapter 9, "A Sartrean Case History: 'Martha the Marvelous Mirror,'" Cannon presents the story of Martha as typical of many clients she has worked with. Certain aspects of Martha's therapy were similar to classical or post-Freudian analysis. For example, Cannon saw an Oedipal triangle in Martha's relationship with her parents. In addition to Sartre's philosophy and traditional Freudian themes, Cannon reports on having used techniques such as empathetic mirroring, interpretation, confrontation, body-oriented psychotherapy, and Gestalt role-playing. Her awareness that the concrete and the particular are significant for the understanding of life, rather than ontological structures behind lived experiences, makes her reject the ontological overgeneralization in therapy. So far her theory is *toward* a Sartrean clinical practice, a prologue to Sartrean studies in Existential therapy: "Later work will have to describe more precisely how . . . techniques come to be modified by an Existentialist conceptualization of therapeutic issues."[114]

In spite of Cannon's excellent treatment of Sartrean metapsychology, she does not ask whether therapy itself is compatible with Sartre's thought. She argues that psychotherapy based on Sartrean metatheoretical principles can lead to a transformation of the self and the world, although she admits that "from a Sartrean perspective, there is something slightly askew about the views of psychoanalytic theorists that the aim of therapy is to repair the ego, find and develop a real self, or coach one's client to finally develop self and object constancy."[115] I agree with Cannon that Sartre's philosophy can lead to a transformation of the self and the world, but not that transformation is therapy, or for that matter, that Sartre's thought is helpful for every person, although many people may be helped through it.

A point of view similar to mine is expressed by Alfred Stern in his study of Sartre's existential psychoanalysis. Stern rejects any identification of Sartrean psychoanalysis with mental therapy, and instead considers it only as moral hygiene.[116] Sartre saw the possibility of change, of conversion, of the redemption of human life, but did *he* consider this therapy? Is not therapy always related to implicit or explicit human norms? In Sartrean "therapy" this norm would have to be pure freedom, which paradoxically is a norm that Sartre considers in its perfect state to be beyond human attainment. In *Life/Situations* Sartre expressed his pessimism about transformations of self and the world; yet "the only thing to do" is not to give up the idea, and to continue working towards a society of free individuals.[117] Freedom can be attained in the domain of the imaginary: in recognizing the illusionary boundaries of objective and subjective consciousness.

It seems to me that the basic contradiction between Sartre's thought and most psychotherapy is that Sartre insisted that human reality cannot be reduced or healed. He refused, for example, to analyze people into original givens or drives or to use other means to diagnose people in his proposed existential analysis. Traditionally, psychological definitions are "emotional prototypes," such as projection, transference, or the Oedipal triangle. These definitions are all disappointing from a philosophical–historical perspective—which is Sartre's—because they are not specific interpretations. Instead of these "given" models of interpretation Sartre suggests the following: "Existential psychoanaly-

sis recognizes nothing before the original upsurge of human freedom. . . . It rejects the hypothesis of the unconscious; it makes the
psychic act co-extensive with consciousness. . . . We are not dealing
with an unsolved riddle as the Freudians believe; all is there, lumi-
nous; reflection is in full possession of it."[118]

Sartre's analysis does not explore libido complexes, but searches
for particular and concrete choices. Human reality is not created
by alleged hypothetical "causes," such as heredity, education, social
class, or temperament. Choice is the "choice of being"; it is identical
with existence. Sartre found special interest in the understanding
of dreams, failures, obsessions, and neuroses, but also in conscious
thought, effective accommodative behavior, and habits. Sartre concluded the chapter on existential psychoanalysis in *Being and Nothingness* with naming as examples of his method certain successful
biographies.[119] In 1948, Sartre wrote about the practical application of existential psychoanalysis (in answer to a question from
Stern): "I tried to apply it twice: once to the study of an individual
(*Baudelaire*), the other to the study of a collective problem
(*Reflexions sur la Question juive*)."[120] In addition, one may add
Sartre's biographies of Genet, Freud (the Scenario), and Flaubert,
as well as Sartre's own autobiography, as instances of existential
psychoanalysis.

I exemplify existential psychoanalysis in a elementary sketch of
Sartre's analysis of Genet. Sartre described Genet's life in three meta-
morphoses: that of the thief, the aesthete, and the writer. The child
Jean became a thief not so much by stealing from his adoptive family as by the look that caught him in the act of theft. "What happened? Actually, almost nothing: an action undertaken without
reflection, conceived and carried out in the secret, silent inward-
ness in which he often takes refuge, has just become objective."[121]
To free himself from having been made into a thief, Genet chooses
evil, that is, he decides to be a thief.

In the aesthetic metamorphosis the will to beauty replaces the ethics of evil. Sartre understands this change as an identification of beauty
with evil. Beauty is constructed out of value—it is an appearance of
reality, it is "being engulfed in nothingness."[122] Genet became an aesthete because of the destructive power of beauty over reality.

The metamorphosis of Genet into a writer is shown in the context of the occurrences of life. Genet was again sentenced to prison.
This time it was his lot to be with prisoners who despised him. In
spite of the humiliating attitude of the prisoners, Genet felt chal-
lenged to compete with an inmate—a "poet." He wanted to show
the inmates that he could write better. When the inmates rejected
his poem "The Condemned Man," he loved it even more. This poem

became a bridge to Genet's prose writing. Genet's masterpiece, *Our Lady of the Flowers*, was written secretly on the paper he received from the prison authorities for making bags.[123]

Sartre was fascinated with Genet because Genet was an example of the philosophical archetype as idealized in the writings of Jean Jacques Rousseau. Genet was born free, yet his chains became obvious in childhood. From a Sartrean viewpoint Genet forced himself to be free by destroying the reality that he disliked and replacing it with a chosen, desired, reality: "Freedom can arise only as being which makes itself a desire of being; that is as the project-for-itself of being in-itself-for-itself."[124] In Flaubert's biography, *The Family Idiot*, Sartre again highlighted human freedom in Flaubert's transcendence of the givens of life. Through his literary praxis Flaubert related "being-outside-himself" to being in the world. Sartre does not describe in Flaubert's life the metamorphosis as he does with Genet. He compares Flaubert's life to a spiral, which returns to the same points but at higher levels of integration and complexity. This upward circular movement is the transcendence of Flaubert's world and self, although, if one looks at each circle separately, the progressive movement appears to be a repetition of the "facts" of life.

Sartre's analysis of Genet and Flaubert had not the intention of providing a psychoanalytic cure, although Genet himself and others reacted to *Saint Genet: Actor and Martyr* as though it were. David Cooper, for example, described the biography of Genet as a kind of "anti-psychiatric cure": "In ten years of writing, in Sartre's view, Genet achieved something of the equivalent of a psychoanalytic cure. Each of his books represents a crisis of catharsis, each is a psychodrama."[125]

Sartre however was actually trying to describe and interpret a particular lived existence: "to review in detail the history of his (Genet's) liberation."[126] This review immediately became the "exemplary cure," which Genet had accomplished himself. Sartre's final chapter in the Genet biography is called "Please Use Genet Properly." The proper use of Genet is in realizing that only a consciousness that is liberated from the boundaries of its objectivity can give a full account of all that a person is. Genet does not speak to us as the specialists do *about* homosexuals or criminals. His records were written by himself *as* a thief and *as* a homosexual. For Sartre, the author is the work. Reading Genet does not give us objective knowledge about ourselves or others; nevertheless, Sartre's portrait of Genet is a mirror in which we can recognize ourselves. The Flaubert biography is also a history of liberation. As Oreste Pucciani pointed out, Flaubert was a historic object for Sartre: "Philosophy as a method of investigation and explanation enlightens Flaubert's history."[127] *The Family Idiot*, like all true historical or biographical writing, received its "being" from its author's subjectivity.

Within my practice I find Sartre's ideas—as philosophical self-analysis—helpful when visitors are "bewitched" by the past and its causal "facts." I find that people often think and talk about their lives from the perspective of the unhappy present, from which they see "no exit." When the past and the present are analyzed from the perspective of a freedom—the transcendence of "givens"—that can be found from the account people themselves give, a feeling of desperation changes into the power to hope and to change. Although Robert Solomon, Albert Ellis, and others have also argued for the freedom to "create" oneself, I see the following reflections as part of Sartre's influence on my practice: reflection on the possibility of making something of the person one has become through life's events, other people, and oneself; reflection on the possibility of choosing oneself, one's emotions and thoughts, and one's future.[128]

Utilizing Sartre's thought in philosophical counseling is different from practicing existential therapy from a Sartrean perspective in the following aspects (although persons who consider all change, influence, and conversation of all kinds to be therapy may find the differences I arrive at dubious):

1. Philosophical counseling is an open, "beyond-method" approach, since the philosopher accompanies the visitor in thinking through, from many different perspectives (including those of Sartre), those problematic issues or questions the visitor wishes to discuss.

2. There is no therapeutic aim, since there are no implicit or explicit a priori therapeutic ideals or values that the philosophical practitioner wants to apply. I do not try to help people change according to a set therapeutic vision. When a client has expectations of being cured through therapy, it is important to discuss whether it is therapy that is needed or whether the client wants to understand his or her life philosophically and may eventually want by him or herself to transform existence. As a philosophical practitioner I can make a Sartrean-like analysis of my client's life, yet this analysis is not presented as therapeutic, objective, or as an expert judgment. It is given to the client as a provocation to arrive at self-analysis, which he or she may perform during the sessions or privately.

3. The content of the sessions is philosophical in that the visitor's conceptual world is investigated by philosophical means. Problems and questions are related to philosophical understanding and knowledge.

An illustration of how Sartre's ideas were made relevant for a counselee in my practice is found in Chapter 7, the philosophical–biographical discourse on Yoni.

CONCLUSION

Not only was philosophy influential in the past as a way to care or to cure, but is so today as well. Various philosophies, from the most ancient to the most modern, can contribute to a cognitive perspective that creates well-being. In sessions with visitors I might not only discuss ideas from Plato, Buber, or Sartre, but also from Aristotle, Plotinus, Philo, Augustine, Hegel, Schopenhauer, G. E. Moore, Russell, Wittgenstein, Derrida, and countless others. Philosophical practice should not be limited to discussing only particular philosophical viewpoints. It is—and should remain—an open, free conversation in which ideas from the entire history of philosophy can be selected to work on, or where one philosophizes without relating it directly to philosophical–historical knowledge.

The recent awareness of cognitive, existentialist, and humanist psychologists and psychiatrists that some aspects of philosophical practice resemble their ways of treatment has lead some to contend that they have been already practicing philosophy, and that they developed it in a way more appropriate for people in difficulty and in pathological situations. Nevertheless, today's philosophical care as the philosophy practice that Achenbach initiated, does differ significantly from the way philosophy is used by psychotherapists, psychoanalysts, and other mental-health workers, in terms of its methodology and content.

NOTES

1. Pedro Lain Entralgo, *The Therapy of the Word in Classic Antiquity* (New Haven, Conn.: Yale University Press, 1970), 97–98.

2. Richard S. Peters, *Brett's History of Psychology* (Cambridge: M.I.T. Press, 1965).

3. Bertrand Russell, *The Will to Doubt* (New York: Philosophical Library, 1986), 83.

4. Elliot S. Valenstein, *Brain Control: A Critical Examination of Brain Stimulation and Psychosurgery* (New York: John Wiley & Sons, 1973); Malcolm Norman, *Memory and Mind* (Ithaca, N.Y.: Cornell University Press, 1977), 271.

5. Nathaniel J. Pallone, "The Phenomenal Self, Person, and the Catholic Counselor," in *Readings in Guidance and Counseling*, ed. J. M. Lee and N. J. Pallone (New York: Sheed and Ward, 1966), 69; Orville Walters, "Metaphysics, Religion, and Psychotherapy," *Journal of Counseling Psychology* 4 (1958): 247.

6. Lawrence Brammer and Everett Shostrom, *Therapeutic Psychology: Fundamentals of Counseling and Psychotherapy* (Upper Saddle River, N.J.: Prentice Hall, 1982), 420.

7. Donald S. Browning, "Introduction to Pastoral Counseling," in *The Clinical Handbook of Pastoral Counseling*, ed. R. Wicks, R. D. Parsons, and D. Capps (New York: Paulist, 1985), 12.

8. Bernard J. Tyrrell, "Christotherapy: An Approach to Facilitating Psychospiritual Healing and Growth," in *Clinical Handbook of Pastoral Counseling*, 62.

9. Dietrich Bonhoeffer, *Spiritual Care* (Philadelphia: Fortress, 1985), 13.

10. Paul Tillich, *The Courage To Be* (New Haven, Conn.: Yale University Press, 1952), 77.

11. Earl A. Grollman, "The Clergyman's Role in Grief Counseling" in *Community Mental Health: The Role of Church and Temple*, ed. H. J. Clinebell, Jr. (Nashville: Abingdon, 1970), 98–99.

12. Gary Almy and Carol Tharp Almy, *Addiction to Recovery: Exposing the False Gospel of Psychotherapy* (Eugene, Ore.: Harvest House, 1994), 10.

13. Stephen R. L. Clark, *From Athens to Jerusalem* (Oxford: Clarendon, 1984), 18.

14. Henri Ellenberger, *The Discovery of the Unconscious: The History and Evolution of Dynamic Psychiatry* (New York: Basic Books, 1970), 42.

15. Jan Ehrenwald, *From Medicine Man to Freud* (New York: Dell, 1956), 18.

16. Richard McKeon, ed., *The Basic Works of Aristotle, Nichomachean Ethics*, bk. 7; ch. 5, 1149a.5 (New York: Random House, 1941), 1045.

17. Brian Inwood, *Ethics and Human Action in Early Stoicism* (Oxford: Clarendon, 1985), 128–152.

18. Russell, *The Will to Doubt*, 110.

19. Martha C. Nussbaum, *The Therapy of Desire: Theory and Practice in Hellenistic Ethics* (Princeton, N.J.: Princeton University Press, 1994), 15, 508.

20. St. Augustine, *The Happy Life* (London: Herder, 1939).

21. David Winston, *Philo of Alexandria* (New York: Paulist, 1981), 42.

22. This section contains a summary of some ideas of Bakan as expressed in a letter to the author. See also David Bakan, *Maimonides on Prophecy: A Commentary on Selected Chapters of the Guide of the Perplexed* (Northvale, N.J.: Jason Aronson, 1991), 46.

23. Martin Heidegger, *Being and Time* (New York: Harper & Row, 1962), 238, 243.

24. Edith Weigert, "Existentialism and Its Relations to Psychiatry," *Psychiatry* 12 (1949): 400.

25. Gerd B. Achenbach and Peter Sloterdijk, "Gespräch über die Lebenskunst, zur Welt zu kommen," *Agora: Zeitschrift für, Philosophische Praxis* 4 (1988): 1–3.

26. Betty Cannon, *Sartre and Psychoanalysis* (Lawrence: University of Kansas Press, 1991), 264.

27. Simone Weil, *The Need for Roots* (London: Routledge and Kegan Paul, 1978), 224.

28. Charles Snow, *The Two Cultures and the Scientific Revolution* (London: Cambridge University Press, 1959).

29. Susan Sontag, *Against Interpretation* (New York: Doubleday Anchor, 1990), 296.

30. Leo Strauss, "Plato," in *Perspectives on Political Philosophy*, vol. 1, ed. J. Dowton (New York: Holt, Rinehart, and Winston, 1971), 49.

31. Anthony Kenny, *The Anatomy of the Soul* (Bristol, England: Basil Blackwell, 1973), 6.

32. Thomas Szasz, *The Myth of Mental Illness* (New York: Harper & Row, 1974), 161.

33. Richard Norman, *The Moral Philosophers* (New York: Harcourt, 1983); Bennett Simon, *Mind and Madness in Ancient Greece* (London: Cornell University Press, 1978).

34. Sigmund Freud, *The Future of an Illusion* (New York: Doubleday Anchor, 1964), 88.

35. Carl G. Jung, *Modern Man in Search of a Soul* (New York: Harcourt, 1933), 118.

36. Rollo May, *Love and Will* (New York: Dell, 1969), 86.

37. B. Jowett, *The Dialogues of Plato*, vol. 1 (New York: Random House, 1937), 330.

38. John M. Heaton, "How Can We Discuss the Erotic?: Plato and Freud Compared," in *Thresholds Between Philosophy and Psychoanalysis*, ed. R. Cooper (London: Free Association Books, 1994), 114.

39. Jowett, *The Dialogues of Plato*, 667.

40. Charles L. Griswold, *Self-Knowledge in Plato's Phaedrus* (Stoughton, Wisc.: Alpine, 1986).

41. Moses Hadas, *The Essential Works of Stoicism* (New York: Bantam, 1961), 81.

42. Edgar Z. Friedenberg, *R. D. Laing* (New York: Viking, 1973), 11.

43. Norman, *The Moral Philosophers*, 35–36.

44. Alfred Taylor, *Socrates* (New York: Doubleday Anchor, 1953), 136.

45. Samuel Scolnicov, "Socrates on the Unity of the Person," *Scripta Classica Israelica* 7 (1985–1986): 19, 20.

46. Jon Elster, ed., *The Multiple Self* (Cambridge: Cambridge University Press, 1989), 28.

47. Nathaniel J. Pallone, "The Phenomenal Self, Person, and the Catholic Counselor," 61–63.

48. Robert Baldwin and James McPeck, *An Introduction to Philosophy through Literature* (New York: Ronald Press, 1950). For more examples of how the concrete and the abstract are joined, see the case histories in Part II of this book.

49. Pierre Grimes and Regina Uliana, *Philosophical Midwifery: A New Paradigm for Understanding Human Problems* (Costa Mesa, Calif.: Hyparxis, 1998), 167.

50. Szasz, *The Myth of Mental Illness*, xiv.

51. Jean-Paul Sartre, *Between Existentialism and Marxism* (New York: Pantheon, 1974), 204.

52. Ibid., 210.

53. Jean-Paul Sartre, *Truth and Existence* (Chicago: University of Chicago Press, 1992), 7.

54. David Heyed, "Psychoanaliza al Sapat Ha Philosoof" (Psychoanalysis on the Philosopher's Couch) (in Hebrew), *Iyyun: A Hebrew Philosophical Quarterly* 35 (1986): 60–61.

55. B. A. Farrel, J. O. Wisdom, and P. M. Turquet, "Symposium: The Criteria for Psychoanalytic Interpretation," *Aristotelian Society, Supplementary*, 36 (1962): 100.

56. Maurice S. Friedman, *The Healing Dialogue in Psychotherapy* (New York: Jason Aronson, 1985).

57. Emmy van Deurzen-Smith, *Everyday Mysteries: Existential Dimensions of Psychotherapy* (London: Routledge, 1997), 196, 231–247.

58. Marius A. J. Romme and Alexandre D.M.A.C. Esher, "Hearing Voices," *Schizophrenia Bulletin* 15, 2 (1989): 209–216.

59. Simon Du Plock, "Smoke without Fire: Towards an Existential–Phenomenological Perspective on Hallucinations," *Journal of the Society for Existential Analysis* 6, 2 (1995): 114.

60. Described in Maurice S. Friedman, *Dialogue and the Human Image* (Newbury Park, Calif.: Sage, 1992), 55.

61. Jowett, *The Dialogues of Plato*, 414.

62. Deurzen-Smith, *Everyday Mysteries*, 171.

63. Hans W. Cohn, *Existential Thought and Therapeutic Practice* (London: Sage, 1997), 6.

64. Shlomit C. Schuster, "Sartre's 'Words' as a Paradigm for Self-Description in Philosophical Counseling," in *Perspectives in Philosophical Practice: The Proceedings of the Second International Congress on Philosophical Practice*, ed. W. van der Vlist (Doorwerth: The Dutch Society for Philosophical Practice, 1997), 20–34; Michel Foucault, *Politics, Philosophy, Culture*, ed. L. D. Kritzman (New York: Routledge, 1990); Paul A. Schilpp, ed., *The Philosophy of Karl Jaspers* (New York: Tudor, 1957).

65. R. D. Laing, *The Politics of Experience* (New York: Ballantine, 1967).

66. Described in Fritjof Capra, *Uncommon Wisdom* (London: Fontana, 1989), 142, 154.

67. R. D. Laing and David G. Cooper, *Reason and Violence* (New York: Pantheon, 1971), 6.

68. Max Charlesworth, "Sartre, Laing, and Freud," *Review of Existential Psychology and Psychiatry* 17, 1 (1980): 28. On the possibility of a Sartrean influence on contemporary antipsychiatry see Shlomit C. Schuster, "Sartre's Freud and the Future of Sartrean Psychoanalysis," *The Israel Journal of Psychiatry* 35, 1 (1998): 20–30.

69. Douglas Kirsner, "An Abyss of Difference: Laing, Sartre and Jaspers," *Journal of the British Society for Phenomenology* 21, 3 (1990): 209–210.

70. Cohn, *Existential Thought and Therapeutic Practice*, vi.

71. R. D. Laing, *The Divided Self* (London: Penguin, 1970).

72. Susan Baur, *The Intimate Hour: Love and Sex in Psychotherapy* (Boston: Houghton Mifflin, 1997).

73. Adolf Guggenbühl-Craig, *Power in the Helping Professions* (Woodstock, Conn.: Spring, 1996).

74. Ad Hoogendijk, *Spreekuur bij een filosoof* (Utrecht, The Netherlands: Veen, 1988), 24–25.

75. Leonard Nelson, *System of Ethics*, trans. N. Guterman (New Haven, Conn.: Yale University Press, 1956), 216.

76. Stephen Palmquist, *Dreams of Wholeness* (Hong Kong: Philopsychy Press, 1997), 231, 234.

77. Warren Shibles, *Rational Love* (Whitewater, Wisc.: Language Press, 1978), 67.

78. Martina Winkler-Calaminus's statement is from her lecture "Freundschaft: Eine Kategorie Philosophischer Praxis" at the Fourth International Conference on Philosophical Practice, Bensberg, Germany, 3–7 August 1998.

79. Chad Varah, ed., *The Samaritans* (London: Constable, 1965), 23–24.

80. Richard Fox, "The Recent Decline of Suicide in Britain: The Role of the Samaritan Suicide Prevention Movement," in *Suicidology: Contemporary Developments*, ed. E. S. Shneidman (New York: Grune & Stratton, 1976), 499–524.

81. Brain McGuire, *Friendship and Community* (Kalamazoo, Mich.: Cistercian, 1988), 418.

82. C. S. Lewis, *The Four Loves* (London: Collins, 1985), 75.

83. Plutarch, *Selected Essays On Love, The Family and the Good Life*, ed. M. Hadas (New York: New American Library, 1957), 143–144, 164.

84. Martin Buber, *I and Thou,* trans. and intro. W. Kaufman (Edinburgh: T. & T. Clark, 1970), 66, 129, 147.

85. Friedman, *Dialogue and the Human Image*, 35–56.

86. Buber, *I and Thou*, 92.

87. Maurice S. Friedman, *The Healing Dialogue in Psychotherapy*; Mordechai Rotenberg, *Dia-logo Therapy: Psychonarration and PaRDeS* (New York: Praeger, 1991); Tamar Kron and Rafi Yungman, "The Dynamics of Intimacy in Group Therapy," *International Journal of Group Psychotherapy* 37, 4 (1987): 529–548.

88. Martin Buber, *Pointing the Way* (New York: Harper & Row, 1963), 94–95, 97.

89. From a dialogue between the author and Maurice S. Friedman.

90. Carl Rogers, *On Becoming a Person* (London: Constable, 1974), 199–225.

91. Ibid., 223.

92. Maurice S. Friedman, "Dialogue between Martin Buber and Carl R. Rogers," in *The Knowledge of Man*, ed. and trans. M. S. Friedman (New York: Harper & Row, 1965), 166–184.

93. Hwa Yol Jung, "Mikhails Bakhtin's Body Politic: A Phenomenological Dialogics," *Man and World* 23 (1990): 86.

94. Buber, *The Knowledge of Man*, 119.

95. Carl Rogers, *A Way of Being* (Boston: Houghton Mifflin, 1980), ix.

96. Buber, *Between Man and Man*, ed. and trans. M. S. Friedman (New York: Macmillan, 1967), 104–117.

97. Maurice S. Friedman, *Martin Buber: The Life of Dialogue* (Chicago: University of Chicago Press, 1960), 180.

98. Friedman, *Dialogue and the Human Image*, 50.

99. Rogers, *A Way of Being*, 42.

100. Gerd B. Achenbach, "Die 'Grundregel' philosophischer Praxis," in *Psychotherapy und Philosophie*, ed. R. Kuhn and H. Petzold (Paderborn, Germany: Junfermann Verlag, 1992), 359; Petra von Morstein, "Breath Life into Philosophy, Professor Urges," *Calgary Herald*, 11 September 1987, F14.

101. Friedman, "Dialogue between Martin Buber and Carl R. Rogers," 178.

102. Carl Rogers, "The Characteristics of a Helping Relationship," in *Readings in Guidance and Counseling*, ed. J. Lee and N. J. Pallone (New York: Sheed and Ward, 1966), 219.

103. Gerd B. Achenbach and Thomas Macho, *Das Prinzip Heilung* (Cologne: Jürgen Dinter, 1985), 49–81.

104. Haim Gordon, *Dance, Dialogue, and Despair* (Tuscaloosa: University of Alabama Press, 1986).

105. Ibid., 235.

106. William E. Kaufman, *Contemporary Jewish Philosophies* (New York: University Press of America, 1985), 55–77.

107. Cannon, *Sartre and Psychoanalysis*, 241.

108. Ludwig Binswanger, "The Case of Ellen West: An Anthropological–Clinical Study," in *Existence: A New Dimension in Psychiatry and Psychology*, ed. R. May, E. Angel, and H. F. Ellenberger (New York: Simon and Schuster, 1976), 315.

109. Amedeo Giorgi, "Sartre's Systematic Psychology," in *The Philosophy of Jean-Paul Sartre*, ed. P. A. Schilpp (La Salle, Ill.: Open Court, 1981), 192–193.

110. Peter Koestenbaum, *The New Image of the Person: The Theory and Practice of Clinical Philosophy* (London: Greenwood, 1978), 6, 7, 21, 60.

111. Ibid., 14.

112. Ibid., 16.

113. Achenbach and Macho, *Das Prinzip Heilung*, 85–192; W. Voois, "Philosophische Praxis: een confrontatie?" *Filosofische Praktijk* 1 (1987): 13–15.

114. Cannon, *Sartre and Psychoanalysis*, 314, 351.

115. Ibid., 349.

116. Alfred Stern, *Sartre, His Philosophy and Psychoanalysis* (New York: Liberal Arts Press, 1953), 203, 207.

117. Jean-Paul Sartre, *Life/Situations* (New York: Pantheon, 1977), 83.

118. Jean-Paul Sartre, *Being and Nothingness*, trans. and intro. H. E. Barnes (New York: Citadel, 1964), 697–699.

119. Ibid., 704.

120. Stern, *Sartre, His Philosophy and Psychoanalysis*, 179; Jean-Paul Sartre, *Baudelaire*, trans. T. Martin (New York: New Directions, 1950); Jean-Paul Sartre, *Anti-Semite and Jew* (New York: Schoken, 1948).

121. Jean-Paul Sartre, *Saint Genet: Actor and Martyr* (New York: Mentor, 1963); Jean-Paul Sartre, *The Words* (New York: George Braziller, 1964); Jean-Paul Sartre, *The Freud Scenario* (Chicago: University of Chicago Press, 1986); Jean-Paul Sartre, *The Family Idiot*, 5 vols. (Chicago: University of Chicago Press, 1991, vols. 1–4; 1993, vol. 5).

122. Ibid., 404.

123. Ibid., 461–481.

124. Sartre, *Being and Nothingness*, 695.

125. Ibid., 695.

126. Sartre, *Saint Genet*, 628.

127. Oreste F. Pucciani, "Sartre and Flaubert as Dialectic," in *The Philosophy of Jean-Paul Sartre*, ed. P. A. Schillp (La Salle, Ill.: Open Court, 1981), 518.

128. Robert C. Solomon, "Emotions and Choice," in *Explaining Emotions*, ed. A. Oksenberg Rorty (London: University of California Press, 1980), 251–281; Albert Ellis and Robert Harper, *A Guide to Rational Living* (Beverly Hills, Calif.: Hal Leighton, 1975).

CHAPTER 4

Philosophical Narratives of Lives

Simeon his son [of Rabban Gamaliel] says: All my life I grew up among the sages and have found nothing better for anybody than silence; not study is the chief thing, but action; and he who is verbose brings on sin.

The Living Talmud

In the classic book *English Prose Style*, Herbert Read recognizes good narrative prose in fiction and in other types of writing such as history, biography, travel stories, and accounts of natural phenomena. Concreteness, speed, and visual clarity are the general characteristics of a good narrative. However, Read recognizes also a different type of narrative in which unity of action, economy, and concreteness disappear for the sake of philosophical reflections. Read finds such philosophical narrative style typical of the eighteenth century: "It is interspersed with the author's commentary, his side glances and quizzings."[1]

Narratives such as the autobiography, biography, and the biographical novel have been and remain oft-practiced literary styles. These narratives of lives are usually analyzed from a psychological, historical, socioanthropological, or literary perspective. Although many philosophers have written autobiographical works, and these narratives have particular philosophical characteristics, exploring the philosophical side of biographical narratives is an almost untouched field of research. George Misch, in his classic book on the history of autobiography, described the use of aphorisms as a confessional method of philosophizing as far back as 500 B.C.[2] When Heraclitus of Ephesus said, "Entering the same river, other and still other waters flow toward you," he was proceeding from a personal philosophical reflection about an experience of life. Michel Foucault, in his article "Technologies of the Self," likewise described a private and experiential form of reflection through which he obtained philosophical self-knowledge. Instead of taking care of the self through an a priori knowledge of it (as is done in most psychotherapies), self-knowledge was the result of care of the self: "It was that need to take care for oneself that brought the Delphic maxim into operation."[3] Foucault gave as examples of self-care the Stoic autobiographical techniques of writing letters to friends and disclosing oneself.

Foucault turned to philosophy and the history of ideas after working for over two years as a psychologist at the St. Anne hospital in Paris. During that time he realized that he identified more with the patients than with the hospital staff. A few years afterward he started writing *Madness and Civilization*, a critical history of psychiatry; here the malaise he experienced during the years he worked in St. Anne took the form of a structural analysis.[4] Though he hardly ever mentions Freud, many of Foucault's alternative interpretations of the self can be read as a criticism of psychoanalysis: "Whereas Freud provides a method for investigating the internal workings of the psyche, Foucault seeks to show how the method itself is an ancient technique of self-fashioning that has over the centuries shaped the mind externally."[5] *The History of Sexuality* is, as it were, a pre-Freudian text—an analysis of sexuality, love, and friendship relations with the intent of creating an "ethics, or at least to show what could be an ethics of sexual behavior." It seems that some of Foucault's readers also suffered from what I call in the introduction chapter "psychopathologization." For example, Foucault complains that he often has been labeled an antipsychiatrist, while he himself has always identified himself as simply a philosopher and historian of ideas.[6] In a similar way, people under the influence of psychopathologization ideals turn all sorts of texts in the fields of history, biography, autobiography, or any other narrative, into psychology texts, or into something with an interdisciplinary flavor, such as psychohistory or psychobiography.

An exceptional figure in our psychoculture is Karl Jaspers. Jaspers employed a philosophical biographical method in his books, *Psychopathology* and *Strindberg und van Gogh*.[7] He understands the connection between the works of August Strindberg and Vincent van Gogh and their mental constitutions, in relation to their philosophical and spiritual life journey. Though Jaspers does not subscribe to a Hegelian phenomenology of spirit, he does consider the whole of the history of philosophy as the growing self-awareness of man. Moreover, he believes that philosophical ideas should be situated in the framework of their own history: "Only through the history of philosophy as a whole can we learn how philosophy developed in relation to most diverse social and political conditions and personal situations." I believe that human beings—those having a philosophical dimension—can only come to self-understanding and the understanding of life and society through knowledge of the history of philosophy. Although technology is the most prominent feature of modern society, this society developed and is currently structured based on the philosophical reflection on the nature of human beings, society, and science. Accordingly, an attitude which is antihistorical and antiphilosophical is a cause of alienation from understanding life and from the philosophical resources and spiritual treasures that such understanding makes available. Much of Jaspers's work aimed at making these philosophical resources available to the average reader. In *Nietzsche* and *The Great Philosophers*, Jaspers created biographic paradigms through which the reader could become an independent thinker: "Our own philosophical thinking twines upward as it were round the historical figures. Through the understanding of their texts we ourselves become philosophers. But this confident learning is not obedience. In this following we test our own essence."[8]

The fact that Jaspers' writings had little influence on psychotherapy—with the exception of his still popular *General Psychopathology*, which he wrote before his conversion to philosophy—might be due to his fierce criticism of psychoanalysis. Marxism, racism, and psychoanalysis were all denounced by him as "pseudo-faiths" disguised as sciences. However, the idea that philosophical thought and reflection in general affects human behavior—and for that reason needs to be emphasized in the understanding of life—did find some recognition in cognitive, existentialist, and social therapies, as well as in logotherapy. Jung, Adler, Frankl, and others were well aware of the dominant influence of worldviews and thought on the lives of their patients. Jaspers—like Sartre, who considered experimental psychology to be psychology "proper," the rest being philosophy—distinguishes the medical science of the psychopathologist from philosophical knowledge. The former is knowable and can be demonstrated by rational scientific processes; one becomes conscious of the latter knowledge by philosophizing from out the whole being of man in the world. Jaspers described his conversion from psychiatry to "philosophical faith" in his philosophical autobiography: "Increasingly . . . genuine philosophy showed itself to me. . . . Nowhere does philosophy render results as means for the planned making of the world. But it does bring the basis of consciousness into clear focus which alone gives limit and meaning to the results of science and the possibility of planned creativity."[9] Accordingly, a scientific, medical, or psychological description of life is seen from a philosophic perspective as limited.

Edmund L. Erde finds philosophy to be essentially different from science, in spite of the commonality between aspects of the two disciplines, because of the role fiction plays in philosophy: "In philosophy we want to UNDERSTAND a BEWILDERING claim p. If we can on the basis of some proposed cases then that is all that we require or desire. All the philosopher need to do is suggest 'Suppose XYZ! Doesn't p then fit?' The scientist can't get away with that." The scientist must explain his theory by applying it to reality—his job is to "fix" theory and reality by establishing methods and facts. Fiction has no role in science, but in philosophy, fictional cases convey as much weight as matters of fact. Erde finds philosophy concerned with concept formation as outlining a form, which must take place, as Wittgenstein also remarked, before new discoveries and inventions can come in existence.[10]

A philosophical description of lives aims at giving an account of the whole being of man in the world, without "fixing it up" with methods and facts. A philosophical narrative will not only accentuate the conscious, intellectual, or philosophical development of a person, but will question how his or her life was shaped—for example, by a quest for meaning, justice, or any other philosophic concept, and by personal confrontation with various ideologies and ethical dilemmas. Narrative representations of lives may be written by psychologists, philosophers, historians, or literary artists. Each narrator will deal with the subject based on his or her professional knowledge; this does not indicate that the professions overlap or are interdisciplinary, but rather that they have a common topic of investigation. In the arts common topics do not lead to any confusion concerning the identity of the artistic profession. A photographer, painter, poet, or sculpturer may all portray the same object without accusations of intruding on the other's art.

The increasing popularity of the narrative in different academic disciplines has already led to the publication of several journals on this subject, such as *The Narrative Study of Lives*. The narrator–

psychologist, Amia Lieblich, shows clearly that her description is a psychological narrative by the existence of the psychological interpretations and understandings woven into the narrative, such as in the following example: "It was easy for Natasha to admit openly that she has changed in her sense of belonging to the Israeli society, because from her point of view this is an external change. From my point of view, however, following Erikson's . . . concept of identity, the change in belonging naturally leads to a change in values, norms, behaviors and choices."[11] In a philosophical narrative the narrator might question if "a change in belonging" naturally leads to such changes; from a Sartrean perspective one would have to decide on one's values in order to become an authentic person. Instead of using psychological interpretations, the philosophical narrator will find philosophical content and developments of which the person involved might not have been aware. An example is the ethics a person was exposed to in childhood and whether this influenced perceptions of good and evil throughout that person's life.

While people have been fascinated by biographers throughout the ages, it was only in the nineteenth and twentieth centuries that autobiography became one of the most popular forms of writing.[12] Augustine's *The Confessions* is the first and most famous example in the history of this genre, followed by *The Essays* of Michel Montaigne and Jean Jacques Rousseau's *Confessions*. The following are some examples of modern philosophical narratives.

In a paper published in 1980, the philosopher Norris Clarke asked whether there is any philosophical importance in writing one's autobiography.[13] He then offered the answer of many great metaphysicians, particularly that of St. Thomas Aquinas: "To be is to be one," that is, one in harmony with him or herself through wisdom. Clarke considers the writing of an autobiography to be an attempt to take full, self-conscious possession of one's being. In his own autobiography he describes how he developed as a philosopher. The key phases of his development are drawn together, and out of them, a pattern is woven. These phases are

1. The first time he remembered being conscious of himself.
2. The role of high places (e.g., trees, bridges, or mountains) as the concrete visual symbols of, and "introduction" to, metaphysical synthesis in philosophy.
3. Crucial readings.
4. Meetings with philosophers, teaching philosophy, and continual philosophical study.

Reflecting on his autobiography, Clarke concludes that the pattern uniting his life is one of guiding illumination and exhortation.

Susan Sontag, the literary critic, writer, artist, and philosopher, considers self-examination to be a trend in French literary culture, which had as its origin the philosopher Montaigne. Sontag is not widely know as a philosopher in spite of her degree in philosophy, and although most of her books on criticism are indexed by philosophy and contain essays on philosophers and philosophical queries. In her introduction to *The Best American Essays 1992*, Sontag states that "two of the century's greatest minds, Kierkegaard and Nietzsche, could both be considered as practicing a form of essay. . . . Of course, to say that a philosopher is an essayist is, from the traditional point of view of philosophy, a demotion."[14]

In line with the French literary tradition, Sontag finds that Roland Barthes's writings ended in autobiography. Sontag's descriptions of the lives of writers, philosophers, and artists, as well as other matters (e.g., *On Photography* or *The Volcano Lover: A Romance*), are enlivened with the philosophical analysis that is characteristic of philosophical narratives. Thus Sontag writes about Barthes: "At the end . . . there was an emergence of a vision of 'wisdom' of the Platonic sort—tempered to be sure, by wisdom of a worldly kind: skeptical of dogmatisms, conscientious about gratification, wistfully attached to utopian ideals."[15] Sontag's analysis of Antonin Artaud is another exemplary philosophical narrative. Through her philosophical knowledge she explicates Platonic, Nietzschean, and especially Gnostic themes in the works and life of Artaud; she finds his principal metaphors typical Gnostic. Artaud's life is presented as the realization of the Gnostic project, that is, a search for wisdom, but not of the ordinary type. Artaud chooses to transcend his work and life in a Gnostic dream of perfect unity; he embodies the alchemic will of transformation directed to body, mind, and world. Sontag describes Artaud as standing at a crossroads that leads in opposing directions: one to the moralist Platonizers and the other to the surrealist lovers of joy and life. His Gnostic escape from the rift between Platonism and surrealism created a new revelation in art and philosophy: "And, for the first time, the Gnostic themes can be seen in evolution. Artaud's work is particularly precious as the first complete documentation of someone living through the trajectory of Gnostic thought."[16]

Jean-Paul Sartre's and Simone de Beauvoir's autobiographical and biographical writings are likewise examples of the philosophical illumination of personal consciousness. Sartre described in his autobiography *The Words* how his life's project, his "existential project," develops through the "original choices" he made during his childhood and later in life. Sartre demonstrated in his autobiographical and biographical narratives that the existential project can always be revised through additional choices.[17]

The biographies by the philosopher Brand Blanshard of Marcus Aurelius, John Stuart Mill, Ernest Renan, and Henry Sidgwick are a rewarding continuation of Blanshard's life work: the analysis of the nature of reasonableness.[18] This attempt to show reasonableness as the most desirable of human virtues, and also as belonging to the lives of men described, is parallel to the chief interest in classical biography and hagiography: the discovery of virtue or vice in the character of the narrative's hero or heroine. Philosophical narrative is obviously not limited to philosophers alone. Jawaharlal Nehru's description of his philosophy of life is particular interesting in that the Indian political leader was not involved in philosophizing until he was imprisoned: "Sometimes they (philosophical or metaphysical problems) come to me almost unawares in the long silences of prison, or even in the midst of an intensity of action, bringing with them a sense of detachment or consolation in the face of some painful experience."[19] About seven years before Nehru's imprisonment, he was called upon to write an essay on his philosophy of life, but he had then "forgotten" about it; although later, he included a chapter on his philosophy of life in *The Discovery of India*, a history of India, which he wrote in the Ahmadnagar Fort Prison.

One may conclude that philosophical self-knowledge and reflection and philosophical narratives of oneself and of others, can come about through various events and intentions. In my philosophical practice I find it necessary to write personal philosophical memoirs of sessions with clients. Thinking and writing about these sessions often leads to additional questions and insights regarding the problematic issue the client has brought to the session. Likewise, I occasionally encourage clients to start or renew a personal dialogue with philosophical texts. I do this by bringing a particular text that is relevant to the visitor's situation into the conversation or suggesting reading philosophical novels, biographies, autobiographies, and philosophy books. Moreover, the writing of philosophical memoirs, a philosophy of life, or a philosophical text might be suggested to certain clients. Within philosophical practice, writing philosophical narrative is not concerned with literary criteria, but with philosophizing as an activity integrated with all situations of life. In actualizing the "literary" aspect of philosophical practice, it is necessary to first observe the visitor's intellectual interests and talents and then suggest some "literary" endeavor. I do not believe that the writing of a philosophical text is suitable for everyone.

The case histories in the second part of this book have to be understood within the tradition of the confessional and biographical method of philosophizing, which seeks philosophical knowledge through self-disclosure. Names and circumstances have been either changed or partly omitted.

In these philosophical narratives there is a proper place for descriptions of physical details, such as Dani's half-unbuttoned black shirt and black hair, as well as his dark face, which had a sad but friendly expression that could change with anger and then have the wild look of a hurt animal that does not understand; all this has significance for understanding Dani's experience and reality philosophically. Another example is the description of the white sport shoes Yoni used to wear; all these exterior details—not to mention the "interior" ones of a persistent stream of thoughts and associations—are of paramount importance to the understanding of philosophical–biographical discourse, but they are to a great extent left out. Presented is only a sketch of the essential contours. The ambience of the setting—in the office, salon, clinic, or café— also has an influence on the conversation. Some clients want to meet with me in a lobby, a café, or at their home. In certain circumstances I find it prudent to honor such requests. For example, it seems appropriate to visit a person at home who is physically incapacitated or in another exceptional situation. The counselees that wanted to meet with me in a hotel lobby or a café had a different attitude about disclosing themselves than those who came to my home office. Meetings in public places may give insecure persons a chance to feel secure and may help them to speak about their questions or problems in a more casual manner.

One of my visitors showed herself to be very sensitive to the "clinical atmosphere" at the psychological institute in Tel Aviv where I sometimes receive visitors. Before she visited me in Tel Aviv, she had been at my consultation office in my Jerusalem home several times. Her criticism made me aware of issues I had not considered myself. She considered the "clinical atmosphere" impersonal and artificial: The reproductions on the walls, the wall-to-wall carpet, and the fluorescent lights all caused her to feel alienated and distracted her from thinking and talking.

This occurrence made me aware that a homelike atmosphere— one that seems "real"—is more suitable for philosophical consultation. I prefer to meet people at my home and to serve them some light refreshments if they wish. The sessions in my practice last about seventy-five minutes, but can also continue longer. My fees are on a sliding scale—according to the financial ability of my clients— and about the same or a bit less than private psychologists charge. I found that giving a certain amount of free counseling to those who really cannot afford to pay has been always very productive; I have often experienced that it is better to give than to receive. Philosophical practitioners should not hesitate to ask reasonable payment for the service they provide, but they also should not let earnings become the most important facet of their work.

During my first three years of practicing philosophy, I talked with about one-hundred people, with a ratio of about 55 to 45, women to men. About 60 percent came for short-term consultation—that is, less then seven visits. The remainder continued over a period of a few months to a few years. The frequency and cessation of the sessions are determined by the visitors. Some come once or twice a week, others once every few weeks. Other visitors find that only one or two conversations are sufficient for clarification and guidance.

The only criterion I have for accepting a client for philosophical counseling is the client's common-sense and ability to engage in dialogue. I have accepted many clients who had previously been in psychotherapy (a few of whom had been hospitalized), others who were critical of psychotherapy without having tried it, and still others who considered their problems to be specifically of a philosophical nature. A large percentage of the visitors have artistic professions or are teachers, students, or work at an administrative job. A smaller percentage are business people, scientists, psychologists, nurses, or manual laborers. The average age of the visitors is around forty, but the range of ages includes teenagers and senior citizens. The majority of my visitors are secular Israelis, but ultra-Orthodox Jews and Muslim or Christian Palestinians have also been among my clients.

In the philosophical narratives, I have mainly described the long-term consultations, but I also mention some remarkable short-term sessions. I view every narrative as a *portrait* of a visitor. It is important that portraits can convey many details and feelings about the person portrayed. However, no matter how lively and true the portrait may be, it obtains its outline through the skill and vision of the portrayer. In his *Confessions*, Rousseau depended only on his memory in portraying "the history of his soul," his self-portrait.[20] Likewise, the portraits in the second part of this book depended upon my recall of the sessions, and not on scientific, objective observations or tape and video recordings. I have to admit and warn that my descriptions try to recapture past events with few words. Imagination is needed to envision what went on in the counseling sessions. What in fact happened cannot be described or known, even if I would have tried to imitate James Joyce and had set out for another *Ulysses*.

NOTES

1. Herbert Read, *English Prose Style* (Boston: Beacon, 1955), 108.

2. Georg Misch, *A History of Autobiography in Antiquity*, vol. 1 (London: Routledge and Kegan Paul, 1949), 90.

3. Michel Foucault, "Technologies of the Self," in *Technologies of the Self*, ed. L. H. Martin, H. Gutman, and P. H. Hutton (Amherst: University of Massachusetts Press, 1988), 20.

4. Foucault, *Politics, Philosophy, Culture*, ed. L. D. Kritzman (New York: Routledge, 1990), 6.

5. Patrick H. Hutton, "Foucault, Freud, and the Technologies of the Self," in *Technologies of the Self*, ed. L. H. Martin, H. Gutman, and P. H. Hutton (Amherst: University of Massachusetts Press, 1988), 121.

6. Foucault, *Politics, Philosophy, Culture*, 15.

7. Karl Jaspers, *General Psychopathology* (Manchester, England: Manchester University Press, 1972); Karl Jaspers, *Strindberg und van Gogh* (Munich: Piper, 1977); Karl Jaspers, *Nietzsche: An Introduction to the Understanding of His Philosophical Activity* (Baltimore: Johns Hopkins University Press, 1998); Karl Jaspers, *The Great Philosophers* (New York: Harcourt Brace, vol. 3, 1993; vol. 4, 1995).

8. Karl Jaspers, *Way to Wisdom* (New Haven, Conn.: Yale University Press, 1951), 135, 170; Karl Jaspers, *General Psychopathology*.

9. Paul A. Schilpp, *The Philosophy of Karl Jaspers* (New York: Tudor, 1957), 79.

10. Edmund L. Erde, *Philosophy and Psycholinguistics* (The Hague: Mouton, 1973), 53, 222.

11. Amia Lieblich, "Looking at Change," *The Narrative Study of Lives*, vol. 1, ed. A. Lieblich and R. Josselson (London: Sage, 1993), 121; E. H. Erikson, *Identity: Youth and Crisis* (New York: Norton, 1968).

12. *Encyclopedia Britannica*, 1971, ed., s.v. "Autobiography"; "Biography."

13. Norris W. Clarke, "The Philosophical Importance of Doing One's Autobiography," *The American Catholic Philosophical Association Proceedings* 54 (1980): 17–25.

14. Susan Sontag and Robert Atwan, eds., *The Best American Essays 1992*, intro. S. Sontag (New York: Ticknor & Fields, 1992), xv.

15. Susan Sontag, *A Susan Sontag Reader* (London: Penguin, 1983), 446; Susan Sontag, *On Photography* (New York: Farrar, Straus, and Giroux, 1977); Susan Sontag, *The Volcano Lover: A Romance* (New York: Farrar, Straus, and Giroux, 1992).

16. Antonin Artaud, *Antonin Artaud, Selected Writings*, ed. and intro. S. Sontag (Berkeley and Los Angeles: University of California Press, 1988), xlix, li.

17. For an analysis of Sartre's autobiographical and biographical projects see Shlomit C. Schuster, "Sartre's Freud and the Future of Sartrean Psychoanalysis," *The Israel Journal of Psychiatry* 35, 1 (1998): 20–30; Shlomit C. Schuster, "Sartre's 'Words' as a Paradigm for Self-Description in Philosophical Counseling," in *Perspectives in Philosophical Practice: The Proceedings of the Second Annual International Congress on Philosophical Practice*, ed. W. van der Vlist (Doorwerth, The Netherlands: The Dutch Society for Philosophy Practice, 1997), 20–34; Jean-Paul Sartre, *The Words* (New York: George Braziller, 1964).

18. Brand Blanshard, *Four Reasonable Men* (Middletown, Conn.: Wesleyan University Press, 1984).

19. Jawaharlal Nehru, *The Discovery of India* (New York: Doubleday Anchor, 1959), 7.

20. Jean Jacques Rousseau, *The Confessions of Jean Jacques Rousseau* (New York: The Modern Library, 1945), 284.

PART II

PHILOSOPHICAL PRACTICE PORTRAYED

CHAPTER 5

Daniel

Daniel visited me over a period of three months at my consultation office in Jerusalem. The following is a description of four philosophical sessions, during which philosophical tactics and strategies were used.

In these sessions I made use of existentialist thought and critical reflections on psychoanalysis (Nietzsche, Kierkegaard, Sartre, and Popper). The tactics and strategies I made use of in Daniel's situation fit Nietzsche's pragmatic understanding of "how to become the poets of our life."

Nietzsche considered philosophical intentions useful even in the smallest matters of everyday life. By analyzing Section 299 of Nietzsche's *Gay Science*, I was able to apply its philosophical ideas to my philosophical discourse with Daniel, as follows.

1. Nietzsche describes the idea of distancing reality and making it comprehensible through a mind that is not limited in its thought. In his second session, Daniel was able to distance his primary judgment, and to instead create and make use of a critical judgment.

2. According to Nietzsche, situations can be understood from different perspectives. In the first session, we exercised a skeptical perspective on the causes of Daniel's insomnia; in the second session, a more pragmatic perspective was utilized, in that forgiveness was justified by its effects.

3. Nietzsche describes the need to apprehend life aesthetically. In the second, third, and fourth sessions, Daniel worked from the assump-

tion that one can compose one's past, present, and future, and that one can choose one's thoughts, feelings, and deeds.

4. Nietzsche advocated an almost prima facie understanding of the world. In the second and third sessions, the causes Daniel gives for his insomnia are also considered as the possible real causes.

FIRST SESSION

Daniel is a man in his fifties. He presented insomnia as his greatest problem. Daniel's symptoms had prevented him from retaining a job for the last twenty-five years. Neither psychiatric medication nor psychotherapy provided him with relief. He usually went to bed at midnight after several hours of watching television and then he could not fall asleep. Then he usually went back to the television, but after watching another few hours of movies, shows, and news he had enough of it. This was the time that troubled him the most, when everybody was asleep, and everything was silent, except for his mind. In these late-night hours, which seemed an eternity to him, childhood memories started to afflict him. He was convinced that his insomnia was caused by obsessive thoughts of taking revenge on his parents, who had died several years before. Though they were no longer alive, he felt that he wanted to destroy both his father and mother, because they had destroyed him.

A secondary cause of his insomnia, nervous tension and headaches, he believed was a result of unconscious memories of the cruel treatment he had received in his youth. I asked Daniel if his complaints might be caused by a physical disorder, but tests he had done to find this out did not reveal any cause for the complaints. His doctor thought that he suffered from a psychosomatic illness.

In this first session, I suggested that Daniel adopt a skeptical attitude toward the causes of his insomnia. My argument was that physical illness or physiological conditions and habits that induce insomnia, such as the excessive use of stimulating drinks, lack of physical exercise, and lack of mental concentration, could all be triggers for his sleepless nights. Daniel was encouraged to replace his habits with others that relax body and mind (e.g., herbal teas, sports, meditation, and classical music). He was asked to concentrate, some hours *before* he usually tried to fall asleep, on what troubled his mind when he was trying to fall asleep, and to write these things down.

SECOND SESSION

Daniel related to me some memories of his youth when his parents sent him to work. His father had friends with fruit and veg-

etable stands at the Jerusalem Machane Yehuda market, where he
was sent to help them out by selling and carrying produce. Instead
of going to school, he was forced to contribute to the household in-
come. He received only a few years of elementary education. Daniel
remarked, "My father used to say, 'You only need to know how to
sign your name on your paycheck.'" Any money earned had to be
given to his father, who scarcely gave him enough food in return.
Daniel recalled an incident when his father said to a friend, "Dani
isn't worth a piece of bread." When the whole family (of ten) were
seated around the dinner table, his father would make hurtful jokes
about him. For example, "Dani, why don't you work a bit harder at
the market? I spoke to Shuki, and he said that if you would carry
twice as many boxes as you do now, he would adopt you. Wouldn't
that be nice?"

Memories like these made him angry and gave him thoughts of
revenge; though Daniel thought it absurd that he wanted to avenge
himself on his dead parents. Apparently he had "kept up good relations" with his parents during their lifetime. Only after their death
was he able to feel, although not express, his hatred for them. My
argument in the second session was that the only "revenge" that
remained possible was to forgive his parents. Though this argument is a rhetorical one, it is one where the soul may be influenced
through words. Obviously, forgiveness is not revenge; but "antilogic,"
as applied in this session, is justified when it ultimately improves
living and the attainment of logic at a later stage.[1]

But, to take revenge by forgiving his parents was impossible for
Daniel: To forgive was to justify what his parents had done! I clarified the notion of forgiveness for Daniel: Is it not the case that only
a person who has done wrong can be forgiven? Thus instead of jus-
tifying his parents' behavior, forgiving them would underline their
guilt. But Daniel continued to feel that his parents should receive
a just punishment. To forgive them was not right. Kierkegaard's
understanding, that "when a sin cries for punishment, then it looks
quite different, far greater than when the same sin is forgiven,"
gave me a solution for the problems of Daniel's tortured soul.[2] I
opposed his rejection of forgiveness with a pragmatic argument: "It
may not be right to forgive your parents, but this should not disturb you if forgiving them will change your life." I suggested to him
that he could still secure something of what his parents, intention-
ally or not, had destroyed. His demand that they be punished made
the past look more grievous. Forgiving could help him overcome
his feelings of hatred and his absurd thoughts of vengeance. From
a practical perspective the sensible "revenge" was not to seek vengeance, but to understand his need for expressing his anger.

To his repeated question, "How could they have been so cruel?" I tried to answer with verses from Kahlil Gibran's *The Prophet*. In these verses evil is described as good "tortured by its own hunger and thirst." I asked Daniel, "Is it always possible to make a clear distinction between good and evil? Is it possible that cruel actions are not always intended to do harm?" I compared his "judgment" with the impartial judgments made in court cases. Could he imagine handing over his case to a court? Could he hear his parents' attorney? Could he lift himself above his prejudices and judge them justly? I thought that if Daniel could distance himself emotionally from his painful past, he would start to understand and find answers to his questions. Daniel was advised to think over what he had to lose by forgiving those who had injured him and to consider what he could gain by it.

THIRD SESSION

At the beginning of this session I asked Daniel if he had come to a different understanding of his past. His answer was "Yes." He had found my arguments convincing and had decided to forgive the cruelties done to him. Still bothering him were "the memories in his unconscious which he could not remember." These memories were the cause of insomnia and headaches. To my question, "How do you know that such memories exist and are bothering you?" he explained that he had read newspaper articles on psychology where his symptoms were described as caused by unconscious memories.

He had visited a renowned hypnotist to enable him to recall these unknown memories, but this specialist had rejected his request without specifying why. Although Daniel had no ideas about the nature of hypnosis, still he had the expectation that hypnosis could help him. We talked for awhile about what hypnosis actually does and about altered states of consciousness. In addition, I thought it worth trying to change his attitude toward forgetfulness, in showing it as a positive faculty. I linked Daniel's problem with how Nietzsche understood memory and history: Nietzsche found "the ability to forget" and "the capacity to feel unhistorically" as being an indispensable prerequisites for a happy life.[3] Consequently, I argued that it was not tragic if he could not recall everything that had ever happened to him. On the contrary, his past might be a "Pandora's box" that might be better if it remain closed. By not remembering all of his youth, he could avoid having a mental crisis. However, I told him, it is best not to be fearful of anything in life, including memories, fantasies, or reality. I asked him think of an abhorrent event that could happen or had happened to him and to confront this event bravely. What was the worst thing he could think of? He replied that he did not know but would think about it.

In spite of his negative attitude toward his parents, Daniel might also have had some positive, loving feelings toward them, and I considered this another possible reason for his inability to recall his memories. Just as repressed love for his parents might cause him not to remember some of his bad memories, it might also cause him to forget the good ones. I contended that it was plausible that self-deception was keeping him from remembering what he could not forget (if there was indeed anything to remember).

The next step was to clarify the scientific status of psychological knowledge about the unconscious. Daniel had acquired information about Freudian concepts of the mind, but criticism of these concepts was new to him. Popper's, Ricoeur's, and Habermas's expositions of Freud's theory have demonstrated that psychoanalysis is unscientific.[4] Likewise, Daniel had never heard of Sartre's rejection of the Freudian unconscious in favor of an all-knowing consciousness.[5] My argument was that none of the theories about the unconscious—or the conscious, for that matter—can be scientifically proven; even Freud's theory is only a hypothesis. I suggested an antithesis of the unconscious: If the mind contains a faculty which represses memories, it may also have a faculty which excludes events from becoming memories. Additionally, why not suppose there is a faculty that erases memories? Past events that had been excluded or erased would thus exist neither in the memory nor in the unconscious. This could have happened in his mind, and then, neither psychoanalysis nor hypnosis nor anything else could help him recall "lost" memories. This interpretation brought a hopeful smile to Daniel's face. He reacted enthusiastically: "Then I am free."

FOURTH SESSION

At the beginning of this session Daniel told me that one evening when he had tried to fall asleep he had suddenly remembered something new. As a boy, when he had gone to sleep, his father had often burst into the children's bedroom in an angry mood and beaten Daniel with a belt—a belt with a metal buckle. Though it was a painful memory, Daniel was pleased that he had recalled it. He also claimed that his condition had improved: His sleepless nights were becoming fewer and shorter. His obsessive interest in "unconscious memories" had disappeared. From then onward we talked about his present situation: how to find a job, how to give his children the best education, and how to solve a problem with his girlfriend.

CONCLUSION

I had no preconceived strategy for change in Daniel's situation. During the talks certain philosophical understandings and ideas appeared to be helpful. Afterward, I found these conceptions congruent with ideas expressed in Nietzsche's *Gay Science*. What I told Daniel resonated in my life experiences, and I could envision putting these ideas into practice myself. I gave him several authoritative perspectives on the topic of memory with the aim of generating an understanding that would facilitate change. Through the dialogue with Daniel I came to consider the possibility of the exclusion and erasure of "memories." This was as new an idea for me as it was for him. Thinking about issues like the memory is a topic of interest in the philosophy of mind. For example, the philosopher Norman Malcolm pointed out that so-called "memory traces" are a "theoretical construct only": "They are not entities, states or processes that neurologists have discovered as dentists discover cavities."[6] In situations like Daniel's the results of long- or short-term counseling are frequently surprising. The positive change in Daniel might have been caused by the therapy-like features of philosophical practice. Nevertheless, I find a more important contribution to the transtherapeutic success of philosophical counseling is the philosophic content of its dialogue, which links the "wisdom of the ages" with actual life situations.

NOTES

1. Friedrich Nietzsche, *The Gay Science*, trans. W. Kaufmann (New York: Vintage, 1974), 239–240; James S. Murray, "Disputation, Deception and Dialectic: Plato on the True Rhetoric (Phaedrus 261–266)," *Philosophy and Rhetoric* 21 (1988): 279–289.

2. Søren Kierkegaard, "Works of Love," in *A Kierkegaard Anthology*, ed. R. Bretall (Princeton, N.J.: Princeton University Press, 1946), 320.

3. Jacob Golomb, *Nietzsche's Enticing Psychology of Power* (Jerusalem: Magnes Press–The Hebrew University, 1989), 86–95; Friedrich Nietzsche, "On the Uses and Disadvantages of History for Life," in *Untimely Meditations* (Cambridge: Cambridge University Press, 1983), 57–62.

4. David Heyed, "Psychoanaliza al Sapat Ha Philosoof" (Psychoanalysis on the Philosopher's Couch) (in Hebrew), *Iyyun: A Hebrew Philosophical Quarterly* 35, 1 (1986): 60–61.

5. Lee Brown and Alan Hausman, "Mechanism, Intentionality, and the Unconscious: A Comparison of Sartre and Freud," and Ivan Soll, "Sartre's Rejection of the Freudian Unconscious," both in *The Philosophy of Jean-Paul Sartre*, ed. P. A. Schilpp (La Salle, Ill.: Open Court, 1981), 539–604.

6. Norman Malcolm, *Memory and Mind* (London: Cornell University Press, 1977), 171.

CHAPTER 6

Simone

This case story shows how concepts of reality, the past, and justice may influence a person's inner well-being. I will not describe the thirty weekly sessions separately, but will give a general description of what occurred.

Simone, a nurse, middle-aged, and divorced, complained about feelings of detachment and emptiness. These feelings had started in her early twenties after an intimate friend died in a car accident. Simone thought something was wrong with her; she was afraid that she might have a mental illness or be going insane. Even though she thought this, she was not interested in psychology or other theories of mental health, because she believed that was the "experts'" business. Since she was not a mental-health professional, she thought it wrong to have her own critical judgment on issues like madness. When she was in her late twenties, she had been in therapy for several years with various psychotherapists, but she did not like their cold manner and formal behavior. Once she had met one of these therapists in town, and he had passed her by without greeting her.

Although Simone had picked up some psychological cliches about herself during the time she had received treatment, she was generally able to describe herself and her life without using psychologist jargon. Her fears were based mainly on what she called "not having contact with reality." I asked her to explain what she meant by that. She answered that she felt separated from others emotion-

ally. It was as if there were a thin glass wall separating her from
life. She said that she was a strong person and usually people did
not notice that she was different, that she was not really like other
people. She did good work at the hospital, but she could never talk
to anybody sincerely. The veil between her and others gave her
"strange thoughts." Sometimes she asked herself questions such
as, "What am I doing here? Is this really my home? Do I live here?
What is this all for?" I asked her if these thoughts were connected
with particular feelings she had had at those moments, but she did
not think they were. In general she did not feel much at all except
for emotional pain, which she explained by saying that she had
suffered in her childhood and youth. Her family had immigrated to
Israel from Kurdistan, and they had kept the religious and traditional ways of the Kurdistani Jews. She had barely known her father, because he was always studying at home or at a religious
institution. When he was studying at home, everyone had to be
very quiet, otherwise he would have rage attacks. The only feeling
she had for him was fear. Moreover, living through several wars,
with a scarcity of food and the lack of other basic needs, made her
feel different from so-called "normal" people. She could not share
in the happiness that other people seemed to have.

I thought it important not to call Simone's problem "not having
contact with reality." As an alternative, I suggested talking about
it as emotional alienation or detachment. We talked about what
reality is. Her perception of reality was similar to that of most people.
She interacted with her surroundings as most people do, without
hallucinations or delusions. We began talking about alienation as
a general human feature, as Hegel, Marx, and Sartre have described
it. Could one see positive sides to alienation as well? Can alienation be transcended? We talked about the detachment of emotions
from a Stoic perspective: The wise person is emotion-free.

One day Simone came to me upset about something and did not
want to talk about anything that had to do with her feelings. This
gave me the opportunity to talk to her extensively about Hegel. I
explained that Hegel's theory of history can be helpful for understanding personal life as well as the historical development of nations. Hegel considered essential in all existence a dialectical
development, in which each topic contains its contradiction in itself. But unlike the idea behind the symbol Yin–Yang in Eastern
thought, there is no harmony between the opposing forces until a
higher state of development is reached. More precisely, the highest
stage of the Absolute Spirit must be realized. This stage is expressed
in philosophy, religion, and art. History is the "progressive incar-
nation of the Absolute Spirit" not just a "tale told by an idiot, signi-

fying nothing."[1] Hegel's dialectical thought opened a new inner world for Simone. The idea that conflicts and difficulties might be considered the fuel for a more advanced future seemed marvelous to her. She then revealed a deeply pessimistic and fatalistic faith: "My therapist told me that early childhood affects the person for the rest of his or her life." I questioned this by stating the following. First, it was the opinion of many psychologists, but not all. Second, there is evidence of people who have made revolutionary changes in their life as adults. For example, there are stories of people who have undergone one or another religious conversion or who had discovered something or had a revelation about themselves or life, and thus become "new" people. Even an ardent atheist like Sartre had a "mystic" streak which allowed him to believe that one can transcend oneself.

Simone then said sarcastically that she wanted to be born again. I replied, "O.K., there are Judaism, Christianity, and quite a few other faiths and ways of life which can teach you how to live so differently that you would feel as if you had been born again. *Birth and Rebirth* by Mircea Eliade is an excellent source book for extensive reflection on this subject. Some faiths even claim that you *are* born again if you fulfill a certain imperative, like saying a prayer."

Simone's wish to be "born again" was the wish to make a radical secular new beginning rather than become an observant Jewess or convert to Christianity or any other religion. I wanted to present an alternative to rebirthing. We discussed the topics memory and imagination, for which I mainly resorted to Sartre's writings. I considered to what extent our memories might actually be fantasies about the past or distortions of reality. I brought up the issue of how imagination could influence our behavior in the present and future. Simone said she had a lively imagination and had been a daydreamer since childhood. She had always dreamed of happiness. I recommended that she read Aristotle's *Nicomachean Ethics* and Russell's *The Conquest of Happiness*. She could not understand how philosophy and ethics could make a person happy, since she understood happiness to be a complete involvement in action. She thought that reflection on happiness had something sad about it. I insisted that this might be the case sometimes, but, according to the experience of philosophers throughout the ages, philosophical reflection could even grant lasting bliss. I advised her to try to think of, or imagine, what could make her happy.

Simone then talked about love, a different job, and "contact with reality." I asked her if and when there had been an emotional involvement in her life. She said this had occurred when she had been in love as a teenager and when she listened to music. She felt

moved by beauty. Sometimes she had burst into tears while listening to a concert. Otherwise, at times when she wanted to cry, she
felt only emptiness inside. I thought that a greater involvement
with art might provide her with an opportunity to unite with her
emotions. Maybe she could take a course in painting, pottery, or
music. She had often thought of this but was too passive—she felt
she was outside life, that life passed her by. I then told her about
Franz Kafka's metaphor in which a man waits and waits in front of
a "closed" gate. He waits for the gate to be opened, while it is really
open all the time. He would have found that out if he had made the
attempt to enter the gate. I encouraged her to *try* to be happy and
to *do* the things she dreamed of.

Simone then acquired information on something that she was
interested in: finishing her art studies at the university. She had
broken off these studies because she had found it too difficult to
finish them within the prescribed time and had been embarrassed to
request spreading them out over a longer period. To be embarrassed,
not to show emotions, and to fear being different from others apparently were connected with events at home with her father. Her father
had been an alcoholic and had often embarrassed and beaten her
in front of her two sisters. She never took friends home because she
was ashamed and afraid of what her father would do next.

This brought the conversation to the subject of authenticity. It
was understandable that Simone's childhood had caused her to hide
her feelings, but now that situation no longer existed and could
never return. I suggested that if she looked back on her life and on
what she had accomplished in spite of her unfortunate childhood,
she had reason to be proud of herself. We then talked for a few
sessions about existentialist views of authenticity and the possibility of choosing to be authentic. Simone started to express her feelings and thoughts about some difficult relationships at work. She
let the head nurse know that there were too many patients to be
taken care of by the nursing team and that she should consider
having more nurses. Since Simone obtained the support of the other
nurses, the head nurse began treating her as the rebel leader and
tried to place her in another department. The situation at work
had changed, because of her new openness, partly for the worse
and partly for the better. Simone's feeling that the head nurse was
treating her unfairly brought us to another issue: justice.

Simone's experiences had taught her that there is no justice in
life. "The just suffer, while the evil flourish," was the religious maxim
underlying her somber attitude. If Simone was not treated as she
liked, she took it as another proof of her hypothesis and would with-
draw into an inner world of agony and pessimism. My advice to her

was as follows: (1) read the book *On Good and Evil in Jewish Thought*;[2] and (2) question good and evil in two of her relationships: with her departed father and with her younger sister. When Simone considered the "evil" actions of these family members in the context of circumstances and intentions, these acts still contained their sting of painful emotions, but they became specified and comprehensible—though not justified—events. For example, in regard to the beatings she had received from her father when she and her brothers and sisters had disturbed him, she found reasons for this behavior, which she had previously considered to only be part of the general evil of life. This more articulated and realistically structured notion of what she named wrong behavior made it possible for her to compare her own behavior with that of her sister. Eventually, after years of estrangement, Simone renewed contact with her sister.

CONCLUSION

Although Simone did not change into a person beaming with happiness, she was helped by talking about her situation. Some of her understandings and attitudes did change through our talks. When she discontinued the sessions, she felt that "not having contact with reality" was no longer a problem for her. She became more active and developed hobbies in which she could express her feelings.

NOTES

1. Henry D. Aiken, *The Age of Ideology* (New York: Mentor, 1956), 81; G.W.F. Hegel, *The Philosophy of History* (New York: Wiley, 1944).

2. Shalom Rosenberg, *Tov ve Rah be Machshevet Israel* (On good and evil in Jewish thought) (Tel Aviv: Misraad Habitahon, 1985).

CHAPTER 7

Yoni

The chapter is drawn from sessions over a period of ten months in 1989 and 1990. I do not include all of the sessions, but rather focus on those talks in which Sartre's thought was discussed. At the beginning of the talks Yoni came once or twice a week, and this continued for about three months, after which he moved from Jerusalem to Tiberias. We then continued the sessions less frequently, about once or twice a month. Yoni had contacted me after having been in psychotherapy for a year and a half. He came to me half a year after he had stopped therapy because of a disagreement with his therapist.

In the first month's sessions, Yoni was feeling depressed and nervous and found it difficult to express himself freely. His hands were sweating, and he had to get up several times to wash his hands or face, drink something, or go to the bathroom. His face frequently turned pale. He was in his late twenties and an artist. He was the only son (he had an older and a younger sister) in an ultra-Orthodox Jewish family. He had wasted his youth, as he put it, in the world of *yeshivas*, or religious schools. He had felt rebellious toward religion from the age of seven. At that age he had wanted to play with the little girl next door, but his parents had forbidden it for religious reasons. He felt as if he had been living in a ghetto; only at twenty-one did he break away from the religious way of life and make contact with secular Israeli society.

The first problem Yoni presented was what he called his weak ego. He explained that if he wanted to buy something or had to decide on some matter, he became confused and started doubting himself. He did not know how to go about choosing anything. For example, the week before he had bought a pair of shoes. In the shoe store he had tried on one pair after an other. He finally bought a pair which were not his size and with a design he did not like. It was the salesperson's fault, he said sarcastically; he had been pressured into buying the white running shoes he was wearing. He wanted to know if philosophical counseling could help him with this problem.

I connected Yoni's problem with Sartre's notion of the other's look. When we do not liberate ourselves from the views of others, their influence is upon us, and we are not living authentically. From a Sartrean perspective, Yoni's problem was a common one. I emphasized that during the sessions we could try to be authentic and not pretend to agree when we were not in agreement. I said I would consider seriously any criticism he had about me or the session, and I asked him to tell me immediately if he thought I was influencing him.

We then talked about various ways of making decisions. Could he think of how to make rational, emotional, or intuitive decisions without being influenced by others? Or were there additional ways of making independent decisions, such as tossing a coin? How can one choose the best way for making decisions? How can one avoid being influenced? He realized then that he had no experience in making decisions. In the ultra-Orthodox world almost everything had been planned for him—what to wear, when, and how. Although he was not religious anymore, he felt as though he was not allowed to choose, and he was afraid to make his own decisions in either trivial and important matters. I considered his fear of choosing as a fear of choosing his being—that is, existential anxiety. This explanation he found comprehensible.

Another question for Yoni was why he had sometimes engaged in petty thievery. He did not steal anymore, but it bothered him that he had once done so and did not know the reason. When he was religious he had stolen money from the charity boxes placed at the entrance of the ritual bathhouse. For that he had an explanation: He stole out of resentment, he hated the bathhouse, yet felt compelled to undergo the ritual purification. What confused him was that on vacation in Greece he had stolen from his travel companion—a student identity card and other things he did not need. He had enjoyed stealing, especially the fear that it caused him. However, he did think that stealing was wrong, and it had just been a temporary aberration.

I connected his stealing with his description of his weak ego. In contradistinction to what goes on in many psychotherapies, the reasons I offered for his thefts were only hypotheses, imaginary possibilities or logical conclusions that I hoped would trigger a new understanding, which would not necessarily be the same as mine. I suggested the following interpretations to him. Perhaps stealing the identity card had been the expression of his desire for his own identity. Perhaps his thefts were a form of revenge for having had his own self "stolen" continuously by others. By feeling afraid while stealing, he could give expression to the fear of being caught in assuming a chosen identity and lifestyle, something forbidden by his religious upbringing. Yoni accepted these suggestions. I recommended that he read Sartre's book on Jean Genet, and we read together a section where Genet's thefts are described as going toward the light—as liberation.[1]

The final issue Yoni wanted to talk about was his painting block. After he left the yeshiva, he had done odd jobs and in his spare time had picked up painting as a hobby. He dreamed of being a professional artist. He had received positive evaluations of his work from professional artists. He wanted to arrange an exhibition of his paintings at an art gallery. His problem was that for about two years he had not been able to paint. After two-and-a-half months of our sessions Yoni reported having picked up his brushes again, and during the remainder of our contact, he continued painting.

The following analysis was crucial in resolving Yoni's painting block. Yoni believed he could not paint because his energies were consumed by thoughts of revenge and fear. As far as Yoni could remember, he always had been attracted to the female sex; but he was a bit shy with girls. He once had been engaged, when he was religious. In the yeshiva, he had been "tricked" into a relationship with a homosexual friend named Bobby, ten years older than he. Yoni denied any inclination to homosexuality or bisexuality; he had been an innocent victim. He had rejected his therapist's suggestion that homosexuality is all too human (something immature, not right and not wrong), but could be sublimated. He could not imagine that he could have homosexual or bisexual interests, and his therapist's insistence on this issue was his main reason for his stopping therapy.

I suggested that although Sartre had found it too early to write an ethic for modern people, nevertheless, as Philip Thody pointed out, Sartre did consider human behavior and "all choices . . . chockfull of ethical values."[2] For Yoni homosexuality was a capital sin. We then examined homosexuality from various ethical viewpoints, such as a subjective account of his own value judgment on the matter as compared with others, such as mine, Genet's, and his ex-friend Bobby's. We discussed whether it was possible to give an absolute value judgment that reflected the truth of the matter. Were value judgments about homosexuality based on feelings, scientific or religious knowledge and beliefs, or a philosophical perspective? In contradistinction to his therapist, I accepted that he might not have homosexual inclinations. I showed him that his point of view on homosexuality was the dominant opinion in Orthodox Judaism and other orthodox religions.[3] I discussed his view that homosexuals need to be cured of their sin and sickness, although I did not conceal the fact that my sympathy lies with liberal views on homosexuality. However, in my opinion Yoni had to take responsibility for having been involved with Bobby, just as he was responsible for all of his actions. He refused this responsibility, since he had been manipulated into a relationship that he hated from the beginning. He felt that if he had been a person with a strong ego it would not had happened. He had thought of several ways of blackmailing his ex-friend, but fear prevented him from putting his plans into action.

The blackmail issue brought our discussion to the topic of law. (According to Yoni, this discussion was essential for him to be able to become creative.) The questions we discussed were as follows: Is there an ethical meaning to the laws of the state or to obeying these laws? Is a community or state possible without laws or agreements among people? Could the anarchist assumption that laws are hindrances to living together be right? I thought that Yoni's problem could be seen as follows: He had rejected the authority of religious laws, but had not consciously replaced these rules with ethics of his own. It seemed to me that a suitable option for his situation could be found in the idea of ethical conduct determined by a contract. Accordingly, we read together a section from Rousseau's *Social Contract*, "On Law," in which Rousseau argues that the laws of the state can teach people how to live. After thinking through these questions, Yoni concluded that laws, as social contracts, are meaningful in community life, and in general that laws should be observed. Accordingly, he rejected his plans for blackmail and decided not to think about the affair anymore.

CONCLUSION

After two-and-a-half months, Yoni's situation had improved dramatically, though he still felt depressed periodically. He had become a relaxed dialogue partner and felt secure in opposing my understandings when he thought them wrong. He decided to buy a house near the Sea of Galilee, and so our sessions were less frequent. He succeeded in making contacts in his new surroundings. After a while he found a girlfriend, who moved in with him. Only then did Yoni discontinue his sessions with me.

NOTES

1. Jean-Paul Sartre, *Saint Genet: Actor and Martyr* (New York: Mentor, 1963), 435–457.

2. Philip M. W. Thody, "Sartre and the Concept of Moral Action: The Example of His Novels and Plays," in *The Philosophy of Jean-Paul Sartre*, ed. P. A. Schilpp (La Salle, Ill.: Open Court, 1981), 433.

3. Norman Lamm, "Judaism and the Modern Attitude to Homosexuality," in *A Psychology–Judaism Reader*, ed. R. P. Bulka and M. HaLevi Spero (Springfield, Ill.: Thomas Books, 1982), 151–183.

CHAPTER 8

David

David is slim, elegant, and graying; he is a well-established architect in his early sixties, with two sons and two daughters. He works for a leading construction firm. His most significant problems involved his family life and his relationships at work. He had been in therapy for several years to overcome the traumatic shock and depression he felt when his wife left him. For twenty years he had thought that his marriage was wonderful. But this splendid relationship with his twelve-years-younger wife had ended suddenly when she left him for a friend of hers from the college where she worked. After a few months, an even greater misfortune occurred. One evening the police came and took David to identify his wife's body. She and her lover had been in a car accident; the lover had survived the crash, but she had died at once.

David felt guilty. He felt as if his wife had been murdered and that *he* had murdered her. It seemed as if her ghost was haunting him. He had contemplated committing suicide, but he did not have the courage to do it. His two years of therapy had helped him recover from the original shock and depression. But he still had many questions and found it difficult to deal with his four children and with people at work, even five years after those traumatic events.

David needed to be listened to and not so much to be given advice or solutions to his problems and questions. He was not looking or even hoping to find a solution. He would talk and talk about anything that had happened during the week. The issues we had decided to discuss philosophically—guilt, ideology, care of the body, death, and education—were often not discussed because of daily events, which seemed suddenly more important to David. He was always too busy working and living. He complained about being torn between the mundane and the philosophical issues of life.

At the beginning of the sessions I was uneasy about David's wandering away from the chosen themes. Only after awhile did I realize that it was important for him to be heard by somebody with a philosophical ear and heart. Philosophical companionship and listening, with few questions and remarks from my side, were typical of most of my sessions with David. Although he and I discussed many issues in the two years of counseling, I will only describe the sessions concerning his problematic relationships with his family and work.

There was much anxiety in David, caused by the unexpected death of his wife. What had happened to her could happen to him, his children, or anyone else. These fears were put in a philosophical framework by talking about various philosophical conceptions of death. David started our discussion on death by saying that he would not commit suicide because he loved his family, and moreover he loved living. In spite of his anxiety, he felt as if he was on life's carousel—he was excited by every dazzling new turnaround. He did not like people to commit suicide but he also did not like the taboo against it. He discussed suicide with his children and with their friends. He found it important that young people could bring their thoughts on this subject into the open, and that by doing so, they might find answers that would prevent them from committing suicide themselves. I agreed with him.

I then asked David what he thought about death. Is it an absolute end, or is there a possibility of life after death? Is death the completion of life, or is it a cruel interruption of something that should last forever? Could there be soul or mind or spirit that is eternal, with the body being just matter, enduring only temporarily? What would life be like if it lasted forever? Could the concept of death be the product of a subjective, human understanding of reality, while death might not exist at all from an objective view of the mind, or God? I brought into the conversation some ideas on death from Spinoza's *Ethics*, such as the idea that the wise person does not occupy himself with death but with life. The higher activity of philosophy, the attainment of higher knowledge, and the intellectual love of God were considered by Spinoza to be the cure for emotional distress, even anxiety about death. I also mentioned the Epicurean view, as well as that of Schopenhauer, which resembles Spinoza's in claiming that reflection offers protection against the fear of death. In addition, we discussed Jaspers's existentialism, which transcends, through philosophy and theology, the confusion and anxiety of disasters and change. Jacques Choron's book, *Death and Western Thought*, in which an attempt is made to help secular "souls" come to terms with the idea of death, seems to me a secular "book of the dead," written precisely for people in David's situation. However, David was not interested in reading this book immediately because he had many others he wanted to read first. He just wanted to tell his story and for me to understand it as it was. David was convinced that death is the end of everything, except that the dead can continue their lives in the memory and imagination of those who knew them, or learn about them through their legacy. He considered himself not afraid to die.

Once he had dreamed about dying. In the dream he saw himself standing in front of a dark tunnel. Suddenly he was drawn into the tunnel by a strong, tornado-like force. It drew him further and further to the end of the tunnel, which then became a submarine diving into the ocean's depth. He suddenly felt as if he were nothing. It was a beautiful and complete rest. He finally felt free of everything he was responsible for and anxious about. Various conversations about death did not free David from his anxiety, but it was clear that he was more concerned with the problem of living with the consequences of death, than with death itself.

It became clear that David experienced emotional dependency. He felt that the existence of his family members and loved ones affected his existence; their lives were his. He needed relationships that would last forever. Reflections on God, a philosophy of religion or philosophical research into the supernatural seemed to me appropriate for our dialogue, but he did not like these topics. He strongly refused to talk about God or an afterlife. I then suggested thinking about developing a relationship with an "eternal subject" or trying to reduce his dependency. He said it was impossible—he had already tried everything. He thought it must be inherited—something genetic that caused this overdependency and involvement of his. However, lasting stability through an "eternal subject" was appealing to him. The examples of apparently never-ending or ever-returning relationships, activities, or hobbies were many: involvement with atheism, philosophy, the arts, or any other pursuit in which he would need only his own presence and talents. Eventually David renewed his love for reading and even started to write poetry.

His anxiety remained—that is, there were times when he felt free of it, but then if anything happened that seemed dangerous, he was back to his usual fearfulness. Nevertheless, he said that philosophical counseling had helped him distance himself from his fears and be less involved with his own feelings. He said that talking to me about his fears made him feel good for at least a couple of hours each week.

Since I thought that the problems with his children were based on a kind of distrust—that is, on the fear that something bad could happen to them—I talked to David about Buber's idea of existential trust and Nietzsche's *amor fati*. I thought it helpful in his situation to think about our planet as a place where "all is well, and all will be well," although this cannot be proven, and there seems to be more evidence to justify the opposite conclusion. However, it might be helpful to think with a confident attitude, with an accepting "Yes," about all the events of existence. I urged him to see life as good, or beautiful, or divine, although, paradoxically, events and situations may be distressing, even evil, and may need to be avoided or altered. Such an *amor fati* attitude was a new idea to him.

David often felt guilty, even when he was proud of himself. He was guilty of existing. He believed that his emotional life, including the guilt feelings, were strongly influenced by the books of Dostoyevsky, Tolstoy, and other Russian writers he had read in his youth. He felt that he had to suffer to redeem existence; consequently, existence could not be good and could not be trusted. Could it really be that Dostoyevsky was responsible for his anxiety? I wondered. Though David was a fourth-generation Israeli of Eastern European descent, he saw himself as having a Russian soul. He did not suffer too much from his guilt feelings because he also could enjoy life immensely. He felt trapped into living, and yet he was intrigued by life. His reasons for living were mostly founded on instincts and feelings, and not so much on an intellectual perception of life.

I did not argue that his instinctual way of life was right or wrong, but I pointed out that it could lead to confusion and conflicts in situations in which he had to give reasons for his actions, such as at his work. When David was in his twenties he had started to work as an architect for a constructing firm that had grown over the years. He liked the security he had gained in working for this company, but he was often agitated over having to compromise because of the demands of the firm's manager. This conflict had alienated him from most of his coworkers, although there were some who understood him and supported his ideas. At a younger age he had been more insistent on his own views, but after his personal tragedy, he found it difficult to continue to work that way. His therapist had taken the problem at work as a "conflict with authority" and had encouraged him to conform to the company's wishes. That was what he did, but he felt that it was wrong and so still often did things his own way.

David said that he had a humanistic inclination; his designs were aesthetic but also had a philosophical content. I tried to understand his aesthetics and philosophy and asked him to explain them to me so that we could discuss his ideas. To my surprise he gave just one argument and no justification or explanation. Things were as he thought them to be, because he conceived them as such. I explained that if he could give good reasons or explanations for his convictions, he would have a better chance of convincing his colleagues. Additionally, he could try to understand the reasons and motivations of the people who rejected his work. I repeated to him the Chinese Maoist proverb: "Know yourself and your enemies, and win a thousand battles." Under this motto we started to analyze his "conflict with authority," which turned out to be an ideological conflict.

David was surprised to learn about philosophical thought similar to his own convictions and eager to find out more about it. These were philosophies that articulated his own intuitions. We also analyzed philosophically the motivations and thoughts of people who opposed his ideas. We tried to find logical arguments against these opposing points of view. The ideological analysis of his work situation showed that often two different concepts of "how to do the job" could both be justified. This gave David more self-confidence. He began to feel less threatened by people he worked with, and his newfound understanding of their point of view even gave him a kind of respect for them. It was David's good fortune that some of the older workers left the company and were replaced by younger people with whom he had more in common.

David then began talking about his smoking habits. He said that while he was in therapy he had often wanted to talk about smoking but had never felt it to be the right occasion. His doctor had told him to quit smoking, but he was not very concerned about his health. He did not mind dying, except that he wanted to continue to live for his children. His children wanted him to stop smoking, and he had made some attempts for their sake, but without any success.

I told David how Socrates thought a "defect in virtue" or ignorance could be corrected. The issue was to be single-minded about not smoking. He was of two minds: He knew he would be better off if he stopped smoking, yet he claimed that smoking helped him to cope with anxiety, and thus protected him. However, he himself knew that this was not true, and we talked about other habits that could reduce his anxiety while not poisoning his body with nicotine.

We then discussed the relationship between body and mind. Is there such a thing as mind over matter? Do bodily habits influence thought patterns? How does one break a vicious circle of unhappy thoughts and bad habits? Did he connect his smoking with events from his past? Is it possible to replace old habits by new ones? It turned out that David linked his smoking with the way he felt, but denied that the need to smoke was connected to his mother's way of breastfeeding or anything else in his early childhood. He thought it possible to change habits but felt he would suffer if he tried. He thought that if he could just feel that he must stop smoking, then he would do so.

During the Gulf War, David got that feeling and quit. In general, he explained later, the war had had a positive effect on him. David had been at home a lot over a period of about two months. He used the war as a good excuse for solitude. He saw almost no one and also stopped coming to the philosophical counseling sessions. When he returned he told me about the diverse changes he had made during that time—of which quitting smoking was one—and how he had suddenly come to confront himself. Interestingly enough, he had not been anxious when the sirens went off. He did not even take the trouble to put on his gas mask during the missile attacks. He and his family did close the windows during the attacks, and they sat in the family's hermetically sealed room, which guarded against biochemical warfare, but that was all. He had stopped smoking because of the lack of air he felt when sitting for hours in their sealed room. He gave as an explanation for his calmness of mind, at a time of great anxiety for people who were ordinarily calm, as the fact that he had grown up amid war. During the Holocaust, most of his family in Europe were killed. War was nothing new to him, and at least during a war, it was more or less reasonable to expect that loved ones could die suddenly.

During these two months at home David had enjoyed reading books, mostly modern Israeli literature and poetry. From a personal perspective, he was even sorry when the war was over and life returned to normal. Those "happy" months had permitted him to think differently about his work. But even though his situation at work had changed, he was still unable to do what he truly wanted. He thought of an early retirement. However, he felt that without work he would have too much freedom and would feel worthless. This brought the conversation around to the value of working, working creatively, or not working. I spoke to him about Russell's theory of idleness, which advocates working only part time.[1] David decided to work less for the company and to start projects of his own. He became quite involved in these projects and his new life of leisure. He gradually came to me less and less often, and finally said that for the present he did not have time to continue with philosophical counseling.

CONCLUSION

In evaluating my talks with David I tried to see if we had made progress on themes like death, guilt, or work, and tried to reach some conclusions. Every two or three months, fifteen to thirty minutes were set aside for this. David did not like these evaluations; they were not important to him. After a year, I stopped trying to review our talks. I came to understand and to accept that what David wanted was for me to share in his way of being, to partake in his existential loneliness. However, I did not give up developing the themes that appeared relevant to his life. Many changes and developments were triggered by the talks, although these became clear only in a total overview of the sessions. David found it interesting to talk about himself and try to understand himself. Because he had been in therapy, it was a relief to him to understand that my interpretations (and those of his ex-therapist) were not "divine truth" or even necessarily right. He had, for example, not agreed with his ex-therapist's interpretation of his guilt feelings (i.e., he had been told that his guilt feelings originated in a death wish toward his children). However, he had never tried to discuss or contradict the therapist because he considered that inappropriate. In philosophical counseling David was encouraged to try self-interpretation, without the assumption that we had reached a final or absolute truth. Both of us found our conversations a rewarding experience.

NOTE

1. Bertrand Russell, "How to Be Free and Happy," in *On Ethics, Sex and Marriage*, ed. A. Seckel (New York: Prometheus, 1987), 323–334.

CHAPTER 9

Yaela

I read the following sentences in *The Simone Weil Reader* while thinking about writing another case history: "Apart from the intelligence, the only human faculty which has interest in public freedom of expression is that point in the heart which cries out against evil. [Next is needed] an attentive silence in which this faint and inert cry can make itself heard."[1] These and other sentences of Weil suddenly reminded me of Yaela.

Part of my philosophical practice is a philosophical hotline—a free first-aid telephone line for ethical dilemmas and existential problems. Its phone number is published in the Jerusalem weekly *Kol Ha-Ir* and by a few other Israeli newspapers. I have been offering this service since 1990, and I have received calls from people with suicidal thoughts, severe depression, loneliness, confusion, ethical dilemmas, and all kinds of other questions. Sometimes people are helped by one phone call, others may call again, and yet others will move from the telephone sessions to private, face-to-face counseling. A person with suicidal thoughts may not start the conversation by saying so, but instead will talk about feeling low, depressed, or anxious. Only later, when the person feels that there is somebody to talk to, he or she might disclose these suicidal thoughts or other thoughts he or she would usually keep to him or herself. Moreover, sometimes these thoughts might not be brought up at all as the reason for calling the first-aid line. In the first chapter I discuss how philosophical practitioners can be helpful in suicide prevention. A philosopher with experience in this field, David Novak, wrote about his research and experiences in *Suicide and Morality*. The book, based on his doctoral dissertation, is about classical suicidology—that is, the arguments presented by Plato, Aquinas, and Kant on the prohibition of suicide. Past suicidology is philosophically oriented, while contemporary suicidology is empirical—an interdisciplinary combination of the social sciences and biology. Novak shows that philosophical arguments have practical importance for contemporary suicidology, but he finds the empirical and the philosophical approaches essentially different. The philosopher considers suicide as a possibility for rational choice, while the "very emphasis in contemporary suicidology on empirical description and therapeutic technique seems to eliminate the factor of rational choice. The assumption seems to be that *all* suicides are what Plato assumed *some* suicides to be, namely, 'compelled.'"[2] Yaela's story is about suicide if one considers—as Bertrand Russell did—alcoholism and other harmful addictions to be concealed ways of killing oneself.

Yaela contacted the hotline in a state of severe depression. After she had expressed her feelings of desperation and hopelessness, I invited her to visit me, and she agreed. Since Yaela's financial situation was as bad as her depression, I did not ask her to pay for the few philosophical sessions we had. There were five sessions, in which I argued for a philosophy of hope and optimism, or for a reasonable pessimism, against Yaela's views of desperation. Most of my arguments did not accord with Yaela's life experiences. Instead of an authoritarian insistence not to be desperate, and to accept an optimistic outlook of life, my arguments served as a catalyst to express, review, and somewhat modify her views. The aim in such open-ended dialectical dialogues is not to have concepts necessarily accepted, although this may occur, even after the sessions are concluded.

Yaela had only a few years of elementary school education, but she was an intelligent young woman with many interests, one of which was writing poetry. Yaela was in her early thirties and unmarried but had three children. She said that the father of her children had been a very important person for her. She had been like a slave to him, and she still would do anything for him, but the relationship had come to an end. She had grown up in institutions and had also lived for some time on the streets. Because of her children she received a small amount of money from the social services every month, which granted them a meager portion of food and housing.

During Yaela's first visit, we arrived at an issue after about forty-five minutes that was difficult to talk about: She had a problem with alcohol. (I had a strong sense that there could have been a problem with drugs as well.) Over the last few months, she had been drinking too much, and she wanted to stop, for her children's sake. She called drinking "a slow but sure way of committing suicide." What caused her to drink more and more vodka and cognac was that she was home all day. She wanted to get a job, but she said it was no good looking for anything. Even though she knew she could find a cleaning job, or she could be referred by the social services for a hairdressing or sewing course, she was not interested. I argued with her that there were other jobs for which not much education is needed, and that she should try to find jobs she might not even have thought of before. She started to look for such jobs but without enthusiasm.

Yaela's pessimism was based on her experiences. In one of the institutions where she had been as a child, she had been abused by some of the people in charge. In her teens she escaped from the institution and worked for awhile at an entertainment palace. She was angry with the welfare establishment. She felt that it was impossible to protest or change anything by speaking up: The underdog does not bark or bite those who supply it with housing and food. She wanted to live a life like other people and hoped that her children would grow up as normal people. Her conception of normality was the typical Israeli middle-class dream: a house, a car, picnics on holidays, good sports shoes, clothing money for the children, occasionally a meal at a restaurant with family or friends, once in awhile a vacation abroad, and savings for an old-age pension.

I could understand Yaela's desire for such prosperity. However, some parts of this dream appeared to me only to be good for tormenting herself, unless she happened to win the lottery. I therefore started to tell her about Herbert Marcuse's conception of created "false" needs. We questioned the following issues: Are all our needs created by our particular society? Are there "universal needs" as there are "universal human rights," and how can false and true needs be distinguished? Do these differ from person to person and from society to society? Are people's true needs only the elementary ones?

I told Yaela of my experience of living and working for half a year in a humanitarian Emmaus community in The Netherlands. This is a period of my life I consider to have taught me some most valuable and happy lessons. The manifesto of the International Emmaus movement is epitomized in the motto, "Serve first those who suffer most."[3] The basic philosophy of this movement is a return to elementary needs and a practical sharing of any surplus with those in need. I found this idea extremely effective in solving personal and social needs. Usually we think that we are the one who is suffering most, but if we look around us for people in worse situations, we do not have to search for long. When we help them, we may discover that we are rather fortunate. The idea of turning away from the self, refusing to be exclusively occupied with one's own inner or outer world, and instead concentrating on somebody or something else—that is, having impersonal interests—was envisioned by Bertrand Russell as a necessity for a happy and good life.[4] Accordingly, I suggested Yaela to look for an interesting volunteer job if she could not find anything else suitable.

In spite of her discouraged and depressed moods and all the difficulties she had been through, Yaela possessed an enthusiasm for life and wanted to be happy. She made jokes—gloomy ones, but jokes nevertheless—about herself, me, and others.

Yaela had the idea that things could not be different than they had been. She considered herself to have been born under an ominous star. There was nothing she could do about her situation. I considered it a possibility that this fatalistic belief was the basic obstacle in her difficulty with breaking the drinking habit. I told her that she could believe in fatalism, but she could not know that it was true. And even if it were, an astrologer would say that every year the constellations may have a different influence on a person's life and every new year brings it own luck. Besides, some astrologers claim that "star-influences" can be changed by a person's character. I discussed the ancient philosophical tradition *against* astrology, although there were also some philosophers who were influenced by astrologers and other diviners; for example, Cicero's *De Divinatione* is an instructive account of this issue in antiquity. I explained and defended the position of free will and self-determination as an ancient but still vital tradition.

Yaela and I enjoyed talking about these and other subjects. Since we were discussing these matters and had become friends, she felt that things were already different from before. That the befriending of a desperate person makes an essential difference in their situation has been shown by the group founded by Chad Varah. In different countries this organization—made up of volunteers and professionals—works under different names, such as "the Samaritans" or "L'Amitie" or "Die Dargebotene Hand." One of their professional members, Mary Bruce, says that people often think that professional consultation is the primary element in helping others, while befriending people is second best, but in her view the latter should be considered the most important thing.[5]

During the third session we talked mostly about Yaela's drinking problem. I thought that Alcoholics Anonymous could be helpful, but she immediately rejected this idea and also all the other ways that could help her to quit drinking. Her argument was that she did not need help from people. It was stupid to trust people— she knew what people were like. She started to tell a fantastic story of how her friend Tony was hospitalized and diagnosed as having cancer. He was supposed to die soon. After she heard this terrible news, she kept saying, "That can't be true, Tony won't die, he won't die, he won't die." She went to see Tony in the hospital and said those words to him. Two weeks later he was out of hospital. I asked Yaela what had happened. How did she explain the sudden recovery? Did she have supernatural powers? Had the doctors made a wrong diagnosis? Or had they cured Tony? She did not know what had happened. It could have been something psychosomatic, or yet again, she thought, maybe the healing had been "an accomplishment of the mind."

I suggested that she try her mind powers on her drinking problem. However, she was convinced that repeating to herself "I won't drink, I won't drink, I won't drink," would not have the same effect. She then told me what had happened this time to get her back on drinking. She insisted that she was not an alcoholic, because she could stop drinking if she really wanted. She was O.K.—she could do all kinds of jobs if she *wanted*. But she did not *want* to work, and now she did not *want* to stop drinking. "People are evil," she said and started to tell me what happened to her during the Gulf War (which had ended about two months earlier). One morning, sometime in the middle of the war, there was a knock on her front door. She opened the door and saw an ugly, shoddy, fat woman. The woman asked her if she could please come in. She was Yaela's mother. At the institutions, Yaela had been told that her father had died and that her mother did not want contact with her. She had never heard of or seen her mother. Now, she let this woman in. This woman wanted to stay because she was afraid to go back to her home in the coastal area, where missiles were landing frequently. Yaela let her mother stay with her. The woman ate all the time, while Yaela drank all the time; they talked very little. After a week the woman left, which made Yaela happy. She did not want any further contact with her.

I remained silent. Yaela then suddenly felt she was a burden to me and told me that she was going. I did not know what to say, but I heard myself say to her, "No, no, please don't go, it is good that you are telling me all this, and I would like to write about you, if that is O.K." That touched her and she started to cry. After a while she said "O.K., lets have a cognac and then I will not drink till we meet again." She had two cognacs, I one, some additional conversation, and then she said she would call me soon to make another appointment.

Yaela did not ask me to write about her, and it is very unusual for me to say to clients that I write about some of them. Retrospectively, it seems that promising to write down a person's sorrows can be helpful sometimes to that person. A similar idea is found in James Hillman's *Healing Fiction*: "Perhaps our age has gone to analysis not to be loved or get cured, or even to Know Thyself. Perhaps we go to be given a case history. . . . This is the gift of case history, the gift of finding oneself in myth. In myths God and humans meet."[6]

Yaela visited again after a few weeks. She said that her drinking was no longer a problem, which I could hardly believe. She asked me if I believed her, and I said that I wanted to believe her. She laughed, said it was true. She explained what had happened. About a week before, she could not sleep and felt very sad. It seemed to her as if she had cried for hours that night "with all of her heart." Suddenly she had become quiet and felt comforted, it was as if somebody, maybe God, had heard her cry, although she usually did not believe in such a being.

She was now optimistic. She had a solution: She was going to have another baby in a few years because the government would pay for her new baby. I suggested to her that to get married might have been a better deal. But marriage meant nothing to her because she wanted to be free and have lots of children by different men.

After that session, I did not hear from her for about half a year. Then around the new year, she called me to wish me a Happy New Year. In contrast to the first time we talked, she now sounded as if she had come to accept her situation and saw life somewhat differently.

CONCLUSION

It seemed to me that my listening to Yaela's heartfelt cry against evil did help her a bit. I understood her complaints as legitimate sociophilosophical criticism. Because of her fatalistic conception of life, Yaela was not at peace with her own criticism of the problems that caused her anguish. Accepting and giving force to her faint voice of protest seemed at least to have helped in getting over some extremely traumatic events.

NOTES

1. Simone Weil, "Human Personality," in *The Simone Weil Reader*, ed. G. A. Panichas (New York: David MacKay, 1977), 316.

2. David Novak, *Suicide and Morality* (New York: Scholars' Studies Press, 1975), 116, 119.

3. Secretariat General D'Emmaus International, *Emmaus International Newsletter* 40 (Charenton, France: Herve Teule, March 1983), 37; Abbé Pierre, *Abbé Pierre Speaks* (London: Lowe and Brydone, 1965).

4. Bertrand Russell, *The Conquest of Happiness* (New York: Bantam, 1968).

5. Mary Bruce, "Befriending the Lonely," in *The Samaritans*, ed. C. Varah (London: Constable, 1965), 143–148.

6. James Hillman, *Healing Fiction* (Woodstock, Conn.: Spring Publications, 1996), 49.

CHAPTER 10

Sarah

I saw Sarah weekly for about half a year. She is a retired dentist who had been working in one of Israel's hospital dental clinics. She had had a lifelong interest in psychology and had obtained, through self-study, considerable knowledge in this field, which she had found helpful in understanding patients and in other life situations. Sarah was born in Germany. As a teenager she and her two younger sisters had been able to leave Germany before the outbreak of World War II.

When they arrived in Palestine, Sarah and her sisters were sent to a kibbutz. Sarah soon got married at the kibbutz to a young man in similar circumstances. In the 1950s she and her husband went abroad to study, and after finishing their studies, they returned and settled in Jerusalem. Her husband later became a professor of law. They had no children, but their lives had always been filled with social contacts and activities.

When I first met Sarah, she had been a widow for about five years. She complained of having no friends with whom she could really share her innermost thoughts. Because of her interest in psychology, she wanted to know about and experience what philosophical counseling as an alternative approach was all about. She wanted to think about her life and wondered if at her age she could develop a philosophy of life.

I always welcome clients' requests for information about philosophical counseling. Usually, I answer such questions in about five to ten minutes and give my clients literature to read on the subject, but Sarah wanted more information. During the first session she told me about herself and asked for written material on philosophical practice and counseling. We began the second session by discussing the articles I had given her on philosophical counseling, and her questions were evidence of a more than superficial interest. I then realized that an important factor in our sessions would be her curiosity about this new type of counseling, but she also had personal questions about herself and her life that she was genuinely concerned about.

Sarah believed in heredity, biological givens, libido, and the unconscious; she found it natural that her understanding of the human soul would be influenced by medical concepts. Yet she felt a need for a philosophy of life mainly as an argument in the midst of what she called her "religious surroundings." Agnostic or scientific answers seemed not helpful when she wanted to answer religious extremists' claims. She was antireligious; she had once heard a lecture on Spinoza's critique of religion, and this had intrigued her. She wanted now to find out if his thoughts could fulfill her need for a philosophy of life.

I thought that Spinoza might help, but I also thought it was good to get a more general and modern perspective on the philosophies of life. I advised her to read *The Meaning of Life* and *Wisdom of the West*.[1] The first of these books presents three philosophical approaches in the quest for meaning: the theistic, the nontheistic, and the approach that questions if the search for the meaning of life is even meaningful. *Wisdom of the West*, a reworked version of Bertrand Russell's book on the history of philosophy, presents a witty and atheist perspective on philosophy through the ages.

One problem she wanted to discuss was her sense of disappointment with friends and family when she talked with them about things that interested her. She thought that this feeling originated in the fact that she had always tried to avoid conflicts. She had her own opinions, which she knew to be right, but if others disagreed with her, she did not oppose them, and the discussion ended. She assumed that through this habit she was keeping up a family tradition and was honoring her upbringing. Her parents had never pressured their children into obeying them, yet everybody always had, and there never had been open conflicts in their family.

She felt that her opinions were always right, and that others should accept them, yet she believed in a plurality of lifestyles. I wondered if her authoritative and detached stance might not originate in her professional life as a physician. After all, her sisters did not find it difficult to squabble about their opinions. She said she would think about that possibility. She also began reading Spinoza's *How to Improve Your Mind*.[2]

In the next discussion, she referred to her authoritative attitude in relation to her profession. It was true that as a dentist she had to be knowledgeable and self-assured and at the same time keep a professional distance. However, she thought of herself in Freudian terms, and thus she could not agree with me that attitudes and habits acquired in her twenties could have such a decisive, lifelong influence on her relationships. Moreover, the absence of unity of mind with others left her disconsolate; and any interference with plans made her feel anxious, to such an extent that it affected her mind and body.

For example, one evening she planned to drive her car to a theater performance, but she could not get the car to start. She took a taxi instead, although the incident had already spoiled her evening. She could not concentrate and had useless thoughts spinning in her head: "Why did the motor not turn on? What happened to it? The car had had its annual check a month ago, all was well then," and so on. After such incidents she was edgy and had difficulty falling asleep. She had acquired a book on self-hypnosis, and when in such mental and physical turmoil, she managed to calm down by following its instructions. I thought that this was a good solution to her problem and encouraged her to continue with it. In addition, I thought some physical exercise or light physical work could be useful to relax her when she was feeling high-strung. She objected to my advice because she found it not to be philosophical. She apparently expected that I would come up with a profound insight about her anxiety based on a particular philosophy of life. Perhaps I should have thought in this direction, but I had sensed that this possibly would not strike well with her Freudian self-concept. She then decided that we would stop talking about her anxiety problem and would concentrate only on philosophy, to which I agreed.

Sarah decided that the topic for the next sessions would be "meaning in life." She began to explain that as a teenager she learned what "meaning" is—she had experienced meaning. After she and her sisters had left Germany, her parents had been asked by the local authorities to disclose how their children had managed to get to Palestine. This would have had endangered the person who had helped them. Her parents refused to cooperate, and accordingly they were put on the blacklist of the secret police. They had also been among the first deportees when the war began. After the war the children learned that their parents had died in a concentration camp.

I considered the integrity and solidarity her parents had demonstrated to be tantamount indeed to a philosophical way of life—a very meaningful and heroic way of life. However, it was one among many ways to contribute meaning to our existence. Since Sarah's intellectual interest was interwoven with psychological understandings of life, I thought that it might interest her to discuss Victor Frankl's theory of meaning.

As a Holocaust survivor, Frankl's views might be considered especially helpful for those with similar backgrounds. Frankl's life seems to have taught him that in therapy—as well as outside of therapy—persons can better cope with that period of mass destruction if they have a purpose or a meaning for living. Understanding survivors' narratives, as they are intended by the survivors to be understood, is unlikely to occur in most types of psychological therapies. According to Jeffrey Masson, the tragic circumstances endured are often not acknowledged as the true reasons for a person's suffering. War trauma psychotherapy mostly deals with the same problematic issues as the treatment of child abuse does. Memories of Auschwitz or the Warsaw ghetto are, in these approaches, "like any other reality, simply the raw clay of our fantasies, of which the master sculptor is the psychotherapist. But it seems that the people who make this claim most vocally are the very people who in their own lives have been furthest removed from traumatic events of this magnitude."[3] Although it is obviously not the conscious intention of the psychotherapists referred to by Masson to deny the Holocaust, nevertheless such treatment actually turns into a kind of therapeutic Holocaust denial.

I suggested Sarah read an essay in which logotherapy is presented as a spiritual therapy that endorses the essential values of the Judeo–Christian tradition. She found the article interesting, but objected to its representation of moral people as "do-gooders." She did not trust such "tiresome" personalities. She disapproved of people finding meaning in a source other than themselves. For her, meaning had to be inherent in being and action. She preferred to find meaning in washing her car or going for a walk with her dog. Was it not enough just to find meaning in the ordinary things of life?

I agreed with her. It seemed to me that if she felt that was enough for her in terms of meaning, that was fine; although, in particular situations, such as when in search for counter-arguments in discussions with religious fundamentalists, she may find that her philosophy of life sounded too meager.

We returned to the study of Spinoza, since other atheist and materialist philosophers did not have the same attraction for her. She had been reading Yirmiyahu Yovel's interpretation of Spinoza's understanding of the psyche and especially liked how it accentuated similarities with Freud's psychology. For example, Yovel states,

"The affinity between them is so great that Freud feels Spinoza could have provided him with philosophical legitimation, had Freud felt the need for one; but as in reading Nietzsche, Freud shuns the unsolicited legitimation . . . from a philosopher much too dangerously akin to himself." However, Yovel also points out that, where Freud's aim was to help people become normal, Spinoza's was to fashion an exceptional, excellent human being—a "non-normal person."[4] In talking with Sarah, I stated that basic differences between Spinoza and Freud nevertheless remain. For example, the former's fundamental belief was that philosophy was a way of personal salvation, while Freud considered philosophy not very helpful in therapy or as a way of resolving emotional conflicts. Although privately Sarah was not interested in philosophical salvation, she was interested in articulating Spinoza's thoughts on this subject, since it appeared to her a valid alternative to religious belief.

After being in philosophical counseling for a few months, Sarah began to argue about Spinoza's concept of God with one of her sisters who had joined a religious group, the Jews for Jesus. Joining these charismatic fundamentalists was evidence for Sarah that something was wrong with her sister. Sarah did have to acknowledge that since her conversion, her sister had become cheerful and balanced and lived a life full of religious meaning. In disputing her sister's newfound faith, Sarah now used Spinoza's explanation of the miraculous as a natural phenomena that we mistakenly understand as a supernatural event. She considered the manner in which her sister had found a new equilibrium to be quite similar to her own achievements in using self-hypnosis in anxious states.

I felt Sarah had made progress in that she had begun arguing with her sister, but Sarah found it disappointing not to be able to convince her sister that God and nature were merely two poles of one axis. I encouraged her to continue debating. It seemed that the philosophical–theological argument of St. Augustine about the final incompatibility between rational knowledge and divine mysteries could cut through Sarah's conflict with, and rejection of, her sister's faith. Augustine understood that rationality and logic could be used partly to understand the world, as well as the supernatural, but the latter—particularly the so-called "divine mysteries"—can only truly be understood spiritually. Spiritual insight comes into being through metaphors—analogous narrations of what is grasped logically.

Since Spinoza explained supernatural phenomena as what we cannot rationally understand, then different theologies can be explained as being imaginative interpretations or spiritual metaphors of what cannot yet be understood. This view is supported by

Augustine's ideas. I thought that interpreting her sister's faith in this way would make Sarah more tolerant of her sister's ideas. Could Sarah understand her sister's faith in Jesus as an imaginative articulation of a natural phenomena and not as the proof that something was wrong with her? Could their conflict then become an issue of semantics only? This seemed a reasonable possibility to Sarah, and such an understanding perhaps could be acceptable by a religious person as well.

However, Sarah's sister thought this attempt to transcribe her faith was blasphemy, since she considered each word written in the Bible as factual. Sarah then decided that it was better to not attempt rational discussion of what she had begun to call her sister's religious imaginations or allegories.

We continued for a while discussing various books and interpretations on Spinoza till Sarah found that she had had enough private instruction and preferred to continue to philosophize by herself.

CONCLUSION

During the sessions one notion became quite clear, something Sarah herself had said at the beginning of the sessions: She had strong opinions about quite a few issues, and she was not interested in modifying these. It seemed to me that next to her curiosity about philosophical counseling, her purpose in the sessions with me was to acquire philosophical skills and a vocabulary through which she could articulate and share her opinions in a better way with others. Philosophical counseling as private study and intimate philosophical discussion sessions did help her achieve her goals.

NOTES

1. E. D. Klemke, ed., *The Meaning of Life* (Oxford: Oxford University Press, 1981); Bertrand Russell, *Wisdom of the West* (London: Bloomsbury, 1989).

2. Baruch Spinoza, *How to Improve Your Mind* (New York: Philosophical Library, 1956).

3. Jeffrey M. Masson, *Against Therapy* (New York: Atheneum, 1988), 5.

4. Yirmiyahu Yovel, *Spinoza and Other Heretics* (Princeton, N.J.: Princeton University Press, 1989), 139, 164.

CHAPTER 11

William

William, or Villi as his family, friends, and others who knew him personally called him, had turned forty the month he came for conversations with me. Reading a newspaper article on philosophy practice had given him the idea that he might be helped by it.

He complained of nightmares that woke him up with goose bumps all over, and of fear of death. His nightmares had began during the three years he had served in the Israeli Defence Forces. At eighteen he had left his parents' home to do his army duty. He had not been taken into the combat unit he had applied to, but rather had been given camp duties, such as being on guard at the barracks, waking up the soldiers, and sometimes helping out in the kitchen. Not being recruited by the combat unit of his choice had given him the feeling that he was not taken seriously as a soldier; consequently, he lost his former interest in being in the military. Instead of focusing on his work during those years, he made the female soldiers the chief object of his interest. He claimed to have had sex with most of the girls of his unit, some of whom he had not even been attracted to. After the army, he found a job at a government office as a clerk, but he had little chance of climbing the career ladder there, since he was not interested in doing the administrative courses that were necessary. He married in his late twenties and had two children.

I asked Villi if he had any idea why he had these nightmares. He thought they were punishment—a punishment which he believed he deserved. One repetitive dream Villi had was that he would sink into the ground and then arrive at an underworld where he saw decayed bodies and talked to spirits. Another horrifying dream is that angels carry him into a room filled with incense where his mother's body is being prepared for burial. In front of his mother's body is a giant silver plate, and he feels as if any moment an angel will sacrifice him on it. In another nightmare he dreams of fighting with black people and of being persecuted by German Nazis, but he always escaped by disappearing in grottos and underground tunnels. His background was Moroccan Israeli, and he did not understand why he always had to fight with blacks and Nazis, since in his personal history, he had never encountered violent relations with these two groups of people. He also dreamed sometimes of being a bird flying through the sky. This pleasant though infrequent dream made him wake up with a good feeling. However, most of the time he woke up screaming, and feeling only fear. What made it all the more frightening was that he also had dreams that came true.

It seemed to me that his dreams were marked with symbols of a religious, spiritualist, ritualistic, and violent nature. Had such rituals and beliefs been part of his upbringing? I asked if he could make associations betweens customs he remembered from his upbringing and scenes from his nightmares. He made an interesting association: When his mother had wanted to make cooking utensils kosher, a hole was made in the ground of their backyard and the pots and pans were buried for awhile in the ground. When they were dug up again, they were considered ritually clean, and after being washed with water and soap, they were again ready to use in their kosher kitchen. I had never heard of this custom (neither could I find it listed in the *Practical Guide to Kashruth*)[1] but found it interesting, as it seemed to relate to his dream experience of repeatedly being buried or "sinking in the ground." Perhaps his disappearing into the earth expressed that he felt guilty, unclean; it might express also the wish to be purified and forgiven, to become free of guilt and punishment. Villi thought that this interpretation may have been valid.

I asked Villi why he felt guilty and whether his fear of punishment could be related to his fear of dying. But before he could answer on this question, I thought it important to tell him that according to Hassidic Jewish tradition, death is the ultimate grace, and through death one makes atonement for one's sins. Villi could not believe this; he was convinced that he would go to hell. He recalled his first encounter with death: It was when his grandfather died. His grandfather had remained in Morocco while most of his brothers and sisters and their children and grandchildren had immigrated to Israel. A sister of Villi's grandfather had later brought them the sad news—that their grandfather had died. His mother started to scream when she heard the news, but Villi (he was about eight when this happened) had burst out into hysterical laughter. His mother's reaction to his laughter had been to beat him till he began to cry. I considered that maybe this incident left him with the association of the thought of death with punishment, but could this also be a cause for his fear of death?

An interesting analysis of a scene similar to Villi's dream in which he is led to a sacrificial altar is presented by Alice Miller in *The Untouched Key*. Here Miller analyzes two paintings of Rembrandt and those of twenty-eight other painters portraying Abraham's intended sacrifice of Isaac. Villi's dream resembles these paintings: His mother's eyes are closed and she is not seeing him, just as Abraham's eyes are turned away from Isaac. Abraham seems to be emotionally as dead as Villi's mother. Miller finds the different portrayals of the biblical story all similar in their symbolic representation of the situation of many people in our time: "They learned to deny their feelings as children. . . . Their souls have become rigid, they have learned to adapt."[2] Moreover, Miller observed in her more than twenty years experience as a psychoanalyst that parental substitutes (e.g., priests, psychotherapists, gurus, philosophers, or writers) often reinforce in these grown-up children the repression of their childhood experiences by not calling into question the so-called "wisdom" of traditional ways of upbringing and education. I fully agree with Miller that understanding childhood experience is made into something that is taboo and mystical. In addition, I find that ordinary people are made to believe that they are not equipped for self-understanding without the professional help of "experts." I even heard about some philosophical counselors who do not dare to touch the subject of a person's childhood out of fear of "damaging" what has become the sacred territory of the psychologists and psychiatrists. I cannot avoid making the assumption that these philosophical counselors must have thought through their own childhood with the help of these "experts," or that they simply never think, talk, or interpret their early years.

In response to my question concerning the spiritualist beliefs of his family, Villi at first could not remember anything, but he asked one of his sisters about it. His sister remembered all kinds of eerie stories, and when she narrated these, he began to remember as well. His mother had often gone to pray at the graves of important rabbis. She also had a collection of charms against the evil eye and against evil spirits. There had been all kinds of superstitious beliefs in the family: The children had been forbidden to jump in the house, because that would cause the ghosts of the dead to return. I mentioned to Villi the idea that these dreams about spirits were possibly related to his upbringing. He found that difficult to accept because he found his parents' faith in ghosts embarrassing and primitive; he was uncomfortable thinking and talking about it. Instead he thought that he had these dreams because God might be telling him that something was wrong with his life. He felt guilty about how he had behaved during his army service and for not living according to the Jewish Orthodox tradition. But on the other hand, he did not want to become Orthodox.

I considered that what he called the "primitive" beliefs of his parents were issues that had also been investigated by parapsychology and philosophy—they were not necessarily only issues primitive people believed in. I shared with him some of the findings of Charles T. Tart, who argued that four fundamental phenomena—telepathy, clairvoyance, precognition, and psychokinesis—have been proven to be real by laboratory experiments. But when researching other phenomena, such as psychic healing, out-of-body experiences, and survival of physical death, major methodological research problems are encountered. Nonetheless, Tart finds that extensive studies in the area of survival of physical death "have also produced moderately convincing evidence of the possibility of reincarnation."[3]

Although I personally have a skeptical attitude toward these matters, the phenomenon Villi experienced, that is, precognition through dreams, is shared by other people. I thought he might relate to it as something paranormal but not necessary as abnormal or primitive. Tart's perspective on Psi phenomena helped Villi to accept a paranormal aspect of his being.

Next, I suggested that he might have something in common with William James. Although James was from a Christian background, he was not a practicing Christian. However, there was something that made him respond to those who seemed to have transactions with God: "Something tells me:—'thither lies truth'—and I am sure it is not old theistic prejudices of infancy. . . . I have grown so out of Christianity that entanglement therewith on the part of a mystical utterance has to be abstracted from and overcome, before I can listen."[4]

It seemed to me that James's philosophical research could be a beacon for Villi's way out of anxiety, and helpful in creating a philosophical understanding concerning the ghost encounters in his dreams. James compares the reality of the unseen, such as religious or spiritual entities, to the nature of other abstractions, such as ideas. James finds that for Plato, abstract beauty is "a perfectly definite individual being, of which the intellect is aware as of something additional to all the perishing beauties of the earth." Although

James does not share Kant's opinion, he refers to the Kantian conception that objects of belief such as God or the soul are not really
objects of knowledge. Though one can conclude from a Kantian theoretical perspective that such words have no relevance, "strangely
enough they have a definite meaning *for our practice*. We can act
as if there were a God; feel *as if* we were free; . . . lay plans *as if* we
were to be immortal; and we find then that these words do make a
genuine difference in our moral life."[5]

I suggested that even though from a Kantian perspective we cannot have any objective knowledge concerning spirits, this does not
mean that these "whatevers" have no definite meaning for our everyday, practical lives, either waking or sleeping. The appearances
of spirits in his dreams meant anxiety and punishment to Villi,
and perhaps it was right not to look for any ulterior meanings.

I did not expect that our talks on his dreams would have a quick
and dramatic influence on Villi's life, but according to him, a great
change occurred after having seen these issues from a philosophical perspective. After three sessions he found that he did not suffer
anymore from nightmares and could sleep without waking up in
the middle of the night. He felt now that it was not his fear of spirits but fear of God that had troubled him.

In addition to James's skeptical–pragmatic approach toward religion, two other ways of pacifying Villi's fears for God were considered. I guided our conversations to include the ideas of the first
Chief Rabbi of Israel, Abraham Isaac Kook. His religious thought
is similar to the philosophical practice movement, in that it focused
on a concern for actual situations and the issues of people in the
"here and now" of life. Kook's view is radically different from Freud's
conception of people. For example, in Kook's *The Lights of Repentance*, people are perceived as inherently good and as striving for a
moral life. Accordingly, fear of God is a form of alienation and can
be overcome by trusting in the goodness of creation. On the other
hand, the rabbi holds that anxiety, such as that which Villi suffered from, expresses the "will for virtue," which is the primary
force of the human personality. However, this positive aspiration
should be given the assurance of conclusive success in individual
as well as communal life: "If man is constantly prone to stumble to
impugn righteousness and morality, since the primary basis of perfection is the yearning and firm desire towards perfection, this desire itself is the basis for repentance which constantly triumphs
over his way of life and truly perfects him."[6] Kook's religious optimism is generally appreciated by both Orthodox and secular Jews
in that its positive approach to human beings unites the religious
and nonreligious through tolerance, hope, and respect for each

group. Although Villi had learned about Kook's religious thought in high school, he never had considered that by believing it he could reduce his anxiety. Next, I introduced Villi to Buber's I–Thou dialogue. Although Buber's philosophy is also based on Jewish thought and religion, unlike Rabbi Kook's vision, the I–Thou encounter does not necessarily lead toward observing Orthodox Judaism. From a Buberian perspective Villi's fear could be analyzed as the lack of an I–Thou relation. Was his relationship to God not similar to a tie with a despotic something or a cult object—an "it"? I suggested he read the book *I and Thou* by himself, but as a preliminary means of finding God and a peaceful relationship with the Thou, I quoted this passage: "It is rather as if a man went his way and merely wished that it might be *the* way; his aspiration finds expression in the strength of the wish. . . . Ready, not seeking, he goes his way; this gives him the serenity towards all things and the touch that helps him."[7]

CONCLUSION

The sessions with Villi were few in number and were spread over a period of three months. It amazed me how much changed in his inner world over this short period of time. Maybe Villi's understanding of Miller's belief that "new Isaacs" can escape the role of being victims and victimizers by seeing the altar that had been prepared by unquestioning, blind authorities explains his transformation.[8] I do not know how Villi's fear of God resolved itself, if it did indeed resolve. Perhaps it did not need to be resolved at all.

Looking back on these sessions, I would have liked to have added another angle in our discussions of Villi's fear of God: an affirmation of this fear as it is found in the books of the Hebrew, Christian, and other religious traditions. The affirmation of this fear is best expressed in the words of the Psalmist: "The fear of the Lord is the chief part of wisdom, and they who live by it grow in understanding" (Ps 111:10). Likewise, James, in *The Varieties of Religious Experience*, points out that although the experience of the fear of God can be a quality of the sick soul, it can have also valuable, practical results for life.[9]

NOTES

1. S. Wagschal, *Practical Guide to Kashruth* (London: G. J. George, 1972).

2. Alice Miller, *The Untouched Key* (New York: Doubleday Anchor, 1990), 139.

3. Charles T. Tart, "Perspectives on Scientism, Religion, and Philosophy Provided by Parapsychology," *Journal of Humanistic Psychology* 32, 2 (1992): 70–100. See also Richard S. Broughton, *Parapsychology: The Controversial Science* (New York: Ballatine, 1991).

4. William James, *The Varieties of Religious Experience*, intro. Martin E. Marty (New York: Penguin, 1986), xxiv.

5. Ibid., 55, 57.

6. Abraham Isaac Kook, *The Lights of Repentance*, trans. and intro. Alter B. Z. Metzger (New York: Yeshiva University Press, 1968), 12, 22.

7. Martin Buber, *I and Thou*, trans. and intro. W. Kaufman (Edinburgh: T. & T. Clark, 1970), 128.

8. Miller, *Untouched Key*, 145.

9. James, *Varieties of Religious Experience*, 259–378.

CHAPTER 12

Natalie

This is a summary of twenty-two sessions that took place over a period of ten months. Anger, love, self-destructiveness, guilt, rebellion, and moderation were some of the topics that were explored.

Natalie was a pleasant-looking woman in her early forties. Her main problem was being overweight and having been so since the age of fourteen. She had to lose eighty to ninety pounds to reach her ideal weight. She had been in psychotherapy for about three years, but had left the therapist because she believed that he had given up on her: He had told her to try a stomach operation.

It had suddenly become urgent for her to lose weight since she developed a problem with the cartilage in her knees, which was possibly caused by her excessive weight. Her doctor had recommended a very strict diet or predicted a knee operation in the near future. She wanted to talk through what might be behind her being overweight because she believed that then she would be able to lose weight.

She attributed her overeating to anger. Her anger resulted in a vicious cycle: It caused her to overeat, then to become more angry that she had eaten so much, and then to eat more. I felt intuitively that her compulsive habits might be related to love and asked if we could maybe discuss the topic of love first. She spoke about not having received any love from her parents, that they had never hugged or kissed her. She married in her late twenties, but she did not believe her husband loved her. Likewise, her friendships were a mere social formality. People seemed unreliable to her: One day they would call each other honey or another nice name, and the day following they would use unpleasant names. I suggested that real love may stand such tests, and people may still love each other after conflicts and disappointments.

In the session following those just described, she said that she had thought about our talk on love, and she thought it would be useful to continue to talk about the relationships of her childhood. As the eldest child in a family of nine, she had been responsible for her younger brothers and sisters. She had to care and worry about the family as if she had been the only parent at home. She felt as if she never had a childhood because of this. The only memory she felt really good about was that there had always been lots of food on the table and the children always could eat without restraint. Even now, so many years later, sitting at a table loaded with food made her feel at home and gave her a safe feeling.

She felt that expressing her anger through overeating was safe as well. Expressing it differently might make her look foolish; she believed that showing one's anger or any other emotion was a weakness in character. I questioned this, but she felt that other ways of expressing anger would not be hers—she would then not be expressing *her* anger.

I considered a possible relationship between her anger, hate, and love. Hate, just like love, seemed not to exist for her. Besides eating, the only expression of anger she approved of was talking about it. Accordingly, in the following sessions she talked about quite a few issues that made her angry: incidents at her work as a secretary or issues at home with her two children. But most of her anger was directed to her own overindulgence. She had diagnosed herself as self-destructive, and I imagined that she might have been so diagnosed in therapy as well. She wanted to explore her self-destructiveness.

In the next session, I suggested that what she viewed as self-destructiveness could have been a result of her sacrificial life as a child. She had been taught "not-to-be" for the sake of her brothers and sisters, and thus could have acquired an adult sense of not being allowed to be, or in other words, a desire to destroy herself for the sake of being herself. Next, was not anger—although hers was a hidden anger—a useful emotion for achieving self-destruction, even to the extent that her anger seemed to blot out any other emotions she might have? These reflections seemed also appropriate in understanding the consequences of a theft she described in another session to be discussed later.

Talking about the issues that she considered to be at the root of her problem and by trying to improve her eating habits, Natalie after ten sessions lost about thirty pounds.

Yet she felt guilty and a failure because of not always keeping up
the diet. I proposed to reinterpret her failures as stepping stones to
success: Is not success often obtained by repeated trial and error? I
took as inspiration for this idea a quotation from Sartre's dialogues
with Benny Lévy: "Moving from failure to failure, would achieve
progress." In Sartre's *Being and Nothingness*, despair and failure
were not confronted with the concept of hope. Sartre contends that
in his early work, hope was always there "as a manner of grasping
the goal I set myself, as something that can be realized." Accordingly, Sartre finds that although action can be a series of failures,
something positive is likely to emerge.[1]

Natalie thought that this was true but felt a need to uncover
different kinds of failures and guilt in her life. She repeated that
one of the most painful failures she had ever experienced was having been referred to a surgeon in order to decrease her stomach,
and that after three years of therapy! She had been deeply shocked,
and she abhorred the therapist's somber advice, since in spite of all
her failures she believed that she would be able to break her bonds
of overeating, guilt, and anger. Considering a stomach operation
was to her surrendering the last bit of self-respect she had.

I urged her to keep this spark of hope and faith in herself burn-
ing. I explained Martin Buber's view of guilt, which is quite different from that of Freud and Jung: "Guilt does not exist because a
taboo exists . . . but rather . . . the placing of taboo have been made
possible only through the fact that the leaders of early communities knew and made use of a primal fact of man as man—the fact
that man can become guilty and know it." Buber finds that the
reality of existential guilt is a reality between man and man and
man and the world: "Existential guilt—that is, guilt that a person
has taken on himself as a person and in a personal situation—
cannot be comprehended through such categories of analytic science as 'repression' and 'becoming conscious.'" Buber finds that in
most instances of psychotherapy, existential guilt is denied. He il-
lustrates what he means by existential guilt in a short case history
about Melanie. Melanie is a middle-aged woman who suffered from
a neurosis after her husband left her for another woman, just as he
had left his first wife for her. The first wife, however, had committed
suicide. Melanie became, through therapy, more socially adept, but
she was not able in her relationships with others to interact authentically because she and her doctor never confronted the particular
situation that had made her feel guilty and sick in the first place.[2]

In the context of Buber's philosophical–anthropological perspective on guilt, I asked her if—with exception of her eating habits—
anything else had occurred in her life that could have made her

feel guilty. She then told of an event that happened when she was about fourteen. She had influenced her nine-year-old brother to steal something, and he was caught while executing this objective. Her father seemed not to know that she had been behind her brother's theft, but nevertheless found her responsible for not watching over her younger brother. After that incident her father had changed the hierarchy at home. He had taken the responsibility from Natalie and given it to her sister who was one-and-a-half years younger. Instead of feeling relieved by no longer having to look after her younger brothers and sisters, she felt very guilty and sad, and that was when she began to overeat. It seemed plausible to me that she had tried to continue a pattern of "self-denial" as self-punishment and destruction when this previous pattern of self-denial was taken away. It seemed to me that she had begun to destroy her physical self by not caring for it, that is, by denying her body its proper care.

Around the same time she herself had begun stealing from her parents, for at least a few years. She thought by doing it, she was proving that she was smarter than they were. She had only stolen small things that could easily have gotten lost, and her parents seemed never to have been aware of her stealing. She had never told anyone about these little teenage misdemeanors. She thought that they were an expression of rebellion against her parent's authority. She claimed that the incident with her brother had made her somewhat anarchistic: Her parents had overturned the hierarchy, the order in her life, without any justifiable reason, so why should not she do the same?

Natalie thought that her anarchistic leanings were another major obstacle in keeping the strict diet her physician had prescribed. She *had* to rebel against instructions about how many grams or ounces she could eat a day. All this brought up the theme of rebellion, anarchy, and morality.

I recommended reading the chapter "Moderation and Excess" from Albert Camus's *The Rebel*. In this chapter Camus discusses the necessity to recognize that "unadulterated virtue, pure and simple, is homicidal." Revolution and rebellion fails when it does not recognize the limits of change; such limits should take shape through principles of moderation. Camus observed that rebellious excess dies or creates its own moderation, since moderation and rebellion do not oppose each other: "Rebellion in itself is moderation, and it demands, defends, and recreates it throughout history and its eternal disturbances. The very origin of this value guarantees to us that it can only be partially destroyed. Moderation, born of rebellion, can only live by rebellion."[3]

Although Camus's book seemed highly relevant for her situation, Natalie did not like reading philosophical books, and she was only interested in hearing about the contents of the chapter mentioned. I had a strong sense that although she always thought seriously about my questions and about what I had to contribute to the conversations, it was of paramount importance to talk endlessly about her difficulties in keeping the diet and to complain about being angry. I continued listening to her with an ever-renewed philosophical wonder and empathy.

I continued to apply Camus's idea of moderation to her situation: During one month, keeping the diet every week for about 75 to 80 percent of the time would be a much greater achievement than keeping it 100 percent one week and only 25 to 30 percent for the next three weeks. Her disappointment with not being able to keep the entire diet, or her anarchistic refusal to do so, should not be a justification for not dieting at all.

In addition, I talked about St. Augustine's philosophy and how he himself experienced and described in his philosophical autobiography, *The Confessions,* a transformation of his mind and will by understanding that his rational chosen ideal was possible to attain through genuinely desiring it. I considered that the way in which Augustine achieved inner harmony could be an example for her and others suffering from compulsive habits. Augustine had changed his mind and will through hearing, believing, and understanding the stories of others who radically changed their lives. Since it was ultimately through grace and by becoming a believing Christian that Augustine's passion-tormented soul achieved inner harmony, she found the example of Augustine's transformation problematic. Such amazing divine influence seemed to her "too Christian." I understood her problem, but I countered by stating that according to other religions as well, divine help is available for all who seek a way out of distress, without it necessarily leading to conversions of one kind or another. However, she liked Camus's ideas better, and she decided to cut back on her high expectations in having to keep the diet.

She continued to come for a few more sessions. She kept complaining, and I kept listening and encouraging her. What can be considered crucial in all this is that she became better at keeping her diet, and kept losing weight.

CONCLUSION

No obvious changes occurred in the way Natalie felt, in her self-perception, or in her concept of life, but sharing the one problem she wanted help with seemed sufficient. Elementary to her successful weight reduction seemed to be her initial belief that by talking about her problems, she would be able to help herself. In addition, her hopeful outlook needed affirmation and philosophical resonance.

NOTES

1. Jean-Paul Sartre and Benny Lévy, *Hope Now,* trans. A. van den Hoven (Chicago: University of Chicago Press, 1996), 54, 66; Jean-Paul Sartre, *Being and Nothingness*, trans. and intro. H. E. Barnes (New York: Citadel, 1964).

2. Martin Buber, *The Knowledge of Man*, ed. and trans. M. S. Friedman (New York: Harper & Row, 1966), 126, 128–129.

3. Albert Camus, *The Rebel*, trans. A. Bower (London: Peregrine, 1962), 260, 265.

CHAPTER 13

Postscript

[Socrates'] last words—he said: "Crito, I owe a cock to Asclepius; will you remember to pay the debt?"

Plato, Crito, 118

In ancient Greece, it was common practice for those who believed they had been healed by the god of medicine, Asclepius, to offer a cock as a sacrifice. That Socrates remembered the god of medicine on his deathbed might have been the last ironic expression of his provocative spirit. But it could also have been an expression of true thankfulness for the swift effectiveness with which the poison he had been given was stiffening his limbs. After all, the sage did not know if it was better to live or to die. Only because his inner voice had not forbidden him to submit to the death penalty the Athenians had sentenced him with did he accept the cup of poison readily and cheerfully.

Not only Socrates, but most human beings owe some sort of debt to medical practitioners. This debt makes it difficult for many people to take the detached stance that would be needed for a critical autonomous view of the medical profession; radically criticizing it is an unpopular and even perilous activity.

The psychoanalyst Jeffrey Masson, for example, as Projects Director of the Sigmund Freud Archives at the Library of Congress, was fired when he disclosed his discovery concerning Freud's attitude toward sexual abuse. In the beginning of the 1980s, Masson's claim that Freud tried to cover up for these matters was not only a cause of controversy in psychoanalytic circles, but antagonistically resounded in the media as well.

Elaine Showalter's critical analysis of recovered memories, multiple-personality disorders, alien abductions, fatigue syndrome, and the Gulf War syndrome was received by the public not only with hate mail, but even with death threats. Criticizing medics and their institutions seems to be quite a common phenomena in modern societies. However, this trend is only acceptable as long as clinical sacred cows remain untouched.

Nevertheless, this book offers not only a critique of clinical psychoanalysis and psychotherapy, but also offers an alternative. Many philosophers, psychotherapists, and psychiatrists have written scholarly criticisms of the helping professions, but without effectively applying these criticisms to promote change of problematic issues. Of course, not all of these critics were only "salon revolutionaries"; Laing, for example, did put his criticisms into action. Radical clinicians face the problem of finding the right surroundings for revolutionary aspirations, which often become subverted by their professional associations. For example, psychotherapists can have academic degrees and be duly licensed or certified professionals. However, if they deliberately reject the common policy of diagnostic labeling, they will lose out on jobs with persons who receive mental health and substance abuse benefits, or on clients belonging to most other health insurances. Free-marketing philosophical counselors can perceive their practice as a free place for discussion and can make various criticisms available to the counselee when appropriate. These critiques of psychotherapy can be applied and realized in the philosophical practice.

I and other philosophical practitioners are aware, in spite of our criticisms, that mental-health workers and physicians often do a satisfying job; there are studies that show that about two-thirds of patients find they benefit from therapy.[1] One should remember not to generalize about therapy and therapists. There are endless theoretical dissimilarities among therapies, and various individual aptitudes among psychiatrists, psychotherapists, and psychoanalysts. Philosophical practitioners do not need only to compete but may also cooperate with clinicians that accept their legitimate criticism and alternatives.

According to Laing, real communication is always a rare commodity, especially in the mental-health profession. The lack of communication in the therapeutic professions can be a factor in patients' subsequent deterioration and misery: "This rift or rent is healed through a relationship with anybody, but it has to be somebody. Any 'relationship' through which this fracture heals is 'therapeutic,' whether it is what is called professionally, a 'therapeutic relationship' or not."[2]

Thinking and talking about problems with a philosopher may help make problematic issues comprehensible and communicable. Philosophical practice is an alternative by talking philosophy in such a way that communication between human beings is evident. Having problems is all too human; nevertheless, imagining life without the difficulties that living includes seems attractive to multitudes of people. Although I believe it is good to be hopeful in all situations, I cannot share the vision that life must or can be cured of all its problems. It seems to me relevant to see human problems as owned or acquired—and sometimes even created—by a specific person in a specific situation. My view is contrary to the one that generalizes human problems into complexes belonging to human nature; these complexes pertain only to psychological theories and research methods.

The various Freudians, Jungians, and Adlerians, for example, have constructed complexes that are assumed to be inherent in people universally. Nevertheless, the Freudian Oedipal complex has very little to do with the specific problems "owned" by the man called King Oedipus, or the difficulties you and I acquire in the course of living. I find that people remain responsible for reaching a personal understanding of themselves and their particular problems, and likewise for finding a unique, personal solution to their difficulties. Persons needing help in this can make use of the skills, knowledge, and experience of a philosophical practitioner. The concepts Achenbach has put forth for practicing philosophy have proven themselves so far—for close to twenty years now—to be reliable and beneficial. There are a considerable number of clinicians who support his ideas.

Though philosophical counselors may want to enrich the life of every person through philosophy, not all persons are attracted to philosophy and its practice. When a person is indifferent or even hostile to a philosophical inquiry into problems, this approach will have no attraction nor will it be beneficial for that person. Consequently, involuntary philosophical aid (one might envision, for example, the possibility of government-endorsed compulsory philosophy practice as rehabilitation for prisoners or treatment in mental hospitals) would only be a pathetic attempt to reeducate people's minds by force. Every method of enforcing philosophy practice would meet the same moral and legalistic barriers encountered when persons aim to enforce religious practices on fellow citizens. Cultivation of the mind, be it through philosophy, art, or religion, is only possible through an interest freely flowing from a person's innermost being. Thomas Jefferson's statement in the *Bill for Establishing Religious Freedom in Virginia* eloquently states the notion of freedom in thought and culture: "Well aware that Almighty God hath created the mind free, and manifested his supreme will that free it shall remain by making it altogether insusceptible of restrains; that all attempts to influence it by temporal punishments, or burthens, or by civil incapacitation, tend only to beget habits of hypocrisy."

In The Song of Songs, King Solomon's advice for relationships characterized by indifference and absent love is patience: "I adjure you . . . that you stir not up, nor awake my love, until it please." A patient, tolerant attitude on the part of the philosophical counselor to those who deny the value of this approach reflects the philosophical counselor's nondogmatic way of practice. Preferring philosophical help instead of psychological counseling should be a matter of personal preference only.

Though I have explained the differences between philosophical and psychological approaches throughout this book, some might still not grasp these distinctions, because the approaches deal with a subject matter that seems to belong only to the psychologist. These people may want to understand philosophical counselors as unlicensed existential therapists, and accordingly in need of supervision by a clinician. However, to me the difference between the disciplines of philosophy and psychology is and remains as clear as, for example, the difference between history and geography. In a historical research, one may want to discuss geographical findings, and vice versa; though neither turn one into the other. The content of the sessions and the "being" of the philosophical practitioner make philosophy practice essentially different from other kinds of practices. Those wanting to obscure the distinctions between these disciplines and practices may find some similarities between philosophy and psychology, or psychotherapy and philosophical practice, and use these similarities to argue that no clear distinction can be made. Indeed philosophical practice and psychotherapeutic or theological dialogue may seem similar in certain aspects, but they are in essence quite different. Could my distinguishing between these disciplines and practices be caused by a blind spot in my understanding of them? Or should I interpret those who cannot see things as I see them as suffering from "psychopathologization–hysteria," or being under the spell of psychotherapy? Maybe it is best not to interpret this matter further, and to follow Solomon's wise advice of silent, patient waiting. Understanding, knowledge, and wisdom are created not only through proper linguistics, arguments, and insights, but also by an attitude of silent waiting for what has not yet been grasped. The proposed silence is not the result of trying to avoid a conceptual conflict; rather, it makes place for the other's thoughts and for the unknown, so that new thoughts may become comprehensible.

In concluding this book on philosophy practice, I want to take a moment to discuss Marcuse's critical theory of society. His observations concerning one-dimensional people are, in an ever-growing measure, applicable to our present society and may be more so during the twenty-first century. One-dimensional forms of thought and behavior are subtly acquired in the realization of the technological worldview. The two-dimensional style of thought advocated by Marcuse is Socratic; it is a subversive discourse, a critical dialogue, a political discussion that points to the person who realizes truth in words and deeds. One-dimensional society is characterized by totalitarian preferences, making feeble the protest against intolerable situations, while creating an illusion of popular freedom and self-determination.[3] An example of this in the mental-health sector are the increasing long-term prescriptions of pharmaceutical drugs to resolve personal and social problems. Depression, sleeplessness, violence, anxiety, and other possible expressions of personal discontent (Are all these "disorders" not often the immediate result and expression of a revolt in one's innermost being against social events or other actual situations?) are easiest, and seemingly with the least expense, resolved by a technological approach: by scientifically indicating the source of these problems in people's faulty genetic makeup or detrimental biochemistry. Many clinicians are so fixated with medical science that they hardly consider it worthwhile to hear in-depth the complaints of those coming to seek their help. So-called "objective medical technology" is deemed that which has the answers. Often physiological tests, like a simple blood test, will indicate if a person is depressed, stressed, or something worse is wrong. Should we than cynically agree with the medical assistant who advised the complaining patients to consult a veterinarian, instead of frequenting the clinic of her employer, a well-known specialist. Well, not really, but veterinarians may teach their colleagues how to prevent and empathize with the violent, animalistic behavior of human patients. Why more and more patients have become violent toward their doctors, psychotherapists, and social workers is not yet comprehended by most of these caregivers.

Marcuse concluded *One Dimensional Man* as follows: "The critical theory of society . . . wants to remain loyal to those who, without hope, have given their life to the Great Refusal. At the beginning of the fascist era, Walter Benjamin wrote: . . . 'It is only for the sake of those without hope that hope is given to us.'"[4] Philosophy practice, through its open-minded and open-ended inquiry into the questions and problems of persons, offers first and foremost *hope*. Instead of limiting possible solutions to the few options provided by certain knowledge (for example, the Freudian, Jungian, Platonian, or the Prozac options), philosophy practice offers the hope that *much more is possible* by not putting boundaries on the limits of thinking and inquiry. I believe I have shown, by describing the theoretical and practical sides of philosophy practice, that there is more hope for human beings than we have thought so far.

NOTES

1. Jeffrey M. Masson, *The Freud Controversy*, Internet publication. http://www.jeffreymasson.com/freud.html (last accessed 20 March 1999). Elizabeth Gleick, "All in the Head," *Time* (7 July 1997), 50–52. Elaine Showalter, *Hysterical Epidemics and Modern Media* (New York: Columbia University Press, 1997). Anthony Storr, "Cure Thyself," *Nature* 377 (1995): 299.

2. R. D. Laing, *Wisdom, Madness and Folly* (London: Macmillan, 1986), 30.

3. Herbert Marcuse, *One Dimensional Man* (London: Sphere Books, 1968), 200.

4. Ibid., 201.

Bibliography

Achenbach, Gerd B. *Philosophische Praxis.* Cologne: Jürgen Dinter, 1987.

———. "Die 'Grundregel' philosophischer Praxis." In *Psychotherapy und Philosophie,* ed. R. Kuhn and H. Petzold, 345–362. Paderborn, Germany: Junfermann Verlag, 1992.

———. "About the Center of Philosophical Practice." In *Perspectives in Philosophical Practice: The Proceedings of the Second International Congress on Philosophical Practice,* ed. W. van der Vlist, 7–15. Doorwerth, The Netherlands: The Dutch Society for Philosophical Practice, 1997.

———. "What Does It Mean to Say: Philosophical Practice Is No Psychotherapy." In *Perspectives in Philosophical Practice: The Proceedings of the Second International Congress on Philosophical Practice,* ed. W. van der Vlist, 16–19. Doorwerth, The Netherlands: The Dutch Society for Philosophical Practice, 1997.

———. "On Wisdom in Philosophical Practice." *Inquiry: Critical Thinking across the Disciplines* 17, 3 (1998): 5–20.

Achenbach, Gerd B., and Thomas Macho. *Das Prinzip Heilung.* Cologne: Jürgen Dinter, 1985.

Achenbach, Gerd B., and Odo Marquard. "'Diese Biene ist ein Lügner': Der Philosoph als Berater." *ZPP: Zeitschrift für Philosophische Praxis* 2 (1994): 4–6.

Achenbach, Gerd B., and Peter Sloterdijk. "Gespräch über die Lebenskunst, zur Welt zu kommen." *Agora: Zeitschrift für Philosophische Praxis* 4 (1988): 1–3.

Achterhuis, Hans. *Arbeid, een eigenaardige medicijn.* Baarn, The Netherlands: Amboboeken, 1984.

————. *De markt van welzijn en geluk*. Baarn, The Netherlands: Ambo-boeken, 1988.

Aiken, Henry D. *The Age of Ideology*. New York: Mentor, 1956.

Almond, Brenda. "Counselling for Tolerance." *Journal of Applied Philosophy* 14, 1 (1997): 19–30.

Almy, Gary, and Carol Tharp Almy. *Addiction to Recovery: Exposing the False Gospel of Psychotherapy*. Eugene, Ore.: Harvest House, 1994.

Arendt, Hannah. *The Human Condition*. New York: Doubleday, 1958.

Artaud, Antonin. *Antonin Artaud, Selected Writings*. Ed. and intro. S. Sontag. Berkeley and Los Angeles: University of California Press, 1988.

Atkinson, Rita, and Ernest Hilgard. *Introduction to Psychology*. New York: Harcourt, 1983.

Audi, Robert. *Philosophy: A Brief Guide for Undergraduates*. Newark: University of Delaware, 1981.

Augustine, Saint. *The Happy Life*. London: Herder, 1939.

Backx, Els. "Filosofie schrikt veel mensen af." *Filosofische Praktijk* 9 (1992): 12–17.

Bakan, David. *Maimonides on Prophecy: A Commentary on Selected Chapters of the Guide of the Perplexed*. Northvale, N.J.: Jason Aronson, 1991.

Baker, Robert, and Frederick Elliston. *Philosophy and Sex*. New York: Prometheus, 1984.

Baldwin, Robert, and James McPeck. *An Introduction to Philosophy through Literature*. New York: Ronald Press, 1950.

Bateson, Gregory. *Steps to an Ecology of Mind*. San Francisco: Chandler, 1972.

Baur, Susan. *The Intimate Hour: Love and Sex in Psychotherapy*. Boston: Houghton Mifflin, 1997.

Berg, Melanie. *Philosophische Praxen im deutschsprachigen Raum: Eine kritische Bestandsaufnahme*. Essen, Germany: Die Blaue Eule, 1992.

Bernstein, Richard J. *Praxis and Action*. Philadelphia: Duckworth, 1972.

Binswanger, Ludwig. "The Case of Ellen West: An Anthropological–Clinical Study." In *Existence: A New Dimension in Psychiatry and Psychology*, ed. R. May, E. Angel, and H. F. Ellenberger, 237–364. New York: Simon and Schuster, 1976.

Blackburn, Simon. *The Oxford Dictionary of Philosophy*. Oxford: Oxford University Press, 1994.

Blanshard, Brand. *Four Reasonable Men*. Middletown, Conn.: Wesleyan University Press, 1984.

Boele, Dries. "In Dialoog met het gewetene." *Filosofische Praktijk* 2 (1987): 7–18.

————. "The 'Benefits' of a Socratic Dialogue." *Inquiry: Critical Thinking across the Disciplines* 17, 3 (1998): 48–70.

Boer, Gert de. "Socrates in Willebadessen." *Filosofische Praktijk* 6 (1989): 21–23.

Bok, Sissela. *Lying*. New York: Vintage, 1979.

Bonhoeffer, Dietrich. *Spiritual Care*. Philadelphia: Fortress, 1985.

Brammer, Lawrence, and Everett Shostrom. *Therapeutic Psychology: Fundamentals of Counseling and Psychotherapy.* Upper Saddle River, N.J.: Prentice Hall, 1982.

Branwyn, Gareth, Stephanie Mills, John Berendt, David Bohm, Cary D. Wintz, Jack Zimmerman, Virginia Coyle, Christopher Lasch, and Beth Lapides. "Salons: How to Revive the Endangered Art of Conversation and Start a Revolution in Your Neighbourhood." *Utne Reader* 44 (1997): 66–88. Internet publication. http://www.utne.com/cafe/caferesources.html (last accessed 11 March 1999).

Broughton, Richard S. *Parapsychology: The Controversial Science.* New York: Ballantine, 1991.

Brown, Lee, and Alan Hausman. "Mechanism, Intentionality, and the Unconscious: A Comparison of Sartre and Freud." In *The Philosophy of Jean-Paul Sartre,* ed. P. A. Schilpp, 539–581. La Salle, Ill.: Open Court, 1981.

Browning, Donald S. "Introduction to Pastoral Counseling." In *The Clinical Handbook of Pastoral Counseling,* ed. R. Wicks, R. D. Parsons, and D. Capps, 5–13. New York: Paulist, 1985.

Bruce, Mary. "Befriending the Lonely." In *The Samaritans,* ed. C. Varah, 143–148. London: Constable, 1965.

Buber, Martin. *Pointing the Way.* New York: Harper & Row, 1963.

———. *The Knowledge of Man.* Ed. and trans. M. S. Friedman. New York: Harper & Row, 1966.

———. *Between Man and Man.* Ed. and trans. M. S. Friedman. New York: Macmillan, 1967.

———. *I and Thou.* Trans. and intro. W. Kaufman. Edinburgh, Scotland: T. & T. Clark, 1970.

Camus, Albert. *The Rebel.* Trans. A. Bower. London: Peregrine, 1962.

Cannon, Betty. *Sartre and Psychoanalysis.* Lawrence: University Press of Kansas, 1991.

Capra, Fritjof. *Uncommon Wisdom.* London: Fontana, 1989.

Cavell, Stanley. *In Quest of the Ordinary.* Chicago: University of Chicago Press, 1988.

———. *A Pitch of Philosophy: Autobiographical Exercises.* Cambridge: Harvard University Press, 1994.

Chandler, Joseph. "Ceci n'est-pas un philosophe." *The Philosophers Magazine* 2 (1998): 10–11.

———. "The Philosophers' Paris: A Walk Through *La Rive Gauche.*" *The Philosophers Magazine* 3 (1998): 12–13.

Charlesworth, Max. "Sartre, Laing, and Freud." *Review of Existential Psychology and Psychiatry* 17, 1 (1980): 23–39.

Choron, Jacques. *Death and Western Thought.* New York: Macmillan, 1963.

Cicero. *Selected Works.* Ed. E. Rieu, B. Radice, and R. Baldic. Harmondsworth, England: Penguin, 1965.

Clark, Stephen R. L. *From Athens to Jerusalem.* Oxford: Clarendon, 1984.

Clarke, Norris W. "The Philosophical Importance of Doing One's Autobiography." *The American Catholic Philosophical Association Proceedings* 54 (1980): 17–25.

Clinebell, Howard J., Jr., ed. *Community Mental Health: The Role of Church and Temple.* Nashville, Tenn.: Abingdon, 1970.

Cohen, Elliot D. *Philosophers at Work.* New York: Holt, Rinehart and Winston, 1988.

———. "Logic, Rationality and Counseling." *The International Journal of Applied Philosophy* 5, 1 (1990): 43–49.

———. *Caution: Faulty Thinking Can Be Harmful to Your Happiness.* Fort Pierce, Fla.: Trace-WilCo, 1994.

Cohn, Hans W. *Existential Thought and Therapeutic Practice.* London: Sage, 1997.

Cooper, David E. "Metaphors We Live By." In *Philosophy and Practice*, ed. A. P. Griffiths, 43–58. Cambridge: Cambridge University Press, 1985.

Cooper, David G. *Psychiatry and Anti-Psychiatry.* New York: Ballantine, 1967.

Delnoij, Jos, and Wim van der Vlist, eds. *Filosofisch Consulentschap.* Best, The Netherlands: Damon, 1998.

Deurzen-Smith, Emmy van. *Existential Counselling in Practice.* London: Sage, 1994.

———. *Everyday Mysteries: Existential Dimensions of Psychotherapy.* London: Routledge, 1997.

Dill, Alexander. *Philosophische Praxis.* Frankfurt am Main: Fischer Taschenbuch Verlag, 1990.

Du Plock, Simon. "Smoke without Fire: Towards an Existential–Phenomenological Perspective on Hallucinations." *Journal of the Society for Existential Analysis* 6, 2 (1995): 97–116.

Durkheim, Emile. *Suicide: A Study in Sociology.* London: Routledge and Kegan Paul, 1952.

Edman, Irwin. "Introduction." In *The Consolation of Philosophy*, ed. I. Edman, vii–xxii. New York: The Modern Library, 1943.

Ehrenwald, Jan. *From Medicine Man to Freud.* New York: Dell, 1956.

Ellenberger, Henri. *The Discovery of the Unconscious: The History and Evolution of Dynamic Psychiatry.* New York: Basic Books, 1970.

Ellis, Albert, and Robert Harper. *A Guide to Rational Living.* Beverly Hills, Calif.: Hal Leighton, 1975.

Elster, Jon, ed. *The Multiple Self.* Cambridge: Cambridge University Press, 1989.

Entralgo, Pedro Lain. *The Therapy of the Word in Classic Antiquity.* New Haven, Conn.: Yale University Press, 1970.

Erde, Edmund L. *Philosophy and Psycholinguistics.* The Hague: Mouton, 1973.

Erikson, E. H. *Identity: Youth and Crisis.* New York: Norton, 1968.

Fanon, Franz. *The Wretched of the Earth.* Trans. C. Farrington, preface J.-P. Sartre. New York: Grove Weidenfeld, 1963.

Farrel, B. A., J. O. Wisdom, and P. M. Turquet. "Symposium: The Criteria for Psychoanalytic Interpretation." *Aristotelian Society, Supplementary* 36 (1962): 77–144.

Foucault, Michel. *Technologies of the Self.* Ed. L. H. Martin, H. Gutman, and P. H. Hutton. Amherst: University of Massachusetts Press, 1988.

———. *Politics, Philosophy, Culture.* Ed. L. D. Kritzman. New York: Routledge, 1990.

Foucault, Michel, David Cooper, Jean-Pierre Faye, Marie-Odile Faye, and Marine Zecca. "Confinement, Psychiatry, Prison." In *Politics, Philosophy, Culture*, ed. L. D. Kritzman, 178–210. New York: Routledge, 1990.

Fox, Richard. "The Recent Decline of Suicide in Britain: The Role of the Samaritan Suicide Prevention Movement." In *Suicidology: Contemporary Developments*, ed. E. S. Shneidman, 499–524. New York: Grune & Stratton, 1976.

Frankl, Victor E. *Man's Search for Meaning*. Boston: Beacon, 1962.

Freud, Sigmund. *The Future of an Illusion*. New York: Doubleday Anchor, 1964.

Friedenberg, Edgar Z. *R. D. Laing*. New York: Viking, 1973.

Friedman, Maurice S. *Martin Buber: The Life of Dialogue*. Chicago: University of Chicago Press, 1960.

———. "Dialogue between Martin Buber and Carl R. Rogers." In *The Knowledge of Man*, ed. and trans. M. S. Friedman, 166–184. New York: Harper & Row, 1965.

———. *The Healing Dialogue in Psychotherapy*. Northvale, N.J.: Jason Aronson, 1985.

———. *Dialogue and the Human Image*. Newbury Park, Calif.: Sage, 1992.

Galant, Debra. "Cream and Sugar? Philosophical Discourse?" *The New York Times*, 1 June 1997, Sec. 13.

Giddens, Anthony. *Durkheim*. London: Fontana, 1987.

Giorgi, Amedeo. "Sartre's Systematic Psychology." In *The Philosophy of Jean-Paul Sartre*, ed. P. A. Schilpp, 179–196. La Salle, Ill.: Open Court, 1981.

Gleick, Elizabeth. "All in the Head." *Time*, 7 July 1997.

Goldenberg, Herbert. *Contemporary Clinical Psychology*. Los Angeles: California State University, 1973.

Goldman, Howard H. *Review of General Psychiatry*. Los Altos, Calif.: Lange Medical Publications, 1984.

Golomb, Jacob. *Nietzsche's Enticing Psychology of Power*. Jerusalem: Magnes Press–The Hebrew University, 1989.

Goodman, Paul. *Nature Heals*. New York: Free Life Editions, 1977.

Gordon, Haim. *Dance, Dialogue, and Despair*. Tuscaloosa: University of Alabama Press, 1986.

Graefe, Steffen. *Was heißt Philosophiche Praxis?* Hamburg, Germany: Privatdruck, 1989.

Griffiths, A. Phillips, ed. *Philosophy and Practice*. Cambridge: Cambridge University Press, 1985.

Grimes, Pierre, and Regina Uliana. *Philosophical Midwifery: A New Paradigm for Understanding Human Problems*. Costa Mesa, Calif.: Hyparxis, 1998.

Griswold, Charles L. *Self-Knowledge in Plato's Phaedrus*. Stoughton, Wisc.: Alpine, 1986.

Grollman, Earl A. "The Clergyman's Role in Grief Counseling." In *Community Mental Health: The Role of Church and Temple*, ed. H. J. Clinebell, Jr., 98–99. Nashville, Tenn.: Abingdon, 1970.

Guggenbühl-Craig, Adolf. *Power in the Helping Professions*. Woodstock, Conn.: Spring, 1996.

Hadas, Moses. *The Essential Works of Stoicism*. New York: Bantam, 1961.

Hadot, Pierre. *Philosophy as a Way of Life*. Oxford: Blackwell, 1995.

Hamlyn, David W. *Being a Philosopher: The History of a Practice*. London: Routledge, 1992.

Hanfling, Oswald. *The Quest for Meaning*. New York: Blackwell, 1987.

Heaton, John M. "How Can We Discuss the Erotic? Plato and Freud Compared." In *Thresholds Between Philosophy and Psychoanalysis*, ed. R. Cooper, 100–119. London: Free Association Books, 1994.

Hegel, G.W.F. *The Philosophy of History*. New York: Willey, 1944.

Heidegger, Martin. *Being and Time*. New York: Harper & Row, 1962.

Heilbroner, Robert L. *The Worldly Philosophers*. New York: Simon and Schuster, 1972.

Heyed, David. "Psychoanaliza al Sapat Ha Philosoof" (Psychoanalysis on the Philosopher's Couch) (in Hebrew). *Iyyun: A Hebrew Philosophical Quarterly* 35, 1 (1986): 57–61.

Hillman, James. *Healing Fiction*. Woodstock, Conn.: Spring, 1996.

Hoffmaster, Barry. "The Theory and Practice of Applied Ethics." *Dialogue* 30, 3 (1991): 213–234.

Holzman, Lois, and Hugh Polk, eds. *History Is the Cure: A Social Therapy Reader*. New York: Practice, 1988.

Hoogendijk, Ad. *Spreekuur bij een filosoof*. Utrecht, The Netherlands: Veen, 1988.

———. *Filosofie voor managers*. Amsterdam: Veen, 1991.

Huisjes, Mariette. "Mensen hebben ideeën nodig." *Cimedart Faculteitsblad van de Centrale Interfaculteit* (1987): 7–9.

Huizinga, Johan. *Homo Ludens*. Boston: Beacon, 1955.

Hutton, Patrick H. "Foucault, Freud, and the Technologies of the Self." In *Technologies of the Self*, ed. L. H. Martin, H. Gutman, and P. H. Hutton. Amherst: University of Massachusetts Press, 1988.

Iggers, Jeremy. "Pensées au lait: France's Latest Cultural Invention—The Philosophical Café—Has Arrived." *Utne Reader* 82 (1997): 12–13. Internet publication. http://www.utne.com/lens/act/82culturecafe.html (last accessed 11 March 1999).

Illich, Ivan. *Medical Nemesis*. New York: Random House, 1976.

Inwood, Brian. *Ethics and Human Action in Early Stoicism*. Oxford: Clarendon, 1985.

James, William. *The Varieties of Religious Experience*. Intro. Martin E. Marty. New York: Penguin, 1986.

Jaspers, Karl. *Way to Wisdom*. New Haven, Conn.: Yale University Press, 1951.

———. *General Psychopathology*. Manchester, England: Manchester University Press, 1972.

———. *Strindberg und van Gogh*. Munich: Piper, 1977.

———. *Nietzsche: An Introduction to the Understanding of His Philosophical Activity*. Baltimore: Johns Hopkins University Press, 1998.

———. *The Great Philosophers*. New York: Harcourt Brace, vol. 3, 1993; vol. 4, 1995.

Jong, Loes de, and Wim van der Vlist. "Socrates op de markt: Interview met Jos Kessels." *Filosofie* 8, 1 (1998): 37–42.

Jongsma, Ida. "Ontstaans geschiedenis van de Filosofische Praktijk in Amsterdam." *Filosofische Praktijk* 1 (1987): 17.

Jowett, B. *The Dialogues of Plato.* Vol. 1. New York: Random House, 1937.

Julien, Mieke. "Veel mensen voelen zich pas gelukkig als ze nuttig zijn." *Filosofische Praktijk* 10 (1992): 6–11.

Jung, Carl G. *Modern Man in Search of a Soul.* New York: Harcourt, 1933.

Jung, Hwa Yol. "Mikhails Bakhtin's Body Politic: A Phenomenological Dialogics." *Man and World* 23 (1990): 85–99.

Kaufman, William E. *Contemporary Jewish Philosophies.* New York: University Press of America, 1985.

Kemp, Peter T. "Toward a Narrative on Ethics: A Bridge between Ethics and the Narrative Reflection of Ricoeur." *Philosophy and Social Criticism* 14, 2 (1988): 179–201.

Kenny, Anthony. *The Anatomy of the Soul.* Bristol, England: Basil Blackwell, 1973.

Kessels, Jos. "Een repliek aan Eite Veening." *Filosofische Praktijk* 6 (1989): 16–20.

———. "Korte Karakteristiek van het Socratisch gesprek volgens Nelson en Heckmann." *Filosofische Praktijk* 6 (1989): 5–12.

———. *Socrates op de markt: Filosofie in bedrijf.* Amsterdam: Boom, 1997.

———. "The Socratic Dialogue as a Method of Organizational Learning." In *Perspectives in Philosophical Practice: The Proceedings of the Second International Congress on Philosophical Practice,* ed. W. van der Vlist, 45–60. Doorwerth, The Netherlands: The Dutch Society for Philosophy Practice, 1997.

Kierkegaard, Søren. *A Kierkegaard Anthology.* Ed. R. Bretall. Princeton, N.J.: Princeton University Press, 1946.

Kirsner, Douglas. "An Abyss of Difference: Laing, Sartre and Jaspers." *Journal of the British Society for Phenomenology* 21, 3 (1990): 209–215.

Klemke, E. D., ed. *The Meaning of Life.* Oxford: Oxford University Press, 1981.

Koestenbaum, Peter. *The New Image of the Person: The Theory and Practice of Clinical Philosophy.* London: Greenwood, 1978.

Kook, Abraham Isaac. *The Lights of Repentance.* Trans. and intro. Alter B. Z. Metzger. New York: Yeshiva University Press, 1968.

Krämer, Hans. "New Paths in Philosophical Ethics." *Universitas* 27, 3 (1985): 209–220.

———. *Integrative Ethik.* Frankfurt am Main: Suhrkamp, 1992.

Kron, Tamar, and Rafi Yungman. "The Dynamics of Intimacy in Group Therapy." *International Journal of Group Psychotherapy* 37, 4 (1987): 529–548.

Laing, Ronald D. *The Politics of Experience.* New York: Ballantine, 1967.

———. *The Divided Self.* London: Penguin, 1970.

———. *Knots.* New York: Vintage, 1972.

———. *Wisdom, Madness and Folly.* London: Macmillan, 1986.

Laing, Ronald D., and David G. Cooper. *Reason and Violence.* New York: Pantheon, 1971.

Lamm, Norman. "Judaism and the Modern Attitude to Homosexuality." *A Psychology–Judaism Reader*, ed. R. P. Bulka and M. HaLevi Spero, 151–183. Springfield, Ill.: Thomas Books, 1982.

Levi, Albert W. *Philosophy as Social Expression*. Chicago: University of Chicago Press, 1974.

Lewis, C. S. *The Four Loves*. London: Collins, 1985.

Lieblich, Amia. "Looking at Change." In *The Narrative Study of Lives*, Vol. 1, ed. A. Lieblich and R. Josselson, 92–127. London: Sage, 1993.

Lindseth, Anders. "Was ist Philosophische Praxis?" *Agora: Zeitschrift für Philosophische Praxis* 8–9 (1990): 12–14.

Lobkowicz, Nicholas. *Theory and Practice: History of a Concept from Aristotle to Marx*. Notre Dame, Ind.: Notre Dame University Press, 1967.

Malcolm, Norman. *Memory and Mind*. London: Cornell University Press, 1977.

Marcuse, Herbert. *One Dimensional Man*. London: Sphere Books, 1968.

Marquard, Odo. *Tranzendentaler Idealismus, Romantische Naturphilosophie, Psychoanalysis*. Cologne: Jürgen Dinter, 1987.

———. "Philosophische Praxis." In *Historische Wörterbuch der Philosophie* 7, 1307. Basel, Switzerland: Verlag Schwabe, 1989.

Martens, Ekkehard. "Sokrates als philosophischer Praktiker." In *Philosophische Praxis*, ed. Gerd B. Achenbach, 131–143. Cologne: Jürgen Dinter, 1984.

———. "Philosophische Praxis ohne Philosophie." *Agora: Zeitschrift für Philosophische Praxis* 8–9 (1990): 17–18.

Marx, Karl. *Selected Writings*. Ed. D. McLellan. Oxford: Oxford University Press, 1977.

Masson, Jeffrey M. *Against Therapy*. New York: Atheneum, 1988.

———. *The Freud Controversy*. Internet publication. http://www.jeffrey masson.com/freud.html (last accessed 20 March 1999).

May, Rollo. *Love and Will*. New York: Dell, 1969.

May, Rollo, Ernest Angel, and Henri F. Ellenberger, eds. *Existence: A New Dimension in Psychiatry and Psychology*. New York: Simon and Schuster, 1978.

McGuire, Brain. *Friendship and Community*. Kalamazoo, Mich.: Cistercian, 1988.

McKeon, Richard, ed. *The Basic Works of Aristotle*. New York: Random House, 1941.

McQuade, Molly. "A Gluttonous Reader: Susan Sontag." In *Conversations with Susan Sontag*, ed. L. Poague, 271–278. Jackson: University Press of Mississippi, 1995.

Miller, Alice. *The Untouched Key*. New York: Doubleday Anchor, 1990.

Misch, Georg. *A History of Autobiography in Antiquity*. Vol. 1. London: Routledge and Kegan Paul, 1949.

Morstein, Petra von. "Breath Life into Philosophy, Professor Urges." *Calgary Herald*, 11 September 1987, F14.

———. "Wittgenstein on Philosophical Methods as Therapies." *ZPP: Zeitschrift für Philosophische Praxis* 2 (1994): 13–19.

Murgatroyd, Stephen. *Counseling and Helping*. London: The British Psychological Society, 1988.

Murray, James S. "Disputation, Deception and Dialectic: Plato on the True Rhetoric (Phaedrus 261–266)." *Philosophy and Rhetoric* 21, 4 (1988): 279–289.

Murris, Karin. "The Baby and the Bath Water." In *Perspectives in Philosophical Practice: The Proceedings of the Second International Congress on Philosophical Practice*, ed. W. van der Vlist, 117–134. Doorwerth, The Netherlands: The Dutch Society for Philosophy Practice, 1997.

Nehru, Jawaharlal. *The Discovery of India*. New York: Doubleday Anchor, 1959.

Nelson, Leonard. *Socratic Method and Critical Philosophy*. Trans. T. K. Brown III. New York: Dover, 1949.

———. *System of Ethics*. Trans. N. Guterman. New Haven, Conn.: Yale University Press, 1956.

———. *Vom Selbstvertrauen der Vernunft*. Hamburg, Germany: Felix Meiner, 1975.

Newman, Fred. *The Myth of Psychology*. New York: Castillo, 1991.

Newman, Fred, and Lois Holzman. *Lev Vygotsky, Revolutionary Scientist*. New York: Routledge, 1993.

———. *The End of Knowing: A New Developmental Way of Learning*. New York: Routledge, 1997.

Nietzsche, Friedrich. *The Portable Nietzsche*. Ed. W. Kaufman. New York: Viking, 1954.

———. *The Gay Science*. Trans. W. Kaufmann. New York: Vintage, 1974.

———. *Untimely Meditations*. Cambridge: Cambridge University Press, 1983.

Norman, Richard. *The Moral Philosophers*. New York: Harcourt, 1983.

Novak, David. *Suicide and Morality*. New York: Scholars Studies, 1975.

Nozick, Robert. *The Examined Life: Philosophical Meditations*. New York: Simon and Schuster, 1989.

Nussbaum, Martha C. *The Therapy of Desire: Theory and Practice in Hellenistic Ethics*. Princeton, N.J.: Princeton University Press, 1994.

Paden, Roger. "Defining Philosophical Counseling." *The International Journal of Applied Philosophy* 12, 1 (1998): 1–17.

Pallone, Nathaniel J. "The Phenomenal Self, Person, and the Catholic Counselor." In *Readings in Guidance and Counseling*, ed. J. M. Lee and N. J. Pallone, 61–73. New York: Sheed and Ward, 1966.

Palmquist, Stephen. *The Tree of Philosophy*. Hong Kong: Philopsychy Press, 1995.

———. *Dreams of Wholeness*. Hong Kong: Philopsychy Press, 1997.

Peters, Richard S. *Brett's History of Psychology*. Cambridge: M.I.T. Press, 1965.

Pierre, Abbé. *Abbé Pierre Speaks*. London: Lowe and Brydone, 1965.

Plutarch. *Selected Essays on Love, the Family and the Good Life*. Ed. M. Hadas. New York: New American Library, 1957.

Poague, Leland, ed. *Conversations with Susan Sontag.* Jackson: University Press of Mississippi, 1995.

Pucciani, Oreste F. "Sartre and Flaubert as Dialectic." In *The Philosophy of Jean-Paul Sartre*, ed. P. A. Schillp, 495–538. La Salle, Ill.: Open Court, 1981.

Quinton, Anthony. "Madness." In *Philosophy and Practice*, ed. A. P. Griffiths, 17–41. Cambridge: Cambridge University Press, 1985.

Raabe, Peter B. "Philosophy in Public." *Elenchus* 2, 1 (1997): 6–8.

Rademaker, P. "Filososofie en bedrijfsleven." *Wijsgerig Perspectief* 29 (1988–1989): 132–136.

Read, Herbert. *English Prose Style.* Boston: Beacon, 1955.

Rieff, David. "Victims, All?" In *The Best of American Essays*, ed. S. Sontag and R. Atwan, 253–267. New York: Ticknor & Fields, 1992.

Rogers, Carl. "The Characteristics of a Helping Relationship." In *Readings in Guidance and Counseling*, ed. J. Lee and N. J. Pallone, 207–221. New York: Sheed and Ward, 1966.

———. *On Becoming a Person.* London: Constable, 1974.

———. *A Way of Being.* Boston: Houghton Mifflin, 1980.

Romme, Marius A. J., and Alexandre D.M.A.C. Esher. "Hearing Voices." *Schizophrenia Bulletin* 15, 2 (1989): 209–216.

Rosenberg, Shalom. *Tov ve Rah be Machshevet Israel* (On good and evil in Jewish thought). Tel Aviv: Misraad Habitahon, 1985.

Ross, Kelley L. "The Foundations of Value." Parts 1 and 2. In *The Proceedings of the Friesian School.* Internet publication. http://www.friesian.com/founda-1.htm and http://www.friesian.com/founda-2.htm (last accessed 18 August 1998).

Rotenberg, Mordechai. *Damnation and Deviance.* New York: Free Press, 1978.

———. *Dia-logo Therapy: Psychonarration and PaRDeS.* New York: Praeger, 1991.

Rousseau, Jean Jacques. *The Confessions of Jean Jacques Rosusseau.* New York: The Modern Library, 1945.

Russell, Bertrand. *The Conquest of Happiness.* New York: Bantam, 1968.

———. *The Problems of Philosophy.* Oxford: Oxford University Press, 1977.

———. *The Will to Doubt.* New York: Philosophical Library, 1986.

———. "How to Be Free and Happy." In *On Ethics, Sex and Marriage*, ed. A. Seckel, 323–334. New York: Prometheus, 1987.

———. *Wisdom of the West.* London: Bloomsbury, 1989.

Sacks, Oliver. *Awakenings.* Harmondsworth, England: Penguin, 1976.

Sandra, Jaida n'ha. *The Joy of Conversation: The Complete Guide to Salons.* Minneapolis, Minn.: Utne Reader Publications, 1998.

Saran, Rene. "How to Prepare a Socratic Dialogue." In *Perspectives in Philosophical Practice: The Proceedings of the Second International Congress on Philosophical Practice*, ed. W. van der Vlist, 293–314. Doorwerth, The Netherlands: The Dutch Society for Philosophy Practice, 1997.

Sartre, Jean-Paul. *Anti-Semite and Jew.* New York: Schoken, 1948.

———. *Baudelaire.* Trans. T. Martin. New York: New Directions, 1950.

———. *Saint Genet: Actor and Martyr.* New York: Mentor, 1963.

——. *Being and Nothingness*. Trans. and intro. H. E. Barnes. New York: Citadel, 1964.

——. *The Words*. New York: George Braziller, 1964.

——. *Between Existentialism and Marxism*. New York: Pantheon, 1974.

——. *Life/Situations*. New York: Pantheon, 1977.

——. *The Freud Scenario*. Chicago: University of Chicago Press, 1986.

——. *The Family Idiot*. 5 vols. Trans. C. Cosman. Chicago: University of Chicago Press, vol. 1–4, 1991; vol. 5, 1993.

——. *Truth and Existence*. Chicago: University of Chicago Press, 1992.

Sartre, Jean-Paul, and Benny Lévy. *Hope Now*. Trans. A. van den Hoven. Chicago: University of Chicago Press, 1996.

Sautet, Marc. *Un café pour Socrate*. Paris: Robert Laffont, 1995.

Schefczyk, Michel. "Philosophische und psychologische Individualberatung," *Agora: Zeitschrift für Philosophische Praxis* 10–11 (1991): 8–11.

Schilpp, Paul A. *The Philosophy of Karl Jaspers*. New York: Tudor, 1957.

Schuster, Shlomit C. "Philosophical Counselling." *Journal of Applied Philosophy* 8, 2 (1991): 219–223.

——. "Philosophy as if It Matters: The Practice of Philosophical Counseling." *Critical Review* 6, 4 (1992): 587–599.

——. "The Practice of Sartre's Philosophy in Philosophical Counseling and in Existential Psychotherapy." *Iyyun: The Jerusalem Philosophical Quarterly* 44, 1 (1995): 99–114.

——. "Report on Applying Philosophy in Philosophical Counseling." *The International Journal of Applied Philosophy* 9, 2 (1995): 51–55.

——. "Philosophical Counseling and Humanistic Psychotherapy." *Journal of Psychology and Judaism* 20, 3 (1996): 247–259.

——. "Philosophical Narratives and Philosophical Counselling." *Journal of the Society for Existential Analysis* 8, 2 (1997): 108–127.

——. "Sartre's 'Words' as a Paradigm for Self-Description in Philosophical Counseling." In *Perspectives in Philosophical Practice: The Proceedings of the Second International Congress on Philosophical Practice*, ed. W. van der Vlist, 20–34. Doorwerth, The Netherlands: The Dutch Society for Philosophy Practice, 1997.

——. "Everybody's Philosophical Counselling." *The Philosophers' Magazine* 3 (1998): 44–45.

——. "On Philosophical Self-Diagnosis and Self-Help: A Clarification of the Non-Clinical Practice of Philosophical Counseling." *The International Journal of Applied Philosophy* 12, 1 (1998): 37–50.

——. "Revisiting *Hope Now* with Benny Lévy: A Note on the 1996 English Edition of *Hope Now*." *Sartre Studies International* 4, 1 (1998): 63–75.

——. "Sartre's Freud and the Future of Sartrean Psychoanalysis." *The Israel Journal of Psychiatry* 35, 1 (1998): 20–30.

Scolnicov, Samuel. "Socrates on the Unity of the Person." *Scripta Classica Israelica* 7 (1985–1986): 14–25.

Secretariat General D'Emmaus International. *Emmaus International Newsletter* 40. Charenton, France: Herve Teule, 1983.

Senge, Peter, ed. *The Fifth Discipline Fieldbook: Strategies and Tools for Building a Learning Organization*. London: Nicholas Brealey, 1994.

Shibles, Warren. *Rational Love*. Whitewater, Wisc.: Language Press, 1978.

———. "Philosophical Counseling, Philosophical Education and Emotion." *The International Journal of Applied Philosophy* 12, 1 (1998): 18–36.

Showalter, Elaine. *Hysterical Epidemics and Modern Media*. New York: Columbia University Press, 1997.

Shusterman, Richard. *Practicing Philosophy: Pragmatism and the Philosophical Life*. New York: Routledge, 1997.

Simon, Bennett. *Mind and Madness in Ancient Greece*. London: Cornell University Press, 1978.

Singer, Peter, ed. *A Companion to Ethics*. Oxford: Blackwell, 1993.

Sloterdijk, Peter. *Critique of Cynical Reason*. Trans. M. Eldred. Minneapolis: University of Minnesota Press, 1987.

———. *Der Zauberbaum: Die Entstehung der Psychoanalyse im Jahr 1785*. Frankfurt am Main: Suhrkamp, 1995.

Snow, Charles. *The Two Cultures and the Scientific Revolution*. London: Cambridge University Press, 1959.

Soll, Ivan. "Sartre's Rejection of the Freudian Unconscious." In *The Philosophy of Jean-Paul Sartre*, ed. P. A. Schilpp, 582–604. La Salle, Ill.: Open Court, 1981.

Solomon, Robert C. "Emotions and Choice." In *Explaining Emotions*, ed. A. Oksenberg Rorty, 251–281. London: University of California Press, 1980.

Sontag, Susan. *Against Interpretation*. New York: Farrar, Straus and Giroux, 1966.

———. *Trip to Hanoi*. New York: Farrar, Straus and Giroux, 1968.

———. *On Photography*. New York: Farrar, Straus and Giroux, 1977.

———. *Illness as Metaphor*. New York: Farrar, Straus and Giroux, 1978.

———. *A Susan Sontag Reader*. London: Penguin, 1983.

———. *AIDS and Its Metaphors*. New York: Farrar, Straus and Giroux, 1988.

———. *The Volcano Lover: A Romance*. New York: Farrar, Straus and Giroux, 1992.

Sontag, Susan, and Robert Atwan, eds. *The Best American Essays 1992*. Intro. S. Sontag. New York: Ticknor & Fields, 1992.

Spinelli, Ernesto. *Demystifying Therapy*. London: Constable, 1994.

Spinoza, Baruch. *How to Improve Your Mind*. New York: Philosophical Library, 1956.

Stern, Alfred. *Sartre, His Philosophy and Psychoanalysis*. New York: Liberal Arts Press, 1953.

Storr, Anthony. "Cure Thyself." *Nature* 377 (1995): 299.

Strauss, Leo. "Plato." In *Perspectives on Political Philosophy*, Vol. 1, ed. J. Dowton, 40–93. Orlando: Holt, Rinehart and Winston, 1971.

Szasz, Thomas S. *The Ethics of Psychoanalysis*. New York: Basic Books, 1965.

———. *The Myth of Mental Illness*. New York: Harper & Row, 1974.

———. *The Myth of Psychotherapy*. New York: Doubleday Anchor, 1978.

————. *Insanity: The Idea and Its Consequences*. New York: John Wiley & Sons, 1987.

Tame, Judy. "Psychotherapy: Philosophy, Not Medicine." In *Psychological Notes*, Vol. 8, 1–7. London: Libertarian Alliance, 1992.

Tart, Charles T. "Perspectives on Scientism, Religion, and Philosophy Provided by Parapsychology." *Journal of Humanistic Psychology* 32, 2 (1992): 70–100.

Taylor, Alfred. *Socrates*. New York: Doubleday Anchor, 1953.

Thody, Philip M. W. "Sartre and the Concept of Moral Action: The Example of His Novels and Plays." In *The Philosophy of Jean-Paul Sartre*, ed. P. A. Schilpp, 422–437. La Salle, Ind.: Open Court, 1981.

Tillich, Paul. *The Courage To Be*. New Haven, Conn.: Yale University Press, 1952.

Tyrrell, Bernard J. "Christotherapy: An Approach to Facilitating Psychospiritual Healing and Growth." In *Clinical Handbook of Pastoral Counseling*, ed. R. Wicks, R. D. Parsons, and D. Capps, 58–75. New York: Paulist, 1985.

Valenstein, Elliot S. *Brain Control: A Critical Examination of Brain Stimulation and Psychosurgery*. New York: John Wiley & Sons, 1973.

Varah, Chad, ed. *The Samaritans*. London: Constable, 1965.

————. "Introduction." In *The Samaritans*, ed. C. Varah, 9–87. London: Constable, 1965.

Veening, Eite P. "Monoloog, dialoog en metaloog." *Filosofische Praktijk* 2 (1987): 19–25.

————. *Denkwerk*. Culemborg, The Netherlands: Phaedon, 1994.

————. *Over de werkelijkheid van drie werelden*. Groningen, The Netherlands: E. P. Veening, 1998.

Verene, Donald P. *The New Art of Autobiography*. Oxford: Clarendon, 1991.

Vonessen, Franz. *Was krank macht, ist auch heilsam: Mythisches Gleichheitsdenken, Aristoteles' Katharsis-Lehre und die Idee der homöopathischen Heilkunst*. Heidelberg, Germany: Haug, 1980.

Voois, W. "Philosophische Praxis: een confrontatie?" *Filosofische Praktijk* 1 (1987): 13–15.

Wagschal, S. *Practical Guide to Kashruth*. London: G. J. George, 1972.

Walton, William M. "The Philosopher and the Psychiatrist." *Philosophy and Psychiatry: Proceedings of the American Catholic Philosophical Association* 35 (1961): 1–11.

Wear, A. N., and D. Brahams. "To Treat or Not to Treat: The Legal, Ethical and Therapeutic Implications of Treatment Refusal." *Journal of Medical Ethics* 17 (1991): 131–135.

Weigert, Edith. "Existentialism and Its Relations to Psychiatry." *Psychiatry* 12 (1949): 399–412.

Weil, Simone. "Human Personality." In *The Simone Weil Reader*, ed. G. A. Panichas, 313–339. New York: David MacKay, 1977.

————. *The Need for Roots*. London: Routledge and Kegan Paul, 1978.

Westphal, Merold. "Briefer Book Reviews." *The International Philosophical Quarterly* 39, 4 (1989): 479–480.

Winkler-Calaminus, Martina. "Similia similibus curantur." *Agora: Zeitschrift für Philosophische Praxis* 5–6 (1989): 13–14.

Winston, David. *Philo of Alexandria*. New York: Paulist, 1981.

Wittgenstein, Ludwig. *Remarks on Colours*. Berkeley and Los Angeles: University of California Press, 1977.

Witzany, Günther. *Philosophieren in einer bedrohten Welt*. Essen, Germany: Die Blaue Eule, 1989.

———. *Zur Theorie der Philosophischen Praxis*. Essen, Germany: Die Blaue Eule, 1991.

Wright, Elizabeth. *Psychoanalytic Criticism: Theory in Practice*. New York: Routledge, 1984.

Yovel, Yirmiyahu. *Spinoza and Other Heretics*. Princeton, N.J.: Princeton University Press, 1989.

Zdrenka, Michael. "Eine Philosophische Praxis in Israel." *Information Philosophie* 2 (1997): 80–85.

———. *Konzeptionen und Probleme der Philosophischen Praxis*. Cologne: Jürgen Dinter, 1997.

Index

ABOUT THE AUTHOR

Shlomit C. Schuster is a practicing philosophical counselor. As the founder of Center Sophon, which promotes the practice of philosophy in all areas of living, she offers private and group sessions in philosophical counseling and instructs philosophers who want to begin their own counseling practice. She has also published several articles on philosophical counseling.

ISBN 0-275-96541-4

HARDCOVER BAR CODE